THE GEORGIAN GENTLEMAN

THE GEORGIAN GENTLEMAN

by
Michael Brander

 SAXON HOUSE

Saxon House, D. C. Heath Limited, Westmead,
Farnborough, Hants, England

© Michael Brander, 1973

ISBN 0 347 00020 7
LOC No. 73–10622

Printed in Great Britain by
Robert MacLehose & Co. Ltd
The University Press, Glasgow

Set in Times by the
MACTAPE SYSTEM

CONTENTS

PREFACE

My thanks are due to those librarians who have supplied me with material for this book, particularly the staff of the National Library in Edinburgh and Mr. William Leslie and the staff of the East Lothian County Library. I am grateful also to the readers in typescript and proof for their invaluable help — my daughter Ann and my wife Evelyn, as ever, foremost among them, also my son Andrew Michael for the index. Without the help of the above it would have been impossible to write this book, but I must acknowledge at once that all the errors of omission and commission are mine alone.

M.B.

To Peter and Celina

INTRODUCTION

Above all, the Georgian Age was the Age of Contrast. It has been called the Age of Reason, but it was also the Age of Riot. It was the Age of the Individual and of the Mob. It was the Age of Elegance and of Squalor, of Experiment and Stagnation, Courage and Fear, Hope and Despair, Freedom and Slavery, Humanity and Cruelty, Scandal and

Changes in gentlemen's fashions between 1700 (left) *and 1800* (right). (Radio Times Hulton Picture Library)

Prudery, Politeness and Rudery, Scholarship and Ignorance, Drunkenness and Abstinence, of improving Agriculture and the birth of Industry, of Horse and finally Steam.

In no sense a history of the period, this book is solely about the Georgian gentleman and as such clearly does not cover large aspects of the age. It is merely a series of sketches depicting various details of his life and how he lived. By quoting various diaries, letters and the comments of visitors to the country, as far as possible a picture of the gentleman's life of the day is revealed in the words of contemporaries. How often he felt it necessary to have a bath, the prevalence of bugs in inns, the drinking and dining habits, the hundred-and-one aspects of everyday life are referred to by people living at the time, giving their own impressions of the day. That these may often have been erroneous is true, but life is made up of impressions erroneous or otherwise, and as far as possible the reader is kept informed of the facts, thus providing a balanced picture.

Admittedly, the Georgian era was lengthy and profound social changes were at work throughout. The world of Lord Chesterfield, the worlds of Horace Walpole and George Selwyn and that of Greville were all subtly different, with changing fashions and viewpoints and attitudes to life. An attempt has been made, however briefly, to indicate something of these changes and how they affected the gentleman of the day.

The diaries of Horace Walpole, Creevey, Greville, and Fanny Burney, in addition to Selwyn's letters and even Boswell's *Life of Johnson*, tend to show a restricted, artificial world, chiefly because they were mostly written round the Court, or in restricted circles of the times with a view to publication. The sources used here have been principally the lesser known, less well-publicised diarists, letter writers and observers of the scene. Thus we have John Knyveton, whose pithy observations from his medical school days to his death at the age of eighty in 1809 tend to be lost when read by themselves; the letters of Henry Purefoy, an obscure Georgian country gentleman in the county of Buckingham; the splendidly reactionary views of Colonel John Byng, who toured the country extensively between 1781 and 1795; the acute, if sometimes biased or confused, observations of François de la Rochefoucauld, a young French visitor to Britain in 1784; and many others. When taken together, these present a pattern of life as lived by the Georgian gentleman.

The Georgian era, of course, must be said to include the reigns of the first four Georges: the one hundred and sixteen years from George I's accession in 1714 (on the death of Queen Anne) to the death of George IV in 1830 at the age of sixty-eight. The early Hanoverians were heavy Germanic characters, speaking poor English with strong, guttural accents and lacking any real understanding of the English. This, combined with the Jacobite rebellion of 1715 and the later more serious rebellion of 1745, resulted in a very understandable ambivalence in many minds, reflected in John Byrom's satirical verse:

God bless the King, I mean the Faith's Defender;
God bless — no harm in blessing — the Pretender:
But who Pretender is, or who is King,
God bless us all — that's quite another thing.

The accession of George III in 1760, the first of his line to be educated in England, marked a very real change. The sordid 'cheap gin' era of the thirties and forties had been characterised by a low birth-rate and general employment. The increasing pace of the enclosures throughout the eighteenth century, resulting in more efficient farming, led to widespread poverty and misery for those who were dispossessed and forced off the land into the towns. A rising birth-rate and high unemployment marked the end of the Georgian era. The way was paved for the Industrial Revolution of the mid-nineteenth century. Yet those clamouring for the abolition of slavery did little for the child mill workers in the newly built Midlands factories.

Throughout the greater part of his long reign from 1760 to 1820, George III achieved a more positive control over Parliament than any monarch since the Restoration. The ruling factions, powerful political families and cliques controlling enough 'rotten boroughs' to ensure a degree of control in Parliament, were unable to sway the 'King's men', those private gentlemen who in the last analysis could always be expected to vote for the King. The monarch, right or wrong, was seen to be above the bribery, place-seeking and political manoeuvring of the House of Commons, or their superiors in the Lords. It was not until the accession of George IV, whom no one trusted despite his curious ability to project a certain air of dignity in all but his very worst moments, that the terms Whig, Radical and Tory began to have real meaning.

In those sixty years, America gained independence, but Captain Cook discovered Australia and New Zealand. Thanks to stringent Game and Criminal Laws, the new colony at Botany Bay was soon being populated with transported criminals guilty, perhaps, of stealing a loaf of bread to feed their starving families. At the same time Canada was the goal for many immigrants from the north of Scotland and the depopulated farming areas of the south. Trade with India, by then almost completely under British rule, was providing an expanding market for industry. The development of the canals, of new turnpike roads and ever-improving stage coach services, was revolutionising communications at home. The Victorian era of industry and commerce was foreshadowed by events in the latter part of the Georgian period.

Lord Chesterfield's definition of a gentleman in *The World* is worth reading in full, since it covers satisfactorily all the various points on which an eighteenth-century gentleman was vulnerable.

'Every man, who with a tolerable suit of clothes, a sword by his side and a watch and snuff-box in his pockets, asserts himself to be a gentleman, swears with energy that he will be treated as such and that he will cut the throat of any man who presumes to say the contrary.

'A gentleman, which is now the genteel synonymous term for a man of honour, must like his Gothic ancestors be ready for and rather desirous of single combat. And if by a proper degree of wrong headedness he provokes it, he is only so much the more jealous of his honour and more of a gentleman.

'He may lie with impunity, if he is neither detected nor accused of it; for it is not the lie he tells, but the lie he is told of, that dishonours him. In that case he demonstrates his veracity by his sword or his pistol and either kills or is killed with the greatest honour.

'He may abuse and starve his own wife, daughters or sisters and he may seduce those of other men, particularly his friends, with inviolate honour, because, as Sir John Brute very justly observes, *he wears a sword.*

'By the laws of honour he is not obliged to pay his servants or his tradesmen, for as they are a pack of scoundrels, they cannot without insolence demand their due of a gentleman; but he must punctually pay his gaming debts to the sharpers who have cheated him, for those debts are really debts of honour.

'He lies under one disagreeable restraint, for he must not cheat at play, unless in a horse match, but then he may with great honour defraud in an office or betray a trust.

'In public affairs, he may, not only with honour, but even a certain degree of lustre, be in the same session a turbulent patriot, opposing the best measures, and a servile courtier, promoting the worst; provided a very lucrative consideration be known to be the motive of his conversation, for in that case the point of honour turns solely upon the quantum.'

Chapter One
BIRTH, CHILDHOOD AND UPBRINGING

'Children, being not reasonable, can only be governed by fear.' — Dr.
Samuel Johnson

Life in the eighteenth century was much nearer to nature than is easily
envisaged today. Throughout the Georgian era the cycle of birth, life
and death was freely accepted with a resigned acknowledgment that
birth not infrequently involved the death of either the mother or, more
often, the child, or sometimes both. Infant mortality was high and the
incidence of death in childbirth was very high indeed. Childbed fever,
or puerperal fever, generally the result of insanitary conditions, was
common and any sort of complication was likely to result in the loss of
the child, if not the mother as well. In an age when disinfectants were
unknown because the reasons for infection were not even remotely
understood, when no form of anaesthetic was available and when medical knowledge was scanty in the extreme (still close to the mediaeval
theories of 'humours'), little more could be expected. When the young
doctors had to resort to body snatching from graveyards to obtain
corpses for dissection, it is scarcely surprising that medical progress
was slow and knowledge strictly limited.

Some idea of the primitive standards prevailing at this time may be
derived from a young doctor who, in 1751, gave this description of one
of London's leading hospitals:

'Dr. Urquehart at the entry changes his peruke for a tie wig and
puts on a short coat as his full-skirted one would brush the walls and
sweep from them the lice and other insects which infect them. The
wards at first sight rather curious; the beds of moderate width and
containing not more than three to four patients, but these placed the
feet of one to the head of another so that each receives not the tainted
effluvium of their respective complaints. In the infants' wards there
were of course any from six to eight in one bed. Pregnant women have
their own ward to which they are taken when the pains seize them. . . .
Those in the earlier stages are frequently put with those about to die so
that comfort is had by both. The air rather foul . . . since the windows
cannot be allowed open. For the safety of those that minister to them it

is customary for them to carry some prophylactic which can be held to the nostrils . . . as a rule a sponge soaked in vinegar. . . .'

Such a hospital, of course, was for the poorer classes only and not for the wife of a gentleman. For her, childbirth took place in the home. In general she would be attended by a midwife only. Throughout the early part of the eighteenth century there was considerable prejudice against the male obstetrician, or man-midwife, as he was termed. When men-midwives were seen going about their task in the poorer districts they were liable to be jeered at and even pelted with filth. With their superior knowledge of anatomy, if little else, they gradually overcame the prejudice against them and by the year 1783 the Royal College of Physicians had accepted midwifery as an art deserving a licence. From then onwards, the Georgian gentleman and his wife increasingly came to accept male obstetricians as part of the scene at childbirth.

Even so, we find General George Hanger enjoying himself at the expense of 'men-midwives' as late as 1814: 'Custom governs and sanctions everything,' he wrote, 'or how could the most delicate and decent woman permit a man-midwife, six foot high and two feet broad, over the loins, to attend them during their pregnancy; taking liberties but *only professionally* to know whether the child lies right &c and after that to deliver them?

'I have often thought that we men have lost a very great benefit and pleasure from women not having studied physic, so as to take out their *diplomas as physicians.* . . . To be sure there are some disorders in man which might put a lady to the blush to examine at first, but if they would but consider what great liberties the fair sex allow men-midwives to take with them, without even blushing, I am of the opinion that with a little time and practice, they might handle any part of a man with the same indifference they would handle a cucumber or carrot.'

The standards of knowledge of the average midwife, or even of the average physician, concerning the obstetric arts were remarkably low, and the number of deaths caused purely by ignorance was great. Considering the treatment to which they were frequently subjected, it is not surprising that our eighteenth-century ancestors had to be tough to survive. If they were not tough they died, but however tough they were the treatment to which they were exposed was sometimes too much even for the stoutest constitution. The following instance, vividly recorded by a man-midwife in 1765, was appalling even by the primitive standards of the day. After being woken by a handful of gravel pattering against his window at dawn one May morning, he noted:

'Stumbling downstairs with that awful sense of premature resurrection inseparable from early calls . . . would I please come *immediate* . . . a wench in the next street screaming the tiles off the roof . . . attended by a spotty faced fat hag of a midwife breathing vinous fumes and a tall thin yellow-visaged physician, Dr. S-. . . . The woman being

Lord Chesterfield, son of the Earl of Burlington, as a boy of six or seven, while still in petticoats. The feminine influence of the Georgian nursery is marked. (Radio Times Hulton Picture Library)

in the second stage of labour all the previous day, and her pains so violent, Dr. S- had administered an opiate and so she got some relief; but the pains ceasing and the midwife unable to deliver, and so Dr. S- again sent for; this at dusk; and applied the fillet, at great pain to the mother . . . but being unsuccessful left the fillet in position and went home for dinner; the patient recovering completely from the opiate and beginning to scream, so that he once more summoned. . . .

'There was but little I could do . . . And so to ease the wretched quean . . . far gone in stupor; kindly Death shall give her peace.'

Even by the low standards of the times such callousness was rare. Due to lack of anaesthetics the usual recourse was to provide laudanum, or opium, to deaden pain, but the commonest cause of death in childbirth was the dreaded puerperal fever, the reasons for which were not understood. The normal remedies of bleeding, purging or blistering, to which the average physician had to resort in turn when in doubt, or on occasions all three at once, proved of little avail in such cases. In his diary the same man-midwife revealed:

'Two women have died from the childbed fever. Am at a loss to understand the reason. In the miasma of hospitals it is to be expected, but not in private houses. . . . In the Hotel Dieu at Paris and other large continental institutes, the disorder at times becomes almost an epidemic, bleeding and purging being powerless to check it.'

In the nature of things Caesarians were very rarely attempted and far beyond the skill of the average practitioner. Due to lack of knowledge of antiseptic treatment they were invariably unsuccessful. When it came to a choice between mother and child the obstetrician normally tried to save the mother, aware that without effective means of contraception another child was likely to be born within a year.

Even when an infant had been safely delivered, the odds against survival were considerable. The hazards of life for the very young were numerous. To start with, the child of the Georgian gentleman was usually suckled by a wet nurse obtained prior to birth. Inevitably such a person was of poor circumstances and background, and though she was doubtless vetted for her health and general cleanliness, the system was clearly open to abuse. As late as 1800 Elizabeth Grant remembered the treatment to which her brother William, heir to a considerable fortune and son of a Member of Parliament, was exposed by his wet nurse — apparently quite a presentable woman. In her memoirs, Miss Grant recorded that the nurse 'had William from his birth and to test the strength of the young heir she gave him, before she washed him, a spoonful of gin . . . which medicine he survived.'

Some contemporary medical advice on children's diet and care makes for startling reading. The suggestions of the well known Dr. Heberden (quoted by Mrs. Charlotte Mason in her *Ladies' Assistant* in 1786) are an example. As Mrs. Mason was 'A professed Housekeeper who had upward of Thirty Years Experience in Families of the first Fashion' and her book ran into several editions, it may be assumed that many families followed her advice. She noted that the 'water of the Thames and that of the New River are very often muddy or taste strongly of weeds and leaves. Dr. Heberden acknowledges that the latter fault cannot be easily remedied; but, he observes, they would soon be freed from their muddiness if kept some time in an open jar; and . . . if the water given to very young children were thus purified, it might prevent some of their bowel disorders and so contribute a little to lessen that amazing mortality among the children which are nurtured in London.'

One must bear in mind that the modern amenity of running tap water, which we tend to take for granted, was non-existent in Georgian times. All water for household use was pumped up from wells, obtained from rainwater kept in cisterns or butts, or else transported to the house in casks. To obtain anything resembling pure drinking water was therefore difficult, especially in or near London where the pump water was usually unwholesome. As Mrs. Mason revealed, pump or spring water in London generally suffered badly from the effects of 'impurities from cellars, burying grounds, common-sewers and many other offensive places,' so that it was often thought preferable to drink the water from the river Thames.

Even on this score, she observed that the 'Thames water . . . is mixed with many impure ingredients. It is said to become offensive in seven or eight days . . . if it be kept in unseasoned casks. In this state it generates a quantity of foul inflammable air, as may be seen by holding the flame of a candle to the bung-hole of a cask, when it is first opened. But by this fermentation it soon purifies itself; and by opening the bung it will often become sweet in twenty-four hours.'

The fact that the navy often filled their casks with Thames water may well account for some outbreaks of dysentry which occasionally swept through a ship. The adult stomach, hardened by practice to drinking impure water, usually survived unimpaired, though doubtless many stomach and bladder disorders were traceable to this source. Few adults, however, drank water without adding wine, spirits or ale. Indeed, only the very young child was likely to drink water by itself and hence was liable to fall victim to water-borne germs from dysentery to typhus. In the circumstances, the high mortality rate among young children is not as surprising as the fact that any survived at all, for germs in drinking water were only one of many hazards.

Elizabeth Grant, referring to childhood friends of 1798, mentioned 'little Johnny Redfearn, who died at five years of age, to the abiding grief of his parents; he was the last survivor of their once well-filled nursery.' Due to lack of effective contraception, large families were the rule and childless couples were rare. Yet once the children had been

5

passed to the wet nurse the parents seem to have paid them scant attention during nursery days, save perhaps to enforce discipline when required to do so.

The nursery régime, of course, differed greatly from household to household, much depending on the number of children, servants and the degree of enlightenment of the nursery maids, governess or other attendants. Maiden aunts, or poor female relatives, to whom the care of the nursery was often delegated, might be overwhelmingly maternal, spoiling their charges out of all reason, or uncaring and negligent, or even sadistically ruthless. Direct contact with the parents was virtually unknown in the nursery and the degree of parental supervision varied enormously.

George Elers later recorded that 'soon after I was born (in 1777) I

An example of bullying common in schools during the Georgian era. Termed cockfighting, the younger boys with hands bound and broom-sticks behind the knees were forced to fight each other with their feet. (Radio Times Hulton Picture Library)

was sent into Hertfordshire to be nursed by a woman named Holmes living at Berkhampstead. . . .' On being weaned, he was entrusted to a childless uncle and aunt in Northamptonshire, 'with whom I experienced every indulgence. I at that early age, little more than four, used to ride, with the groom, the horses to water in the village, without a saddle, and accompany my uncle shooting when I grew bigger. Nothing delighted me more than carrying home the game . . . (but) my education was not neglected. I was taught . . . by an old schoolmaster . . . and by the time I was six years old could both read and write.'

Petted and pampered by his aunt and uncle and their servants and friends, George Elers looked back with pleasure on his childhood days with them. When his mother finally came to take him to school at the age of eight, the wrench must have been considerable to him. Until then

Tossing smaller boys in blankets. Fear of hitting the ceiling or floor made this a considerable ordeal for nervous boys. (Radio Times Hulton Picture Library)

he had barely seen his mother, and she was virtually a stranger to him. Added to that, one of his earliest memories was of receiving a severe whipping from his father at age three. It is scarcely surprising that he subsequently felt himself lacking in filial affection for his parents.

Elizabeth Grant, her brother William and sister Jane were not sent away like this, but she commented: 'My mother never had such an idea as that of entering her nursery; when she wanted her children or her maids she rang for them.' In their upbringing the young Grant children were less fortunate than George Elers. Their nursemaid, Mrs. Millar, though highly regarded by their mother, was a psychopathic tyrant, finally dismissed for striking the children against their father's orders. Despite this dismissal their mother's testimonial gave her such a fine character that she went on to the Duke of Roxburgh's household where, for some childish fault, she punished the young Duke by holding him under water in a cold bath. Luckily, when quite insensible, he was rescued through the fortunate intervention of a footman. Not unexpectedly, she was committed to a lunatic asylum where she ended her days.

A nursery tyrant of this kind, unless properly supervised, could turn childhood into a nightmare. Elizabeth Grant wrote bitterly how in 1806 the 'nursery breakfast was . . . dry bread and cold milk the year round. . . . In town a large long tub stood in the kitchen court, the ice on top of which often had to be broken before our horrid plunge into it; we were brought down from the very top of the house, four pairs of stairs, with only a cotton cloak over our night gowns. . . . How I screamed, begged, prayed, entreated to be saved, half the tender-hearted maids in tears beside me; all no use, Millar had her orders. . . . Nearly senseless I have been taken to the housekeeper's room, which was always warm, to be dried; there we dressed, without any flannel, and in cotton frocks with short sleeves and low necks.'

In such circumstances, it is astonishing that the children ever survived, although not all households were quite as spartan as this. Yet throughout the eighteenth century, on the whole little attention was paid to child care. In the nursery, upbringing was extremely haphazard and comfort or wishes were seldom studied. The best that children could expect was to be reared in the manner of George Elers, an only child, the centre of attraction.

Of course, even in such a household as that, all boys until the age of six or eight were dressed in frocks and wore long hair like girls. In this respect, there was little difference between the sexes at first glance, although in practice the difference was generally obvious in more ways than one. Thus one learns from George Hanger, writing in 1814, that 'custom is prevalent and custom establishes everything; for the same nurse, who looks after little miss and little master, tells little miss provided she shows only one inch of her ancle — "O fie miss, for shame, you shew your ancle; that is very indelicate!" and with the next breath she tells little master to take up his (petti)coats and *piss like a man!*'

Colonel John Byng, while at Oxford on the first of his frequent tours of England between 1781 and 1794, also describes juvenile dress — in this case that of a child with unusual musical talent: '. . . we went to tea at Mr. R.'s, where we had been invited to hear an infant in petticoats play tunes upon the violin, taught him by his father, a watch-maker. . . . On being asked if he could play by note; Why aye, says he, give me the book, and then you'll see. . . . Master Cobham (aged 5 years, 3 months) knew all his notes perfectly well, and could play anything at sight with tolerable grace. . . . He retired highly pleased with a golden sixpence . . . tho' being puny, it is probable that great attention to musick may destroy him.'

George Elers also remembered his younger brother Edward at the age of four as 'a fine little fellow in petticoats . . . very saucy . . . and daring — in short, a boy any mother might well be proud of.' Despite the fact that he himself wore petticoats, this does not seem to have prevented him from indulging in boyish pursuits and he recalled with pleasure 'the delight I took in beating the covers after game, riding, fishing, etc.' He also records that when aged seven in 1784, or there-abouts, he was presented with the first boy's suit of clothes he ever wore and '. . . how impatiently I lay in bed the morning they came from the tailor's, waiting for my favourite maid to dress me in them.' Small wonder that he looked back on those childhood days as among the happiest of his early memories.

Inevitably life was not so pleasant in the Grant household under the domineering Mrs. Millar. The children were locked in a small room 'reserved for the purpose' on a diet of bread and water for minor transgressions. When this solitary confinement was not considered suf-ficient, they 'were flogged . . . boys and girls alike' by their father. Yet despite all this, Elizabeth Grant maintained:

'. . . we had very happy hours as well; despotically as we were ruled in some respects, we were left in other ways to our own devices. We disposed of our time very much according to our fancies, subject to certain rules. We were always to appear at the breakfast table of our father and mother some time between ten and eleven o'clock; the last of the three regular ringings of my father's dressing room bell was our signal for leaving our plays; we ran off to brush our hair, wash our hands and seize our books, with which provided we repaired to the breakfast-room, where our duties were to run messages; in summer to amuse ourselves quietly until called upon to stir; in winter to make the toast. Breakfast over, we said our few lessons to my mother, and read in turns.'

The amusements of the day were simple and the children had in general to occupy themselves. The lessons they received depended greatly on the individual households. They might vary from the hapha-zard teaching the Grant children received to the more formal tuition of the retired schoolmaster who taught George Elers. Sometimes the ser-vices of the local parson were sought, or a governess, or even a tutor employed. More rarely some parents might even take a hand in teaching their children, prior to their sons' education either at the hands of a tutor or increasingly at one of the public schools taking fee-paying pupils.

Of course, the greatest exponent of the art of teaching and advising his offspring was Philip Dormer Stanhope, fourth Earl of Chesterfield, whose definition of a gentleman has already been quoted. His letters to his illegitimate son, Philip Stanhope, born in 1732, started in 1739 when the wretched child was a mere seven-year-old. Admittedly these letters were never intended for publication, since they were aimed at forming the boy's character as his father watched him developing. Published at the instigation of his daughter-in-law in 1774, the year after Chester-field's death, they quickly ran through many editions. Their frank cyni-cism and worldly attitudes invited ridicule and lampoons, which were not lacking, but it must be realised that they were never intended for other than his son's eyes.

Two of the livelier lampoons are worth quoting in part as showing the kind of advice Chesterfield impressed on the youngster in the early stages. The first, entitled *The Graces,* by William Woty, was mainly a burlesque of the style of the letters:

> 'Adieu and let the Graces be your text,
> But I'll be more explicit in my next:
> There I will teach thee, with a sire's concern,
> All that is proper for a son to learn;
> In pleasing segments how to pare your nails,
> Segments must please, as long as taste prevails . . .
> And how to cut and eat a currant tart,
> Nor let your napkin, or your chin have part.'

The other lampoon — *By a Lady (Anon)* and dated 1776 — was more deadly and spiked with malice, as this extract shows:

> 'Form friendships, but let it be only with those,
> On whose fond credulity you may impose;
> Their confidence gain'd, unsuspected you'll soon,
> Discover their secrets, and make them your own:
> 'T'is of honor no breach, to betray thus a friend,
> If you find to you Int'rest 'twill visibly tend:
> These maxims, thro' life, I would have you pursue,
> I practis'd them once, and now hand them to you:

Children playing at marbles in the latter part of the Georgian era. The schoolboy on the right is presumably the elder brother in this family scene (aged about 12). The young child in petticoats, centre, could be either male or female. (Radio Times Hulton Picture Library)

Successful they were, they brought honors and fame,
For still I had art to preserve my good name . . .
In your person be cleanly, I humbly intreat,
And attend to your teeth, that your breath may be sweet,
Your nails too keep par'd, I outrageous should be,
If them, tipt with black, I should happen to see . . .
A father I am, to your faults nothing blind,
And claim a free licence for speaking my mind;
By this lecture on cleanliness, all I propose is,
That you may not offend people's eyes, or their noses.

Dr. Johnson's indictment of the Chesterfield letters — as liable to 'teach the morals of a whore and the manners of a dancing master' — is of course one of his sweeping exaggerations with a sufficient kernel of truth to make it arguable. Later he qualified this, observing that they 'might be made a very pretty book. Take out the immorality and it should be put in the hands of every young gentleman.' True. Chesterfield's tastes were not those of the average Georgian gentleman of his time, for he himself was more at ease with the attitudes then current on the Continent. In fact, like many another witty and worldly wise man, Chesterfield knew little about children and never really understood his son.

Three boys aged about seven or eight in the late Georgian era playing at whipping a wooden top. (Radio Times Hulton Picture Library)

Although in parts tedious, prosy and repetitive, some of the letters — especially the later ones when his son was touring Europe — possess both charm and interest. Some are also informative and witty. Yet their success — especially that of the numerous editions published in the nineteenth century — was due not to style or content, but to the aspirations of middle class parents who naively imagined that the letters must be the ideal guide to gentlemanly behaviour because they were written by an earl.

Chapter Two

SCHOOLS, UNIVERSITY AND GRAND TOUR

'The rod produces an effect which terminates in itself. A child is afraid of being whipped, and gets his task, and there's an end on't' — *Dr. Samuel Johnson*

Throughout the eighteenth century the education of a gentleman's sons was liable to be haphazard, although as the century progressed a certain pattern began to emerge. In the earlier years, during the reigns of the first two Georges, the private tutor was frequently regarded as the best and simplest solution to the problem. It was easy enough to engage a poor graduate in holy orders unable to secure a living, who for a modest fee, would take on a boy's education. Such a tutor was not expensive to keep while the advantages accruing to the tutor could be substantial. On the successful conclusion of the boy's education, he was often expected to 'bear-lead' his charge on a tour of Europe. Thereafter, if his employer had influence, he might help in securing a living. The patronage of a living was frequently within the power of a modest country gentleman and the arrangement admirably suited both parties to the bargain.

As the century progressed, fee-paying schools emerged as convenient and desirable places in which to educate a gentleman's sons. The more prominent of them were originally founded as grammar schools for local poor scholars. Where their foundations allowed it, naturally enough the principal ushers, or headmasters, eagerly increased the number of fee-paying pupils as a source of revenue. Throughout the century certain schools — notably Eton, Harrow, Rugby, Westminster and Winchester — slowly built up their reputations, their fortunes fluctuating according to the principals' degree of skill at attracting the sons of the nobility. Frequently, the fee-paying pupils far outnumbered the local scholars for whom the foundation was originally intended. Thus, for instance, as early as 1718 there were 144 boys at Harrow, of whom 104 were 'foreigners'.

In the first part of the century the boys, who were often accompanied by their tutors, generally lived in lodgings near the school, but even so were usually far beyond the control of their ineffectual, underpaid ushers. The introduction of boarding houses, as a rule superintended by 'dames', was the first administrative step towards greater control. Another was the institution of 'praeposters', or prefects — older boys placed in charge of the younger ones, with power to make them 'fag' or serve them in menial ways.

Despite these innovations, most schools suffered occasional rebellions, or mutinies, resulting in mass expulsions or floggings; so much so that when George III met an Etonian he invariably asked, 'Have you had a rebellion lately, eh, eh?' In 1797, Dr. Ingles, headmaster of Rugby, had his door blown open by gunpowder. The boys at Harrow were even more ambitious, setting up a road block and blowing up one of the governor's carriages.

Flogging with a birch, or caning with a rod until blood was drawn from the bare buttocks, was the normal and accepted punishment for transgression. Dr. Samuel Parr of Harrow considered himself humane because he never flogged a boy twice in the same lesson. Some masters were little more than sadists and gloried in their powers to punish. Thus Dr. Keate, the headmaster of Eton, was said to have flogged eighty boys in one day, merely regretting that he had not flogged more.

In his reminiscences, Captain Gronow mentions the case of the young man who was promoted to the command of a frigate. Having suffered under such maltreatment, he invited his old master to dine with him. As soon as the tyrant stepped unsuspectingly on board, the young captain ordered the grinning bosun to tie·him to the mast and give him two dozen lashes, informing the protesting usher that he had promised himself this treat ever since leaving school. In general, however, floggings were looked upon as part of school routine, though if overdone resentment could readily turn into rebellion.

As a rule, schools were so crowded that two or even more boys usually slept in a bed. Fighting, both internally and 'town versus gown,' was also commonplace, and the food was generally so poor and insufficient that it had to be supplemented in the school tuck shop. Bullying and initiation ceremonies, such as blanket tossing and other forms of torture, were an accepted part of scholastic life, in which Latin translation dominated the classroom for years, although in the latter part of the century, French, writing, drawing, dancing and fencing were added to the curriculum in the more enlightened establishments.

In the circumstances, it is surprising that useful work was accomplished at all, yet there were notable exceptions. Cowper, the poet, for instance, while at Westminster School between 1741 and 1749, read a large part of Milton and the whole of·Homer in Greek for his own pleasure and on his own initiative. Ten years later — in 1759 — he wrote:

'Would you your son should be a sot or dunce,
Lascivious, headstrong, or all these at once;
That in good time the stripling's finished taste
For loose expense and fashionable waste
Should prove your ruin, and his own at last;
Train him in public with a mob of boys . . .'

Chesterfield echoed these sentiments in a letter to his son Philip in January 1750, when he admitted, 'You have, hitherto I confess, had very few opportunities of keeping polite company. Westminster School is undoubtedly the seat of illiberal manners and brutal behaviour.'

There was little difference between any of the major schools. It was certainly easy for a boy to go astray in many ways. An example of the type quoted by Cowper was John Mytton, famed in his brief hey-day for his eccentric exploits and for hardly ever drawing a sober breath. He acquired his taste for drink at Rugby and never looked back, dying eventually in the debtors' prison.

With almost total recall, George Elers gives us a first-hand account of how he felt on going to school in 1785 as a boarder at an establishment in Chiswick. With him went his brother who, four years his senior, had been there some time.

'One fine winter morning,' he recalled, 'my father and mother took us both in a glass coach to Mr. Crawford's school at Chiswick. I had but one consolation; my little pockets were stuffed out with oranges, nuts, apples and sweetmeats, and a large purse filled with half-crowns, shillings and sixpences. In the course of the first hour on my arrival in the schoolroom the head usher, a tall, pale-faced young man in the last stage of consumption, by the name of the Reverend Mr. Lancaster, took me by the hand, opened his desk, and pointing to a large rod, hoped I never should be better acquainted with it. The schoolroom was a large one, capable of holding 100 boys; folding doors divided it from the dining room, which was also devoted to dancing, drawing and fencing — twice a week . . .

'The dwelling house, a very large one, was devoted to the parlour boarders and as sleeping rooms for the rest of the boys. In the room in which my brother and self slept were about eight beds, each containing two boys; among them some very big ones. Among the oldest of the boys was one by the name of Holdroyd and he gave me to understand that I was to be his fag and that among other things I was to do for him was to clean his shoes and fetch his water in a large pitcher to wash himself with and to do other jobs that he might require. At first the novelty of the thing amused me, but afterwards being obliged to get out of my warm bed half an hour earlier than the usual time of rising proved to be a hardship and source of annoyance.'

Clearly Mr. Crawford's school at Chiswick was a well-run estab-

An usher about to flog an idle scholar in the mid-eighteenth century. By their dress and background this was probably a fee-paying establishment, such as Westminster, and the pupils are taking their turn to construe a Latin exercise. (Radio Times Hulton Picture Library)

lishment by the standards of the times. Elers, referring to the weekly routine with mixed feelings, mentions that a 'clean, respectable, middle-aged woman attended the school twice a week with a wicker basket covered over with a white napkin, containing apples, oranges, ginger bread, nuts, elecampans and nice lollipops. Every Sunday a friend of my father's called upon my brother and myself and took us into the village to a pastrycook by name Rabbinell and stuffed us with good things, afterwards bringing us home and invariably dismissing us with a shilling piece in our pockets, which as constantly found its way into those of our friend Molly.

'Every Saturday night the junior part of the school underwent a thorough good scrubbing from two damsels standing and presiding over a large tub of water, with yellow soap and towels coarse enough for a mainsail of a man-of-war. These two nymphs used to scrub us most unmercifully. My skin was particularly tender and delicate, and the rough and pitiless Hannah caused me to roar out most lamentably. The other girl was called Peggy — pretty though slightly marked with the small pox.'

He appears to have been involved in a number of fights, in 'the playground, in front of a high wall where we used to play fives,' but nothing very serious. On one occasion the elder brother of his opponent, 'seeing us quarrelling, took one in each hand and declared we should settle it as gentlemen.' He mentions the inevitable bullying almost as a matter of course and does not seem to have suffered unduly:

'Among other methods of tyranny which the elder boys practised upon the younger ones was to force them to strip themselves naked, go downstairs, and when the frost and snow had been on the ground to run round the playground three or four times while they lay snug in their warm beds. Tossing the little boys in blankets was another favourite diversion; pulling off the bed clothes and giving them what they called "cold pigs" another. All these freaks, they said, were to make them hardy and tough. It appeared to me very severe discipline brought up as I was from my earliest recollections with so much care and indulgence.'

He wrote much more feelingly on the subject of a drunken usher, who was probably fairly typical. The standards of the day were not high and unqualified teachers were the rule rather than the exception, but in every way — with this one exception — Mr. Crawford seems to have been responsible for a well-run establishment. On the subject of the masters, Elers recalled:

'I endured much cruelty from an Irish usher by the name of Sullivan. He had the charge of the little boys and used to teach them Latin grammar. This brute used to walk into the country of a Sunday afternoon and amuse himself with cutting from the hedges ash sticks sufficient to last for the week until they got broken on our little backs and arms. He then concluded his evening by getting drunk at some hedge ale-house, the effects of which were visible on the next day, Monday; for he was always half asleep the whole of that day, and being afflicted with an inveterate asthma, he had a most disgusting way of expectorating on the floor. . . . The undermasters . . . were in general kind and good tempered, particularly Mr. Crawford, who wore a large, bushy Johnsonian wig, and in person was not unlike, but not as tall as, the great lexicographer.'

George Elers remained at the Chiswick School until that autumn, when he was sent home with measles. In his absence, the kindly Mr. Crawford died of dropsy. He was then sent in the spring, as a half boarder, to the Reverend Dr. Barrow's school in Soho where, out of eighty to a hundred boys, he specifically mentioned: 'A boy called Boys, who left school for two or three months to go to sea and joined as a jolly "mid" the *Queen Charlotte* just before Lord Howe's victory on June 1. He got his leg shot off in the action and immediately he got well he returned to school to finish his education. You may suppose how all the boys stared when he stumped into school on his wooden leg, for he was so short a time absent he was scarcely missed.'

Elers seems to have been of a philosophical turn of mind, and to have taken life as it came. All the same he was more fortunate than many schoolboys of his time. Elizabeth Grant's reference in her memoirs to her brother's schooldays makes this plain:

'In the Spring of 1808 William was sent to Eton, not ten, poor child! very unfit for the buffetings of that large public school, where the little boys were utterly neglected by the masters and made mere slaves and drudges by the elder boys, many of whom used their fags unmercifully. William was fortunate in this respect, his first master was the present Duke of Leinster, a very good natured lad; his dame, too, Mrs. Denton, was kind to all her boys in a sort of way; but poor William was far from happy, as he told us in confidence at mid-summer, though it would have been incorrect to allow this publicly. We were proud of having a brother at Eton then, now I look back with horror at this school of corruption, where weak characters make shipwreck of all worth.'

The cost of such schooling, whether good or bad, was by no means prohibitive. An outline of the expense involved in educating a boy named James Powell is to be found in the *Shardeloe Papers*. In 1753, at the Reverend Richardson Wood's school in Northampton, his schooling and board for the second half of the year — from July to Christmas — was only £2.10s., with extras valued at £1.14s. On going to Harrow in 1755 his half-year's board was £7, which, with the addition of books and other extras, finally amounted to £12.8s.7d. His pocket money started at 4d. a week and advanced to 6d. weekly after two years. He finally left Harrow in 1763, by which time the boarding fees had risen to £8 a half-year, but, even so, the total cost of his seven-and-a-half years' education was only £206.17s.8d. Even including the cost of all his clothes and general maintenance for the period the grand total was still only £367.10s.2d.

Unfortunately this schooling does not seem to have prepared him well for Oxford, for, though he entered Queen's College, it was noted: 'James Powel went to Oxford 21 March 1763 and left that Place 26 July following.' Among the bills marked 'unpaid' which he incurred was one from a vintner, Edward King, for 65 bottles of port, 7 bottles of Mountain (or Malaga), 5 bottles of rum, 2 bottles of Madeira and 1 bottle of claret, amounting to a total of 81 bottles drunk over a period of 85 days. His outfitting for the university cost £30 beforehand and £85 on arrival, of which about £5 was spent on books.

Clearly not studious, he was sent out as an ensign in the East India Company's service to Madras. His new outfit for this venture cost £192.7s.2d. The last we hear of him was his promotion to captain on the coast of Coromandel in 1771. It thus appears that the expense of rearing a young man from birth to command an outpost of the Empire was around £800.

James Powell seems to have missed the chance to travel on the Continent. A visit to Europe — customarily termed 'The Grand Tour' — was regarded as an opportunity to acquire polish and taste, as well as a certain knowledge of the world, before going on to the university. In some cases, as with Charles James Fox, a visit to the Continent actually took place while at university and in some instances it was postponed until afterwards. In any event, the spectacle of young Englishmen touring Europe in groups and earnestly imbibing culture from their tutors, or else misbehaving in the worst possible fashion, was apparently common. Although in some cases the benefits were outstanding, in general it appears to have been a complete waste of time. Sir Joshua Reynolds, for example, noted: 'Some Englishmen while I was in the Vatican came there and spent above six hours in writing down whatever the antiquary dictated to them. They scarcely ever looked at the paintings the whole time.'

Chesterfield, writing to his son while he was touring the Continent with his tutor, Mr. Harte, warned him as follows:

'May 15 1749 . . . I am informed there are now many English at the Academy in Turin; and I fear those are just so many dangers for you to encounter. Who they are I do not know, but I well know the general ill-conduct, the indecent behaviour, and the illiberal views of my young countrymen abroad; especially where they are in numbers together. . . . There are degrees in vices as well as in virtues; and I must do my countrymen the justice to say they generally take their vices in the lowest degree. . . . Their pleasures of the table end in beastly drunkenness, low riot, broken windows and very often (as they well deserve) broken bones. They game for the sake of vice, not of the amusement; and therefore carry it to excess . . . they come home, the unimproved, illiberal and ungentlemanlike creatures that one daily sees them . . . they become the disturber of the playhouse; they break the windows, and commonly the landlords, of the taverns where they drink; and are at once the support, the terror and the victims of the bawdy houses they frequent. . . .'

Mr. Harte and Philip soon reached agreement that they wished to stay longer in Rome. Despite reminders and hints from Chesterfield, they remained there far longer than he had intended. In January 1750, there appeared in his correspondence a querulous note which (had he but appreciated the point) was common to many fathers with sons on the Continent. 'It is so long since I heard from you,' he wrote, 'that I suppose Rome engrosses every moment of your time.'

In April, Chesterfield returned to the attack on the subject of the English abroad, writing:

'London April 30 1750: Mr. Harte . . . told me . . . that at Rome you had constantly preferred the established Italian assemblies to the English conventicles set up against them by dissenting English ladies. That shows sense and that you know what you are sent abroad for. . . . Pray continue this judicious conduct . . . especially at Paris, where,

Cricket in Marylebone Fields about 1745 after Hayman, The Royal Academy Club, afterwards the Marylebone Cricket Club. Note the curved bats and two stumps only, also the underarm bowler. (Radio Times Hulton Picture Library)

instead of thirty, you will find above three hundred English herding together and conversing with no one French body.

'The life of *les Milords Anglais* is regularly, or if you will, irregularly this. As soon as they rise, which is very late, they breakfast together, to the utter loss of two good morning hours. Then they go by coachfuls to the Palais, the Invalides, and Notre Dame: from thence to the English coffee house, where they make up their tavern party for dinner. From dinner where they drink quick, they adjourn in clusters to the play, where they crowd up to the stage, drest up in very fine clothes, very ill made by a Scotch or Irish tailor. From the play to the tavern again, where they get very drunk, and where they either quarrel among themselves, or sally forth, to commit some riot in the streets and are taken up by the watch. Those who do not speak French before they go are sure to learn none there. . . . Thus they return home more petulant, but not more informed than when they left it; and show, as they think, their improvement, by affectedly both speaking and dressing in broken French.'

Chesterfield's querulous tone on not hearing from his son when abroad was rather exceeded by Lord Auchinleck on writing to the young Boswell on his 'Grand Tour' of Italy and Corsica in 1765. His letter of August 10 began: 'My dear Son — I received a letter from you dated from Rome the 4th of June and your mother received another from the same place dated the 12th of that month; and these are the last letters we have had from you. This is really inexcusable neglect. . . .'

His next letter was even stronger making his views plain: 'Edinburgh. 1 October 1765: Dear Son, Your conduct astonishes and amazes me. You solicited liberty to go for four months to Italy. I opposed it as altogether useless; but upon your pressing importunity, contrary to my own opinion, I agreed to it and thereafter allowed you one month more. You went there January last. . . . If you have any view of returning home, I desire . . . you may do so speedily; that you don't stop in France, except about ten days or a fortnight about Paris and its environs, that you may say you have been there, which is all the benefit travellers have over others. . . .'

It is not surprising that young men with these experiences behind them behaved somewhat wildly at their universities. Colonel Thomas Thornton, himself educated at Charterhouse and Glasgow University, observed in 1784 that the opportunities for vice both at Oxford and Cambridge were 'so great as to make it next to an impossibility for lively young men to resist the temptation.'

In the same year, Colonel John Byng, later fifth Viscount Torrington, entered in his diary during a visit to Oxford: 'I was up at 7 o'clock and had a most precious regale of buttermilk from Whey-Hall, a fashionable & wholesome resort of the scholars for whey and buttermilk. A most particular impertinence towards women and strangers reigns amongst these gentry, owing (as everywhere else) to a relaxation of discipline; or else I had not seen them last night roaring drunk about the streets, which is called being fresh.'

A Cambridge undergraduate of the mid-1790s, John D'Oyly, kept a diary of his activities, of which the following entries are fairly typical. Incidentally, his inclinations were more scholarly than most; indeed, he became a fellow in 1798. Since in those days there were no organised games, much of his time was spent 'lounging', drinking, playing whist or billiards, shooting in the Fens or surrounding countryside, or fishing, boating and skating on the Fens. He recorded: 'Monday 13th July 1795. Got up at six thirty and went shooting in the Fens. Breakfasted at twelve thirty. Rowed down to fish, but caught nothing. Cold weather continuing. Sailed back at five thirty. Laid out nets. Returned and drank milk. Cursed stuff. Gave me a pain in the stomach for three days.'

Another entry reads: 'Got up early and set off by the Stamford Coach from the Blue Boar at $5\frac{1}{2}$. Drove it to Huntingdon. Met and breakfasted there. . . . I drove the gig back to Cambridge. Thrown out of it by the horse's kicking, but not much hurt. Dined at Jesus. . . .'

It is possible that D'Oyly was one of a group of undergraduates who offended Colonel Byng on May 29, 1794, when he recorded in his journal: 'The Cock at Eaton a pleasant spot . . . Observing from our window, with dread and detestation, the outrageous behaviour of some Cambridge bucks, who were abroad on a route of dissipation — The waiter was shock'd! At length off they went in their gigs and tandems, at 9 o'clock to drive 19 miles to Cambridge — arm'd with broomsticks more to encourage than to repell insults; But I sadly fear discipline is lost in our schools and that our young men start blackguards and democrats.'

He went on to quote a story current at Cambridge in 1790 where a scholar, turning out his horse in the college meadow, was threatened by the master that he would cut off his nag's tail. 'Let him do it at his peril,' answer'd the scholar, 'for if he shou'd cut off my horse's tail, I vow I will cut off *his* ears.'

There was remarkable latitude about this time and on occasions degrees were awarded with little merit involved. A French visitor to this country, François de la Rochefoucauld, who toured East Anglia in 1784, quoted the extraordinary case of 'Cock' Langford, the vicar of Great Massingham in Norfolk: 'He was asked,' he wrote, 'whether the sun turns round the earth or the earth round the sun. Not knowing what to say and wanting to make some reply, he assumed an emphatic air and boldly exclaimed "Sometimes the one, sometimes the other." This reply produced so much amusement that he was made a doctor on the strength of this piece of fatuous stupidity.'

Then, as now, medical students differed from other students, being inclined both to play and work harder than their fellows. In certain respects, however, the medical student of the Georgian era had a more varied education than his modern counterpart, as the following evocative entries from the diary of John Knyveton — who in due course became a highly respected physician — reveal:

'November 4 1751: This day George Blumenfield and I to see a hanging at Tyburn of a woman who stole three loaves. Was ready enough for some diversion for have kept close to my business these last days and the stench of the Infirmary though one grows accustomed to it is tiresome for long times. Doctor Urquehart himself, though pompous, has a real mind to the Instruction of his pupils and had kindly taken seats in a nearby house for self, Grge. Blumenfield, St. Clair, Mr. Pope and three other of his young gentlemen. On taking our seats found a crowd already gathered such occasions being quite a holiday for the poor people who live in Oxford Street, and also for those in the villages of Paddington and the hamlets along the road leading to Edgware. A number of the gentry present, standing on the roofs of their coaches both the gentlemen and the ladies very fine, the bucks dressed as for a route and the ladies all powdered and patched, monstrous pretty with their scarves and great hats and flowered pannier skirts.

'The gallows a big one to take four at once but this day only the woman to be hanged and with her a boy who is to be half hanged and then cut down and whipped through the town as a warning to him against begging. George Blumenfield very merry and quizzing the ladies on the coaches and Mr. Pope kindly sends out to a drawer for cans of liquor for us all, which puts us quite happy to watch the Turning Off. The woman arrives after we had waited some twenty minutes, a young wench not ill-favoured driven in a cart tied on to a board so that she might not leap over the side; the hangman greeting her with much cheer and she answering him in kind, so that the crowd and the gentry were Highly Diverted, one buck near me with a vast wig I thought would swoon with mirth, and so she to the Tree and the hangman makes her mount upon a bucket, she being a Vagabond and of no importance, and then fastens the rope about her neck and she blowing him a kiss his assistant pulls away the bucket and she fell with a force that must instantly have deprived her of Her Vital Faculties. Was intrigued to see how the body did jerk so that I thought the rope would break.'

This educational outing was by no means finished. Knyveton, an ardent chronicler with a keen eye for detail, continued:

'Then the boy aforesaid, who had been brought there very early so that the execution might prove of instruction to him, was taken up, he squalling in a fashion that made the gentry cry Shame upon his Cowardice and proving near frantic the hangman did not trouble to tie him to the tree but threw him to the ground and encouraged by the shouts from the crowd did kneel upon his chest and strangle him with a cord,

The aftermath of debauchery and student riot (by Cruikshank, 1824). Compulsory matins was part of the undergraduate curriculum on Sundays. (Radio Times Hulton Picture Library)

removing same before the boy was dead. Then the rogue was pulled to his feet and a bucket of water splashed over him, and so he was taken to the cart in which the woman came and tied to its tail, two gentlemen nigh our window shouting themselves hoarse with admiration; and the hangman's assistant takes up his whip and the cart moves on the assistant wielding the rope right shrewdly. The woman was cut down and delivered to her father who had been waiting for her corse with a barrow and so the crowd disperses and the gentry drive off, one lady laying her whip about the ears of the father with his barrow for not being out of the road of her coach. And so to dine with my friends and a very pleasant hour of music and talk afterwards on divers topics. Did learn that the woman hanged was the mother of the boy aforesaid which I trust will be a lesson to him on the Penalties of An Evil Life.'

It transpired that Doctor Urquehart, their tutor, had hoped to obtain the dead woman's body for dissection, but failed to do so much to their disappointment. She had, however, been buried in the neighbouring graveyard and the following entry speaks for itself:

'November 9: Vastly tired this morning as a result of a Hazardous Escapade from which I count myself lucky to have escaped without Grievous Harm to Life and Limb. Mr. Blumenfield did yester eve put to me that we should disinter the body of the hanged woman for the Advancement of our Art and the Glory of Medicine and so after some talk I agreed and we approached our worthy teacher who warning us of the Dangers — for hanging is not the least penalty, one is likely to be torn to pieces by the mob should they learn of it — did then commend our Diligence and whilst saying that he would have no hand in it and would know nothing of it should it come to light did call his huge manservant to him and gave him instructions that he was to help us. So home to an early supper and to acquaint Mr. Hunt that that night I was to a meeting of Physicians and because of the dangers of the streets would after lie at the house of a friend, this because I thought it imprudent to return home mired in the early dawn. Then to take up my small sword and so to Doctor Urqueharts to enter it by the small gate to find the Doctor gone out but his man and George Blumenfield and Messrs. Pope and St. Clair gathered in the Anatomy room and very comfortable before a fire smoking and discussing a flask of wine and

An early nineteenth-century rag (by Cruikshank, 1824) in Tom Quadrangle, Christchurch, Oxford. (Radio Times Hulton Picture Library)

they very merry at my sword. So with them to pass the evening in pleasant discourse, I growing somewhat drunk on the wine, very potent; and when the clocks are struck the half after twelve to collect spades and grapples and to muffle ourselves in thick cloaks.'

Understandably, the young students were very tense, unlike the 'huge manservant'. It was rumoured that he had been a highwayman and that Dr. Urquehart employed him mainly because he could haul a coffin from a grave singlehanded. He took charge of the expedition. Knyveton continued:

'I was given a spade but betwixt the Wine and the Excitement of My Spirits did so catch it in my cloak that Doctor Urquehart's man did take it from me and give me the sack in which they carry the bodies this having a most foul and dismal charnal house odour. And so in to the lane and to the graveyard, where Mr. Pope was inspired to Belch loudly, this causing Doctor Urquehart's man to swear vilely vowing that he would rather have a School of Apes to help him than such young turnip heads. The grave not easy to find there being very many in a small place and the moon did come out from behind the clouds the which I did not care for as we were more likely to be seen, but with its aid to find where the mould had been newly turned. George Blumenfield very vehement to dig up the coffin only on this being opened did prove to contain an old woman very foul and I to pray with all my heart that Venus Cloacina the Goddess of Sewers would watch over us this

A drunken indoor scene by Cruikshank. Foils and boxing gloves in the background, as well as sporting prints on the walls indicate the undergraduates' sporting proclivities. (Radio Times Hulton Picture Library)

night so that we caught not some enervating distemper; then Mr. St. Clair on sitting down did find the ground give way beneath him and so we found the hanged wench and dragged her out and put her into the sack which Mr. Pope and I did then carry between us and with great haste to the lane and so to the Doctor's again, all mired and sweaty. George Blumenfield did brew us a bowl of punch and we certainly in need of such a Specific. Lord what a business this be, this Quickening of the Aweful Dead, at night when the powers of evil be abroad, amongst the tombs and the earth and the dreadful worms! Fit work only for men of Brutish Minds! Did resolve then to have no more of it, but on reflection realise that nothing is gained without labour and so as Medicine be the most noble of the Arts so the gateway is correspondingly difficult and arduous to pass. Slept on a couch at the Doctor's and so home this morning to Mr. Hunt's and with him and Mrs. Hunt to church, where I heard a tolerable sermon aptly enough on the Resurrection and wonder what his Reverence would say to my night's activities. Shall to bed early this night.'

Life was not all high drama of this nature. There was light relief as well, as the following account of a battle between two rival medical schools indicates:

'March 19th 1752: With my three friends to St. George's Hospital there to hear a lecture by one William Hunter on the Generation of Animals, Dr. Urquehart having expressed a wish that we should do so. . . . After the lecture, which was most instructive, to take a squint at the Hospital, to which one of its young gentlemen, a tall fellow with a pimply face and three-cornered hat, takes exception; likening us to Maggots crawling to a Fresh Cheese; at which George Blumenfield snorts and strikes him in the belly (he being too short to reach his face) and the tall youth's friends fall upon us, and we being hard pressed the other gentlemen of Doctor Urquehart's class to aid us, and a right merry fight ensued. Mr. Pope was trodden down and near throttled by two fellows and I to snatch the arm off a preparation of a Skeleton that stood near, and to beat them over the head with it; so that one was temporarily deprived of his wits, and Mr. Pope gets to his feet very fierce and throws off the other; and then more students hurrying out from the class-rooms the medley became Very Strenuous; only we being possessed by a Most Persistent and Obstinate Courage did force them back and back, catching up on our way very curious a Visiting Physician who did cry Shame! until some wight wielding a cane did knock his wig over his eyes so that he was deprived of Speech. The Hospital Porter to fight us also, rushing out with a cudgel with which he did much damage, until Mr. Blumenfield snatches the Skull off the Skeleton and throws it between his legs very adroit; so that he crashed down like a wind-blown tree and was no more seen. I did catch sight of the yellow poll of Mr. St. Clair very valiant at the front using a tendon

A midshipman about 1799, shown here with his sextant, sword and full uniform, including breeches, stockings, uniform coat, and tricorn hat. (Radio Times Hulton Picture Library)

with a piece of muscle attached to it after the manner of a Spanish lassoo, and did join him, catching one fellow who did oppose me with a very clean Cross Buttock throw, so that he joined the Porter on the floor and was also no more seen. And so we fought, George Blumenfield crying joyous "Into your Cheese you maggots!" until the press broke and we not wishing to disturb the Patients in the Wards, whom we could hear crying dismally in fear of a Riot and subsequent Fire, did retire. All Flushed with Victory, carrying with us the Tall Pimply Gentleman the cause of the trouble, whom we did throw into a Pond at the gates for the Healing of his Distemper; the Wig of the Physician, this upon Mr. Pope's cane; and the major portion of the breeches of the Porter, over whom Mr. Blumenfield had stumbled as we retired and snatched off as Token.'

The sequel was rather what might have been expected. A report of the riot reached Dr. Urquehart, and two days later the entry reads: 'March 21st, Doctor Urquehart very stern this morning, and to deliver a Homily on Manners, instead of a Lecture on Anatomy; interrupted by a messenger who brought . . . a bill from the Governor's Secretary of St. George's Hospital, for the following items:

> One Wig for Doctor Ramsden   £3
> Eleven windows broken   30s
> One Anatomical, Osseus, preparation ruined   £1
> One Anatomical, Muscular, preparation ditto   £1
>   (The source of Mr. St. Clair's lassoo)
> One pair of britches for the Gate Porter   £2
> To damage to wits of same   £5
> One table deprived of a leg   10s
> Four stools broken beyond repair   £1
> Damage to walls and ceilings   £2
>   (From we presume one gentleman's nose having bled all over
>   the wall, and Mr. Pope having thrown an ink pot at the roof on
>   departing.)
> Wear and tear to Nervous Composure of Patients   £10
> Five spittoons and a pot cracked   £3
> Paint off three doors   24s
> Split in panel of Anatomy Room   5s
> Loss of water and paint from gardener's tank in front gar-
>   den   11s
>   (This being we suppose the pond into which we threw the
>   pimply gentleman)
> Medicines for the revival of two Hysterick Ladies   5s
>   (Two fusty old faggots who were in the Porter's Lodge when
>   the fight commenced.)
> TOTAL   £31.3s.).

'At which the Doctor did first frown and then smile saying that he would settle the matter for us for £10; this to be collected among us, adding that he hoped we had had ten guineas worth of Fun, the which we assured him was the case, our brows being Laurel Bound with Victory; at which he did laugh outright and look strangely pleased.'

Chapter Three
CLOTHING, FASHION AND TASTE

'He did not love clean linen and I have no passion for it.' — Dr. Samuel Johnson, of Kit Smart.

The abrupt swing away from the austerity of Puritan dress to the colour-consciousness of the Restoration continued throughout the greater part of the Georgian era. As a matter of course Georgian gentlemen showed considerable interest in clothes, colour and fabrics. In part, this may have been due to early upbringing in the nursery where the rule was feminine and boys wore petticoats. An early acquaintance with fabric and colour impinging on their consciousness at an impressionable age could well have played a part in their later attitude to clothes and fashion. Certainly the Georgian gentlemen were in general far more fashion conscious than the drab products of the industrial age of Victoria, or the first half of the twentieth century. Colour and richness of material, fit and style were all points carefully considered — not merely by the town beau, but also by the obscure country gentleman, even if he rarely visited London.

An example of just such an obscure country gentleman was Henry Purefoy, of Shalstone Manor, near Aylesbury in Buckinghamshire. Many of his family letters have been preserved which, together with their accounts, provide a revealing picture of the early part of the century. Despite their extraordinarily erratic spelling, which brings to mind Chesterfield's remark about an acquaintance of his who 'never recovered from the ignominy of spelling wholesome without the "w",' the letters demonstrate the Georgian preoccupation with mode of dress. They also reveal that, although Henry visited London only once or twice a year, he was particular about his clothes.

Both he and his mother appear to have ordered clothes for each other and were freely critical of their tailor's efforts, as the following shows:

'Ffor Mr. John Boys, London, May 11th 1736. Shalstone: I received Mr. Boys's letter of ye 6th instant & have sent you enclosed the pattern of cloath that I will have my coat & Breetches of, with

Buttons & Trimmings of the same colour, the coat to be lined with a shagreen silk, & to be half trimmed & but one pair of breetches pockets on each side, but no flap to the codpeice. The wastcoat to be a very good unwatered Tabby the same green to ye pattern trimmed with silver buttons & a silver lace about the breadth of the gold lace I had last year on my wastcoat & to have pockets to it. I would not bestow anything extraordinary in the ounce for the making the lace, but let it be a showy lace of the common price by the ounce.

'The Gold laced wastcoat you made mee last year has done you no credit in the making, it gapes so intolerably before at the bottom when I button it at ye wastbone of my breetches & everybody takes notice of it. As to my size I am partly the same bignesse as I was when in Town last, but you made the last cloths a little too straight.

'Pray let this be all done perfectly well & send mee some coat and wastcoat & breetches buttons & mohair & a naill of cloath the same to ye coat & a quarter of a yard of silk the same to ye wastcoat for I han't a bitt left to my last wastcoat — if I had ye gaping might be rectified.

'My mother would have 3 yards of the white peeling if you can get it. The Breetches are sent this week by Webster. . . . My mother's & my service & respect waits on you & Mrs Boyce & I am Your humble servt. H.P.

'P.S. I desire I may have my cloaths as soon as possible & send your Bill with them & a letter by the post so that they may not lie at ye Carriers.'

Henry Purefoy's letters to tradesmen were a curious mixture of business, gossip, friendliness, cajolery and hauteur perhaps because he lived his entire life under the domination of the powerful personality of his mother. She was an extremely sharp business woman, little escaped her eye. The endless procession of servants indicated by the constant change of names in the account books showed that she was almost impossible to please. Her domination almost certainly explains Henry's lifelong bachelorhood and his uncertain business style. Yet they were devoted to each other, and he lived a very comfortable if retired life with her at Shalstone Manor until he died at the age of sixty-five in 1762. It was a measure of her toughness of mind that, although aged ninety at his death and bereft of his company, she survived for another three years.

His letter on receipt of the clothes he had ordered is typical of his business style, and reads:

'ffor Mr. John Boys, Londo: Shalstone, June the 6th, 1736. I received Mr. Boys's letter & the sute of cloaths wch fit tolerable but I was forced to have an inch cut of(f) the coat before at ye bottom & the breetches are too short at the knee. But wee must see & alter them; the green wastcoat is a very poor silk & my mother has bought a better for 4s. I doubt your man did something to it for sure you yourself would

A gentleman's dressing room in 1771 by J. Golder. The gentleman is sitting in his 'powdering gown' while his hair is dressed and powdered by his 'friseur'. (Radio Times Hulton Picture Library)

not put such a silk in any wastcoat. I have sent you a bit of my wastcoat & a peice of the 4s silk. The Sattin won't match with the other so shall have no occasion for it. The sleeves of the coat come quite down to my wrist & are a great deall longer than the wastcoat sleeve, let mee know if they wear their coat sleeves longer than they did last year, then I shall know how to alter it. Wee thank you for the mustard seed & the list & the book & I have ordered Mr. Webster ye Bucks carrier to pay you £13.15s. Pray date & sign the receipt underneath & leave it out if you should not be in ye way it will (be) ready for Webster who will pay you either this week or the next. My mother & my service & respect is with yourself & Mrs. Boys & I am Your humble servt. H.P.'

In 1740 he was writing to a Mr. Baxter, a draper in London, demanding: 'I desire you will send mee ffive and thirty yards of Irish Holland of about three Shillings a yard to make mee night shirts, it must be yard wide cloath & very good at the price. . . . And send two yards of Cambrick for shirt rufles; the last you sent was too thin. Send these by the Buckingham carrier. . . . I am your humble servt. H.P.'

As the years passed it seems that Henry Purefoy put on weight, for five years later — on the 14th of May 1745 — we find him writing to another tailor in extremely strong terms:

'Mr. ffel senior/ I admire you never took measure of mee when you was here; my cloaths are all too little about the belly, I am grown much fatter than I was. If you bring them and they don't fit mee I won't have them; so I desire next Sunday when you come to Tusmore, instead of bringing the cloaths come & take measure on mee. I beg you would not come in such a hurry another time so as to forget to take measure; I can't help taking it amiss of you. Yours in hast. H.P.'

A letter to a Mr. Meredith in London was concise to the point of brevity on the subject of hats. He wrote: 'This desires Mr. Meredith to send mee a fashionable sized Beavor hatt of the very best sort, it must be 26 inches and a half round the outside of the Crown. The last you sent they tell mee was not all Beavor. Send it with your bill by the Buckingham carrier . . . and I will order you payment for it forthwith & am Your hle servt. H.P.'

Two final extracts from letters to his draper, Mr. Baxter, are worth quoting as examples of this typical Georgian preoccupation with dress. patterns, colours and materials. He wrote:

'September 21st, 1742: I desire you will send me 8 yards of the same vermilion or Dimmothy that you sent mee before for night capps, and send my mother for under petticoats 16 yards of tufted Dimmothy to wear under an Hoop . . .'

'October 29th, 1749: I desire you will send mee nine yards of flowered Cotton with a brown ground & coloured flowers (a) yard wide; it is for my own morning gown so that if half of it be of one sort and

'*The Barber's Shop*' (*Henry Bunbury*), *dating from about 1780 and demonstrating the absurdity of the fashion for wigs. The various stages of preparation are clearly shown.* (Radio Times Hulton Picture Library)

half of another it will do, but both of them must have brown Grounds . . .'

The 'morning gown' referred to was, in effect, what today would be termed a dressing-gown. Various forms of these were commonly in use — all differing slightly, but essentially the same garment. They might be termed bed-gown, dressing-gown, or powdering-gown, but there was little difference between them.

The latter was used to cover the clothes while the hair, or wig, was being powdered. Although wigs were almost universal, some people for one reason or another kept their own hair. John Knyveton, for instance, while still a medical student in 1751, noted that 'Henry Augustus St. Clair . . . despite his name a bucolic looking fellow with a snub nose, red face and yellow hair that he ties in a queue behind, he complaining that no wig can be found to suit him; the which I can readily believe.'

Reverting to Henry Purefoy, we find him in May 1747 writing to Mr. Thomas Garrett, Junior, a barber at Buckingham, with even more erratic spelling than usual:

'Mr. Garrett/ The new Periwigg you made mee has some Hair on the top of the Crown that don't curl & when I put on my Hat or the wind blows it stares & rises all up. I have minded other folks periwigs &. I think it should have another row of Curls higher towards ye Crown. Pray don't make my other wigg so, ffor you must alter this that I have. I hope I shall see you here soon. . . .'

Periwigs, perukes, or wigs were of many varieties, from the full-bottomed wig — which went out of fashion about 1730 except in professional or court circles — to the short or long Bob wig (worn by all classes), the smaller Scratch wig (for riding or business), the Ramillies, Bag, Tye, Queue, Major, Brigadier, Caxon and many others. The materials used varied from human, horse, goat, or cow hair, to mohair, worsted, thread or silk, even to wire (either copper or iron) and such unexpected sources as feathers and cork.

It is small wonder that around 1765 the younger men began to wear their own hair. The immediate result seems to have been a petition from the master peruke makers to the King alleging distress 'from the decline of trade occasioned by the present mode of men in all stations wearing their own hair.' Whether or not the petition had any effect, the fashion for wearing their own hair did not last long.

Certainly the early 1760s appear to have been a time of revolt among the young. The Macaroni Club was formed initially as a protest against the crude fashions of the day, but eventually the club members — inevitably known as Macaronis — became more extreme than any, as the following description from the *Town and Country Magazine* in 1772 makes clear:

'They make a most ridiculous figure with hats an inch in the brim that do not cover but lie upon the head, with about two pounds of fictitious hair formed into what is called a "club" hanging down to their shoulders. The end of the skirt of their coat reaches the first button of their breeches which are either brown striped or white; their coat sleeves are so tight that they can with difficulty get their arms through their cuffs. . . . Their legs are covered with all colours of the rainbow. Their shoes are scarce slippers and their buckles are within an inch of the toe. Such a figure, essenced and perfumed, with a bunch of lace sticking out under *its* chin, puzzles the common passenger to determine the thing's sex.'

A month's hairdresser's bill for an Oxford undergraduate in 1778 ran:

4 Sundays dressings	4s
2 net caps	5s
4 prs roulers	2s
(Sausages of baked clay round which the hair was curled)	
2 pounds powder	2s
swansdown puff	2/6
4 yards ribond	2s
(For tying queues)	
hair cutting	1s
hair comming	1s
10 pounds Vilet powder	15s
2 pots oringe pomatum	4/6
pr cold irons	1/6

The expense and convenience of wearing wigs or hair powder caused endless argument as to the respective advantages or otherwise of each fashion. Colonel Byng wore his own hair and used hair powder on occasions, but there is an echo of the controversy in his diary of his tour of North Wales in 1793. He observed: 'I took my way to Mr. Wells's More Hall Farm and found him, happy man, in a night cap; his large wig being laid aside; Now here the Wiggists have the advantage (and probably in winter too) by wearing cool night caps and washing their heads.'

With constant applications of powder, heads and wigs were often verminous. When a tax on hair powder was introduced in 1795, it misfired badly. Instead of paying the tax, everyone gave up what was clearly a tiresome fashion, quite apart from the sheer discomfort of it. Already many individualists, such as Colonel Thornton, had taken to wearing their own hair comparatively short for a decade or more.

By the end of the century scarcely anyone outside the professions wore wigs. Vain young men like Byron might continue to curl their hair 'en papillotte', but hair either grew naturally to the shoulders, or was neatly tied in a queue. A fashion for cropped heads did not last long.

In the latter half of the century the transformation of the word 'breeches' was interesting, mirroring the growing prudishness of the times. By 1756, it was regarded with some disapproval and by the 1770s the term 'small-clothes' had become the accepted euphemism. This in turn was superseded by 'inexpressibles' or 'unmentionables'.

Thus, George Elers, recalling his childhood, explains that in 1790 among 'other fashionable parts of my clothing was a pair of leather unmentionables that I had the greatest of difficulty in getting into — a feat I accomplished not without assistance. Our servant . . . fairly lifted me off the ground in the operation. And then the buttoning of them and, once buttoned, the difficulty of undoing.' (This complaint is echoed in the suicide note of a Mr. Boothby, who could no longer endure the ennui of buttoning and unbuttoning.)

George Elers went on to become a lieutenant in the 12th Regiment of Foot in 1796, his colonel being the famous Henry Harvey Aston, noted duellist, buck and man of fashion. Of their first meeting Elers wrote: 'I was dressed in black coat and waistcoat, white worsted pantaloons and neat Hessian half-boots, with a crape hat band. . . . He eyed me critically from head to foot, said I *turned out well* and finished by asking the name of my tailor. I was ashamed to confess it was an obscure one by the name of Weston, then not known, but afterwards the celebrated artiste for the Prince of Wales. . . .'

Elers himself had 'six regimental jackets, dress coats, greatcoat, shirts about twelve dozen, and everything in the same proportion.' Even so, this was nothing in comparison with Colonel Aston. 'His stock of clothes was immense; from fifty to one hundred pairs of boots.' Lending Elers a jacket on board ship, when the latter pointed out that it might be ruined, he replied: 'Never mind; I have two hundred more.' According to Elers: 'His tailors — Croziers of Panton Street — used to take him home thirty coats at a time. And if they did not fit exactly he used to kick them out of the room.'

A noteworthy fashion change in the 1780s was the introduction of umbrellas when gentlemen gave up carrying swords. The Duke of Wellington did not wholly approve and, during the Peninsular War, issued the order: 'The Guards may in uniform, when on duty at St. James's, carry them if they please; but in the field it is not only ridiculous but unmilitary.'

The reactionary Colonel George Hanger wrote in 1814:

'I remember many years ago if a person had walked down St. James's street with an umbrella and strings in his shoes, it would have occasioned much censure; but now all the priests and footmen wear and carry both.'

Umbrellas, of course, were soon common to both sexes, as was snuff taking, though this was more prevalent in males. Snuff was often taken for effect, with the use of different ornamented snuff-boxes for each day of the week and a ritual observed about taking or offering it. On the other hand, it could readily become a vice of no mean proportions. Special mixtures were made up for individuals by such established firms as Fribourg and Treyer, and sometimes a small spoon, or silver shovel, would be used to ladle sufficient quantities into the nostrils. Smoking was less common, generally in clay pipes out of doors or in taverns, and was not a fashion often found among gentlemen of the day.

No chapter on fashion in the Georgian era would be complete without mention of George Bryan 'Beau' Brummel. His grandfather was a shopkeeper, but his father was secretary to Lord North and later High

Drawn and etched by Deighton in 1800, this illustrates clearly the changes in gentlemen's fashions between 1700 and 1800. Particularly noticeable is the absence of wig and sword. (Radio Times Hulton Picture Library)

Sheriff of Berkshire. Sent to Eton in 1790, aged twelve, young George was extremely popular and gained the name of 'Buck Brummel' by virtue of his attention to dress. Briefly at Oxford, he maintained his reputation as a wit, but in 1795, aged sixteen, under the aegis of the Duchess of Devonshire, he was introduced to the Prince of Wales, who gave him a cornetcy in his own regiment, the 10th Hussars.

Brummel soon became an intimate of his royal patron and spent most of his time on leave, failing even to recognise the men in his own troop when on duty. By 1798 he had secured a captaincy by purchase but, on learning that the regiment was being posted briefly to Manchester, resigned his commission on the grounds that 'he was not prepared to go on foreign service.' Having by this time inherited £30,000, he was able to set up a bachelor establishment and with the Prince's backing soon established himself as the 'arbiter elegantarium'.

In an age not conspicuous for personal cleanliness, he was regarded as slightly unbalanced. His morning toilet took as long as five hours: two hours bathing in water, milk and eau de cologne, a further hour inching himself into skin tight buck-skin breeches, another hour with his hairdresser and as much as two hours discarding as many as a dozen cravats before he was satisfied with the result. 'Use fine linen, plenty of it, and country washing' was his dictate. His boots were polished with the finest champagne and, to ensure a perfect fit, the fingers of his gloves were cut by one firm and the thumbs by another. He had a different snuff-box for each day of the year and even Byron, not readily given to praise, said of the fit of his coat that 'it seemed as if the body thought.'

His dictum on clothing was that a gentleman's clothes should be inconspicuous in material, but exquisite in cut and fit; hence the only material possible was cloth. In effect, this decreed the end of silks, satins and brocades, and the resulting more sombre hues of evening dress were to form a lasting fashion. His saying was: 'If John Bull turns round to look after you, you are not well dressed; but either too stiff, too tight, or too fashionable.'

Brummel's extravagance and the gambling — inevitable in the Prince's circle — exhausted his fortune. His impudent tongue proved too sharp for his royal patron and eventually he was reduced to bankruptcy. In 1816, finally discredited, he fled the country to Calais, the traditional resort of debtors. On his desk he left behind the secret of his perfect cravats — a scrawled note saying simply: 'Starch is your man!'

We catch a final glimpse of him in Greville's memoirs: 'March 6 1830 . . . Calais . . . There I had a long conversation with Brummel. . . . I found him in his old lodging, dressing; some pretty pieces of old furniture in the room, an entire toilet set of silver, and a large green macaw perched on the back of a tattered silk chair with faded gilding; full of gaiety, impudence and misery.'

A Macaroni in 1773. The exaggerated wig and ridiculous hat combined with highly decorative dress make him the height of absurdity. (Radio Times Hulton Picture Library)

The erstwhile arbiter of fashion was to live on another ten years, supported by old friends, but lapsing finally into abject poverty and madness. In matters of taste in clothing and fashion, he revolutionised the end of the Georgian era. Although no fashions change overnight, he might be said to have bequeathed to the Victorians not only trousers and stiff collars, but the sombre evening dress by which the nation has ever since been held in thrall.

Chesterfield, as always, was ready to advise Philip, his son, on the subject of dress and fashion. He wrote to him in 1750: 'When you come to Paris, you must take care to be extremely well dressed, that is, as the fashionable people are. This does by no means consist in the finery, but in the taste, fitness, and manner of wearing your clothes; a fine suit ill-made, and slatternly or stiffly worn, far from adorning, only exposes the awkwardness of the wearer. Get the best French tailor to make your clothes . . . and then wear them; button them, or unbutton them, as the genteelest people you see do. Let your man learn of the best friseur to do your hair well, for that is a material part of your dress. Take care to have your stockings well gartered up, and your shoes well buckled; for nothing gives a more slovenly air to a man than ill-dressed legs. In your person you must be accurately clean; and your teeth, hands and nails should be superlatively so. . . .'

Of course Chesterfield admired the French to the extent that he preferred nearly anything French to anything English. In 1739, in a much earlier letter to Philip, then aged eight, he wrote: 'The English are generally apt to be bashful; and have not those easy, free, and at the same time polite manners which the French have. . . . A gentleman . . . comes into company with a graceful and proper assurance, speaks . . . in a natural and easy manner. . . . This is . . . good breeding . . . most necessary and important . . . in . . . life.'

Among the maxims he urged on his son was the dubious advice 'to strive to acquire that great and uncommon talent to keep his own temper and artfully warm other peoples . . . hate with good breeding and love with prudence.' Philip himself commented on this and other worldly pieces of advice that it was 'excellent . . . but more calculated for the meridian of France or Spain than of England.'

In many instances Chesterfield displayed a bias against his own countrymen which betrayed a lack of basic understanding, as in a letter of May 1749 when he inveighed against the young Englishmen of the time: 'With the manners of footmen and grooms, they assume their dress too; for you must have observed them in the streets here, in dirty-blue frocks, with oaken sticks in their hands, and their hair greasy and unpowdered, tucked up under hats of enormous size.'

It was typical of the freedom of Georgian society that, throughout the latter half of the era at least, there was often difficulty in distinguishing at first sight the gentleman from his groom or coachman. At frequent intervals it was the fashion to dress similarly. Thus the many-caped coats of professional coachmen in the 1820s were a common sight both on the box of a coach and in the fashionable purlieus of Piccadilly. There was a free interchange throughout the Georgian period at cockfights, pugilistic encounters, cricket matches and similar public events between the highest and the lowest in society. This was completely lacking on the Continent where the rigid barriers between lord and peasant led to the bloodbath of the French Revolution.

In 1786 John Knyveton, by this time a respected physician, noted that it was essential in his profession when mixing with the highest society to have at least a nodding acquaintance with the classics as well as with English literature. Often finding himself invited to inspect a 'collection of china, or objects d'vertu, or fine library,' he wrote:

'The tastes and refinements, the culture and intellectual accomplishments of gentlemen of society are the more remarkable when one has hitherto seen them only at a distance, driving a coach race down the Kent road, or backing the Fancy round a close packed ring — aye and stripping off their coat if in any way insulted and standing up to a bargeman or noisy Johnny Raw, and giving better than they receive.'

Conversely, with an insularity entirely opposed to Chesterfield's urbane Francophile views, he noted:

'I must confess the French version of our English gentleman is a creature very hard to stomach. I could not restrain my laughter this morning when at Vauxhall Stairs an illustrious exquisite from St. Cloud took his cane to a sturdy British coachman unable to comprehend his Gallic chatter; and who opened his eyes in amazement, slowly climbed down from his box, took away the beau's cane as if removing a baby's rattle, and, handing it to a grinning porter, rolled up his sleeves, spat on his hands — and knocked the beau flat in the gutter. Nothing will ever convince me that a Frenchman understands an Englishman, or an Englishman a Frenchman; nor for my part do I wish to.'

Dr. Johnson went even further in his condemnation of the French, stating emphatically: 'The French are a gross, ill-bred, untaught people; a lady there will spit on the floor, and rub it in with her foot. What I gained by being in France was, learning to be better satisfied with my own country.'

In such a robust age as Georgian England, the overall standards of politeness were remarkably high. That this may have been partly due to an inbred caution, at a period when the unwary could find themselves suddenly challenged to a duel with the daunting prospect of pistols at dawn for two and breakfast afterwards for one, is by the way. Not only were manners generally good, but serious crime was also remarkably infrequent considering that there was no organised police force. Even by 1811, when Brighton had grown under the Prince of Wales's patronage to a respectable size with a population of 14,000, not only was there no watch patrolling the streets but everyone left doors unlocked with perfect safety. (It was only at the very end of the Georgian age in 1829 that Sir Robert Peel, then Home Secretary, introduced the first police force in London, known as 'Peelers' or 'Bobbies'.)

Dress and manners were but two aspects of fashion. Art and architecture were also capable of mirroring the age. The formation of the Royal Academy in 1768 under the Presidency of Sir Joshua Reynolds reflected the increasing countrywide interest in the arts. As early as 7 June 1757, Hogarth had launched forth in a letter to the *St. James Post,* attacking the picture dealers in vigorous terms for the spurious and low standard foreign art flooding the country.

'There is,' he wrote, 'another set of gentry more noxious to the Art than these, and those are your picture-jobbers from abroad (an abuse grown to such a height that the Legislature had endeavoured to put a stop to it, by laying a duty on the importation of foreign pictures) who are always ready to raise a great cry in the prints whenever they think their craft is in danger; and indeed it is in their interest to depreciate every English work, as hurtful to their trade of continually importing shiploads of dead Christs, Holy Families, Madona's, and other dismal dark subjects, neither entertaining nor ornamental on which they scrawl the terrible cramp names of some Italian masters and fix on us poor Englishmen the characters of *universal dupes.'*

Hogarth, whose satires on the age are still a source of tremendous interest, was born in 1697 and died in 1764. His early life was spent in an unavailing struggle against the type of work produced by men like William Kent. Hogarth was for reality rather than for the grand school epitomised by Kent, which represented almost all the aspects of bad taste of his time. Kent, created Court painter in 1739, did not die until 1748, when he left a considerable fortune. With a dangerous facility he turned his hand from landscape gardening, with elegant vistas, to architecture, building Holkham House in Norfolk and Devonshire House in London, as well as painting. As Hogarth with his trained eye was well aware, the results were second rate at best.

The latter part of the century saw the uninspired, heavy work of Kent give way to the more pleasing influence of the Adam brothers and Wyatt. The Palladian porticoes and evenly spaced, red brick, balanced frontages are well known features of the period. Throughout the country the urge to modernise resulted in many fine old Elizabethan over-sailing frontages being carefully extended and refaced in brick, to provide the appearance of a modern building of the period.

With obvious approval, Colonel John Byng included a satire from *The World,* dated 26 October 1787 and entitled 'Modern Taste', as an appendix to his tour of 1787. It reads:

48

'*Monstrosities of 1819 and 1820*' (*Cruikshank*), *showing some fashions of the later Georgian period.* (Radio Times Hulton Picture Library)

'If you should have purchased a good Old Family Hall, seated low and warm, encircled by woods, and near a running stream, pull it down, and sell all the materials; on no account preserve any carving, old wainscotting, painted glass, or lofty mantle-pieces; because all these things are entirely out of fashion and shew a Gothic taste — Your first thought, then, must be to burn brick and tiles, never think of stone or slate, as nothing looks grander, or is seen further, than a Red Brick House, with long wings: — this done; chuse the Most Excellent Spot on your estate, whence you may command a view of several counties, at which expanse your friends will wonderfully admire, and commit comical mistakes about distant objects.

'Cut down All Trees that are near your house, as they will spoil the prospect, and *obstruct the sun.* Should a few be left, shove them to the very top, for the benefit of the herbage.

'*Grub up all the* Hedges around you to make your grounds look Parkish; and your outside hedge keep well clipped, for it looks neat, and will shew you any passing objects or travellers upon the road.

'Make the Approach to your house as meandering as possible, as better to discover the views, and make your friends eager to arrive. Front all your rooms to the South and West, for the benefit of the sun, and have your *bedchambers* well aired; and let these be *low* and *small* for comfort and health.

'In cutting down all the wood around, you will add finely to the prospect; and in place of nasty decaying old oaks, you may Plant, either singly or in clumps, the large, the Scotch Fir, or the Lombardy Poplar. Our foolish ancestors delighted in trees of gloom, serving only as harbours for rooks, squirrels and woodpigeons, but we prefer these of neatness and quick growth. If there are any old formal Avenues, cut them quite down, and leave not one tree standing to disgrace your taste. . . .

'It were well to make numberless *ha-ha's,* and sunk fences, for as you increase in territory, you may go on laying open, and catching views of the distant counties, never thought of before. . . .

'Keep numbers of *Peacocks and Guinea Fowls,* who will make delightful serenades, adding to the cheerful sounds of the *geese and poultry;* but this is all in the way of rural propriety and simplicity.'

After this heavy satire, it is pleasant to turn to John Knyveton's description of the house he and his wife chose in Golden Square, London, in 1772. He described it thus, on 12 June:

'. . . It is a pleasant airy old-fashioned stone and red brick structure, with long formal windows and a Palladian porch; a square of narrow sooty garden behind, and a coach house backing onto a mews. On the ground floor, two rooms divided by a broad passage, a closet and a kitchen . . . on the first floor, two large rooms and two small; the two large will be a dining room and salon — for one has a fine copy of

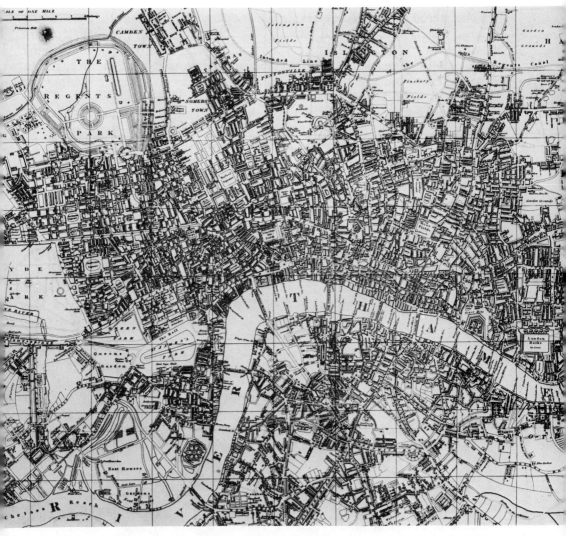

Leigh's New Map of London, dated 1818. Note Chelsea still a village and beyond Regent's Park and Finsbury Fields still countryside. (Radio Times Hulton Picture Library)

a fireplace by the Adam brothers. . . . The two small rooms are to be our bedroom and a nursery; above are garrets for the domestics. All is in good repair, the roof sound, plenty of additional water from a deep well in the garden, and little redecorating to be done. . . .

'August 4th. We are settled in our new house and it is very fine. There is a shelf for books in a cupboard, a fine broad table and strong mahogany chairs in my office, but the chief glory lies in the two rooms on the first floor — the drawing room with a steel fire grate, two tall gilt mirrors, a red and blue carpet, a settee and armchairs of mahogany

51

upholstered with needlework; a glass chandelier! and on the walls, two large panels of china wall paper . . . painted by hand in brilliant colours with flowers and birds; a very rare and precious novelty; the curtains . . . of silk damask in crimson, blue and green with a gilt border, rather an expense! but a good long term investment as the mercer assures me they will stand years of wear.

'Our dining room has a fine mahogany table, a mahogany sideboard with a marble top, and a folding leather screen, whilst the bedroom is all gold and green with a figured velvet overspread and white satin curtains with pink ribbon bindings!!

'The pine panelling in the hall, its lantern, and the pine panelling of the ground floor rooms all scrubbed and polished; the floors waxed, plenty of candles in the candle-cupboard in the hall, and everything of brass or metal, from door handles to kitchen pans, scrubbed and polished till they gleam like silver, I consider it a prodigious fine home. . . .'

A little over twenty years later, when he was older and more successful, Knyveton had a more experienced eye for furniture and knew exactly what was in the best taste of the day. By then he was accustomed to visiting the finest houses in London. For instance, on a professional visit to Lady Ursula Blackett's house in Cavendish Square, he described the furnishings as 'heavy hangings, crystal chandeliers, and furniture designed by Robert Adam and executed by Mr. Chippendale.'

The latter half of the eighteenth century saw a Gothic revival in architecture started by Horace Walpole when he retired to Strawberry Hill at Twickenham in 1747 and built himself a fantastic villa in the style of a Gothic abbey. This was much admired and such monstrosities as Beckford's abbey at Fonthill, with a tower three hundred feet high, were the direct result. Indeed, much of the worst of Victorian Gothic building can be traced to this house which Walpole erected for his own amusement. Perhaps one of the finest examples remaining is the vast house at Allerton Mauleverer in Yorkshire built by Lord Moubray and Stourton in the early part of the nineteenth century.

During the Regency period, Nash was the architect favoured by the Prince of Wales and responsible for designing not only Regent Street and other parts of London, but for completing the Pavilion at Brighton — perhaps the finest specimen of bad taste of the age. The Reverend Sydney Smith referred to it as looking 'as if the dome of St. Paul's had gone down to Brighton and pupped.'

Cobbett was even more elaborate: 'The Kremlin . . . lies in a gorge. . . . Take a square box, the sides of which are three feet and a half. Take a large Norfolk-turnip . . . put the turnip in the middle of the box. Then take four turnips of half the size . . . and put them on the corners of the box. Then take a considerable number of bulbs of the crown-imperial, the narcissus, the hyacinth, the tulip, the crocus and others . . . put all these, pretty promiscuously, but pretty thickly, on top of the box. Then stand off. . . . There! That's a *Kremlin!*'

Of course the Prince of Wales found Brighton a useful retreat from London. Despite Dr. Johnson's famous statement, 'No, Sir, when a man is tired of London he is tired of life, for there is in London all that life can afford,' not everyone was in agreement. As early as 12 June 1767, Knyveton confessed:

'I grow weary even of the pageant in the Mall, the bucks and dandies, and the Society beauties tripping with their Abigails to Betty's famous fruit shop in St. James' Street, a fashionable lounge more to the taste of the frivolous than the celebrated Chinese drawing room of Mrs. Elizabeth Montagu in Hill Street, where gather Dr. Johnson, Mrs.

'Mermaids at Brighton' in the 1820s. The women who 'dipped' their charges looked after the bathing machines. (Radio Times Hulton Picture Library)

Thrale, the Burneys, Joseph Reynolds, etc., and the conversation, if nourishing, is somewhat indigestible.'

Towards the end of the eighteenth century, with improved travelling conditions Londoners had accustomed themselves to 'the season'. The months from July to September were spent in the country, or at the seaside, where sea bathing was considered extremely healthful, or else in taking the waters at one of the spas. Colonel John Byng in 1792 referred scathingly to 'the herd, the silly, the vain, the vicious herd of fashions in London . . . to what a pitch must folly and fashion have arrived, when they have changed day into night, summer into winter, and will suffer no gentility to quit London till August.'

This was not strictly accurate, for in July 1796 we find Knyveton recording: 'London is empty, the tide of fashion has ebbed away to the Spas, to Bath and to the seaside, Scarborough, Lyme and Weymouth are crowded, but Margate I hear is not so popular this year for fear of impudent landings from French privateers . . . with increasing years I find it pleasant to rest awhile during the hot summer months.'

In 1804, however, he observed that Weymouth was really becoming more than a little tiresome. As late as October he wrote: 'I think we shall have to find another resort for our annual holiday — now the King favours Weymouth so much, the noise of the bands grows tedious; and I do not care at my time of life to be started out of a dose to rise hastily to my feet grabbing my hat off my head, every time the National Anthem is played as His Majesty takes a dip. Nor, as a physician, do I consider it at all beneficial to His Majesty's delicate balance of mind to be continually trumpeted at. The poor gentleman already suffers from exhausting sensations of hurry and distress.'

The Gallery at Strawberry Hill, the interior of Walpole's famous Gothic extravagance at Twickenham. (Mansell Collection)

Chapter Four
COOKING, EATING AND DRINKING

'I look upon it that he who does not mind his belly will hardly mind anything else.' — Dr. Samuel Johnson

In the Georgian era in England, the gentleman was well supplied with food of surprising variety and high quality, in quantities which were gross by today's standards, but all too often it was not as well, or as imaginatively cooked as it might have been. Even when well cooked it was often badly served and presented, so that instead of being hot it was at best lukewarm. It was, naturally, a Frenchman who produced the popular and slanderous Continental myth that the English had but two sauces — mint and bread. In fact, as reference to the cookery books of the day indicates, there were many more, but, as ever, all depended on the cook.

Mrs. Elizabeth Purefoy had enormous trouble finding a cook, but considering the numerous duties she expected a cook to undertake in her household perhaps this is not strange. Apart from everyday cooking they were expected to milk the cows, feed the pigs, pluck the fowls and clean the house. Obviously, from the great variety of food ordered and the increasing girth of Henry Purefoy's belly, they ate well at Shalstone Manor. It may thus be inferred that Mrs. Purefoy herself superintended the cooking, as well as the winemaking and other household duties. Under her dictatorial eye few cooks, or indeed any other servants, seem to have survived for very long. Even in those days Mrs. Purefoy was expecting a great deal, as the following letter dated 2 November 1743 indicates:

'Mrs. Sheppard/ I have missed the Opportunity of getting servants and if you can Hire mee a maid servant that can roast & Boill & dresse ffowlls & Rabbitts wee will teach her the Rest & she must do the Dairy of 4 Cows. If it is such an One as has lived in a Clergyman's House & can do as above & has a good Character she may do very well if she is sober & will Stay at Home in the ffamily. She milks at the Gate by the House & her Wages is to be three pounds or three pounds ten shillings a year. If you should meet with one who can dresse Victualls well & should not care to milk I should be glad of a young healthy girl to help her who can stand at the Buck (i.e. heavy wash) Tubb & milke the Cows & serve (i.e. feed) a couple of Hogs & pluck ffowlls & to help clean the House and Scald the milk vessell or any other Thing she may be set about & I will give her 40 shillings a year.

'If they han't had the Small Pox they must set their Hands to a paper to provide for 'emselves in such case because wee have never had it ourselves, tho' wee never had any ffall here of that Distemper. . . . Your ffriend to serve you. E.P.'

It seems that Mrs. Purefoy had no success with these extravagant demands, and by the following year she offered more while playing down the amount of work involved. There is a distinct note of desperation beginning to enter her letters:

'Wensday 26th September 1744: I received Miss ffrewen's letter, am very sorry the maid won't undertake to clean part of the house, for my maid must & must clean the eating parlour every morning; I hope you will hear of one that will, & likewise a cook-maid which will oblidge Your humble servant E.P.

'This was to have waited on you yesterday, but the bearer was gone to Brackley by noon. I received your last this day & if you will hire ye cookmaid, if she won't come here under 4 pounds, you may hire her as you can. She milks but 3 or 4 cows & that just by the yard gate / In hast.'

'October ye 1st 1744: I received Miss ffrewen's letter & am much oblidged to you for your care about the cookmaid; she was here on Saturday last & I hired her & gave her half a crown earnest & am to send for her on Wensday next. With our compliments to you all am in hast. Your oblidged humble servant E.P.'

'October the 2nd 1744: This acquaints Miss ffrewen that this morning the cookmaid sent her earnest again & sais she is to be married. I entreat ye ffavour of you to enquire mee out another cookmaid if you can, which will oblidge, Your humble servt. E.P.'

Throughout the eighteenth century, it was a familiar complaint that young country girls were attracted to London, where they hoped for domestic work, rather than staying at home. The *Gentleman's Magazine* of 1793 commented on 'vast numbers continually drawing off from the country . . . to the metropolis to the service of noblemen and gentlemen.' How many of these were cooks is another matter. François de la Rochefoucauld, the son of the famous philosopher, visited England in 1784, and while staying at Euston in East Anglia with the Duke of Grafton, made some pungent comments on English cooks.

'English cooks,' he wrote, 'are not very clever folk and even in the best houses one fares ill. The height of luxury is to have a Frenchman, but few people can afford this luxury since apart from the cost of the servant in wages and food, the government has imposed a tax on male servants of one guinea per head. . . . Accordingly . . . the cooking and the house work that is not seen are usually done by women and the men servants are only employed for such duties as are performed in the presence of guests.'

He was either biased or else unfortunate in his choice of hosts, for he repeated the myth that there were no sauces. Of course to French tastes the food was different, but English meat was incomparably superior to the French and fresh fish were readily available. Such delicacies as sugar-cane and live turtles from the West Indies, ginger and spices from the Far East, reindeers' tongues from Lapland, caviare from Russia, olives from Spain, truffles from France and similar additions to the menu were readily available. Even Monsieur Ude, *ci-devant* chef to Louis XVI and subsequently chef to the discriminating Earl of Sefton before progressing to the Duke of York's household, was moved to comment: 'I will venture to affirm that cookery in England when well done is superior to that of any in the world.'

Unfortunately there were many hazards and pitfalls for the ignorant. Mrs. Charlotte Mason, writing in 1786 in her *Ladies Assistant . . . Being a Complete System of Cookery*, particularly noted methods for purifying water, because: 'Almost all the water used in cookery is tainted with impure ingredients; rainwater with a great variety of volatile bodies, fuliginous particles, exhalations, invisible seeds and insects; river, ponds and well water with a mixture of soil and mud, decayed vegetables, and the spawn of vermin. It will be very proper to purify it, before it is used for drinking, or any kitchen purpose.'

So far so good, and she went on to add this sound advice: 'Rain water when grown putrid, may be easily rendered wholesome again, and may be drunk without being offensive, by only boiling it a few minutes; for by this expedient the animals that are in it will be destroyed and with the rest of the impurities will subside to the bottom.'

Rather astonishingly she then added a completely conflicting suggestion: 'Some obscure notion of the unwholesomeness of pump-water induces many persons to boil it, and let it stand to grow cold . . . by which it will . . . become more strongly impregnated with the saline matter and therefor it will be worse. . . . But the best way of avoiding the bad effects of pump-water would be not to make a constant use of it; and in a place so well supplied with river water as London, there is very little necessity to drink of the springs.'

It was not only tainted water which was likely to affect the cooking. Mrs. Mason stressed the dangers of using 'Copper Vessels' which were commonly used in the kitchens of the time. She blamed them for a great deal:

'. . . Verdegris is nothing but a solution of this metal (copper) by vegetable acids. And it is well known that a very small quantity of this solution will produce cholic, vomitings, intolerable thirst, universal convulsions and other dangerous symptoms. . . . We are daily exposed to this poison by the use of copper vessels for dressing our food. . . . Verdegris is one of the most violent poisons in nature; yet rather than quit an old custom, the greater part of mankind are content to swallow some of this poison each day.

'Our food receives its quantity of poison in the kitchen by the use of copper pans and dishes. The brewer mingles poison in our beer by boiling it in copper. Salt is distributed to the people from copper scales covered with verdegris. Pickled cucumbers are rendered green by an infusion of copper coin. The pastry cook bakes our tarts in copper pastry pans. But confections and syrups have greater power of destruction for they are set over the fire in copper vessels which have not been tinned; and the verdegris is plentifully extracted by the acidity of the composition. And though we do not swallow death in a single dose, yet it is certain that a quantity of poison, however small, which is repeated with every meal, must produce more fatal effects than is generally believed.'

Another hazard in the average kitchen appears to have been quite simply dirt, or lack of hygiene. Although de la Rochefoucauld admitted that to outward appearances the English were clean about the house, the cleanliness was more apparent than real. He wrote:

'. . . everything that you are supposed to see partakes of this most desirable quality, but the English contrive to neglect it in what you are not supposed to see.

'To give a single instance, I need only mention the kitchen . . . which ought to be spotlessly clean. But the worst thing that could befall you would be to go into the kitchen before dinner — the dirt is indescribable. Women are usually employed and are as black as coal; their arms, bared to the elbow, are disgustingly dirty; to save time, they handle the portions of food with their hands. You may go into the kitchens in a great nobleman's house and see perhaps ten women at work, but I will wager you will not see a couple of napkins or dishcloths, and if you do see one in use, you will have no desire to wipe your hands on it, since it is used for everything.'

The kitchen itself, of course, still tended to be primitive, and the cooking was done over an open fire, with spits and griddles. A brief glimpse of a typical kitchen is to be had from Pastor Karl Philip Moritz's account of his travels in England in 1782. He recorded: 'they shewed me into the kitchen . . . where they were roasting and boiling. . . . All round on the sides were shelves with pewter dishes and plates, and the ceiling was well stored with provisions of various kinds, such as sugar loaves, black puddings, hams, sausages, flitches of bacon, etc.'

The height of culinary science was attained in 1819 in the Brighton Pavilion in the vast kitchens designed by Nash. There the combined genius of Nash and the Prince of Wales had provided the most modern 'contrivances for roasting, boiling, baking, stewing, frying, steaming, heating.' Not everyone, however, could afford to retain the couple of dozen or so staff needed to run it. There and at Carlton House prior to 1820 Marie Antoine Careme, acknowledged as one of the finest French chefs of his day, employed his imaginative skill to produce menus which were masterpieces of gastronomic art.

A great deal of the finest English food, it should be explained, consisted of specialised local dishes. Thus larks tongues were a famous Dunstable delicacy, wheatears on the Sussex Downs were caught and potted in Brighton, Weymouth was noted for red mullet, ruffs and reeves were specially fattened in East Anglia, salmon came from the Thames, oysters from Whitstable and pork pies from Melton Mowbray, eels from Richmond and John Dory from Devon, to name only a few. Thus we find Colonel John Byng at the Castle Inn in Brighton in 1788 writing: 'Nothing could be better than our dinner and the 2 bottles of claret, and port, that W. and I soon suck'd down; and then sigh'd for more wheatears after the many we had eaten dress'd to perfection.'

England was not lacking in good victuals and eighteenth-century gentlemen were not slow to take advantage of them. Lord Alvanley, an intimate of Brummel's and of the Prince of Wales, insisted on having an apricot tart on his table every day of the year. When his *maître de cuisine* once deprecated the expense, he was promptly sent out to buy the entire stock at Gunter's, the confectioners.

What eighteenth-century gentlemen could not obtain in England was usually brought in from the Continent or farther afield. Some idea of how they fared may be gleaned from the Purefoy letters:

'To Mr. Willson, London, ffebruary the 6th, 1747: Mr. Willson/ I desire you will send me

> One pound of the best Bohea Tea
> Half a pound of the best green Tea
> Two pounds of the best Coffeeberries
> A quarter of a pound of nutmegs
> Two ounces of mace
> A quarter of an hundred of the best treble refined Loaf Sugar
> A quarter of an hundred of Household sugar about 6 pence a
>   pound
> Half a quarter of an hundred of Poland Starch
> Half a quarter of an hundred of Rice

Send these by the Buckingham carrier . . . send your Bill with them & will order you payment. The last Bohea Tea was so ordinary I could not drink it, my neighbours had as good for six shillings a pound. The last hundredweight of Raisins you sent were so bad they spoiled the Liquor they were made on. I hope you will send no more bad Goods. I have had no reason to complain till now, tho' I have dealt at your shop forty years & am Your humble servt. E.P.'

Apart from the advantages of country life — with its ready access to game, poultry, eggs and meat — the Purefoys also enjoyed plentiful fish, as the following extract indicates:

'Mr. John Knight, a ffishmonger in Honey lane market near Cheapside, London. January ye 21st 1747: Mr. Knight/ I received a barrell of oysters from you which I have desired Mr. Moulson to pay you for, & desire you will send another Barrell by the next return of Mr. Jones ye carrier . . . & send a Barrell of oysters once a fortnight till you have orders to the contrary. Pray let them be good firm oysters as these were & if you should have any fresh Herrings that are full of Roes I desire you would send a dozen or a dozen & a half of them when you send the oysters, which will oblidge Your humble servant. E.P.'

There is little doubt that the eighteenth-century gentleman ate very well indeed. 'A very elegant dinner' enjoyed by Parson Woodforde in Oxford in 1774 consisted of 'part of a large cod, a chine of mutton, some soup, a chicken pye, pudding and roots, etc. Second course; pidgeons and asparagus, a fillet of veal with mushrooms and high sauce with it, roasted sweetbreads, hot lobster, apricot tart, and in the middle a pyramid of syllabubs and jellies. We had a desert of fruit after dinner, and Madeira, white port and red to drink as wine.'

Perhaps the meals experienced by de la Rochefoucauld in East Anglia fell below this standard. Nevertheless, his observant accounts of the English eating habits of the day are enlightening:

'Throughout England it is the custom to breakfast together. . . . Breakfast consists of tea and bread and butter in various forms. In the houses of the rich you have coffee, chocolate and so on. The morning newspapers are on the table and those who want to do so, read them during breakfast, so that the conversation is not of a lively nature. At 10 o'clock or 10:30 each member of the party goes off on his own pursuit, hunting, fishing or walking . . . but at 4 o'clock precisely you must present yourself in the drawing room with a great deal more ceremony than we are accustomed to in France. This sudden change of social manners is quite astonishing and I was deeply struck by it. In the morning you come down in riding boots and a shabby coat . . . you behave exactly as if you were by yourself . . . and it is all extremely comfortable. But in the evening . . . you must be well washed and well groomed. The standard of politeness is uncomfortably high — strangers go first into the dining room and sit near the hostess and are served in seniority in accordance with a rigid etiquette. In fact for the first few days I was tempted to think it was done for a joke.

'Dinner is one of the most wearisome of English experiences lasting, as it does, for four or five hours. The first two are spent in eating and you are compelled to exercise your stomach to the full in order to

The Great Kitchen at Windsor Castle in 1800 (Fyne). The number of staff required are clearly shown as are the primitive cooking facilities. (Radio Times Hulton Picture Library)

please your host. . . .

'The courses are much the same as in France except that the use of sauce is unknown in the English kitchen and that one seldom sees a ragout. All the dishes consist of various meats either boiled or roasted and of joints weighing about twenty or thirty pounds.'

The young Frenchman seems to have overlooked the fact that laying the table was an intricate process conforming to a carefully set plan and custom. For instance, it was the practice for the gentleman seated nearest a dish to carve it for everyone, and dessert was often served in a separate room.

Some idea of a dinner table plan can be derived from a domestic booklet for young women written by a Mrs. Copley in the early nineteenth century. 'For plain family dinners,' she relates, 'soup or pudding is placed at the head of the table and meat at the lower end; vegetables straight on each side of the middle and sauceboats in the middle, boiled meat at the top, roast meat at the bottom; soup in the middle. Then the vegetables and sauceboats at cross-corners of the middle dish, poultry or veal at top, ham or bacon in the middle; roast beef or mutton at the top — roast poultry or game at bottom; vegetables and sauces so disposed that the whole table shall present a covered appearance without being crowded.'

De la Rochefoucauld became a trifle muddled over the use of finger bowls, which he had not encountered in France:

'After the sweets you are given water in small bowls of very clean glass in order to rinse out your mouth — a custom which strikes me as extremely unfortunate. The more fashionable folk do not rinse out their mouths, but that seems to me even worse; for, if you use the water to wash your hands it becomes dirty and quite disgusting. The ceremony over, the cloth is removed and you behold the most beautiful table it is possible to see. It is indeed remarkable that the English are so much given to the use of mahogany. . . . After the removal of the cloth, the table is covered with all kinds of wine and even gentlemen of modest means always keep a large stock of good wine. On the middle of the table there is a small quantity of fruits, a few biscuits (to stimulate thirst) and some butter, for many English people take it at dessert.'

Describing with a note of disbelief the drinking that followed dinner, he mentioned one instance where the Duke of Grafton's nephew retired to bed for several hours because he was so drunk.

Of the normal routine he wrote: 'At this point, all the servants disappear. The ladies drink a glass or two of wine and at the end of half-an-hour all go out together. It is then that the real enjoyment begins — there is not an Englishman who is not supremely happy at this particular moment. One proceeds to drink — sometimes in an alarming measure . . . for the bottles make a continuous circuit of the table. . . . After mere thirst has become an inadequate reason for drinking, a fresh stimulus is supplied by the drinking of 'toasts', that is to say, the host begins by giving the name of a lady; he drinks to her health and everyone is obliged to do likewise. After the host . . . everyone drinks to the health of everyone else's lady. Then each member of the party names some man . . . fresh toasts are always ready to hand; politics can supply plenty — one drinks to the health of Mr. Pitt, or Mr. Fox, or Lord North. . . . This is the time that I like best . . . everyone expresses his political opinions with as much frankness as he would employ upon personal subjects. Sometimes conversation becomes extremely free upon highly indecent topics — complete licence is allowed and . . . I have heard things mentioned in good society which would be in the grossest taste in France. The sideboard too is furnished with a number of chamber pots and it is common practice to relieve oneself whilst the rest are drinking; one has no kind of concealment and the practice strikes me as most indecent.

'At the end of two or three hours a servant announces that tea is ready and conducts the gentlemen from their drinking to join the ladies in the drawing room, where they are usually employed in making tea and coffee. After making tea, one generally plays whist, and at midnight there is cold meat for those who are hungry. While the game is going on there is punch on a table for those who want it.'

During the Regency and towards the end of the Georgian period matters were often carried a stage further, as we find from an account of the period:

'When the ladies left the dining room, fresh bottles of port would be brought in, the host would arise and lock the door, and almost every man drank until he was under the table. With the exception of one or two men who kept sober, they never joined the ladies again, and a page, towards the end of the drinking, as the men slipped from their seats, would loosen the neck-cloths of the prostrate guests, and it was a regular custom for the valets to come in, carry out their masters, put them in their coaches, and escort them home. Some curious incidents arose when some of the valets were not themselves too sober, and substitutes had taken their place, and some of the masters were put into the wrong coaches and carried to the wrong houses about midnight or later, much to the astonishment . . . of the wives and other members of the households.'

There were, of course, some people — such as Horace Walpole, the diarist and architect of the Strawberry Hill fantasy — who deplored the eating and drinking habits of the day. The fifth son of Sir Robert Walpole, the Prime Minister, he was probably the illegitimate son of Carr, Lord Hervey, a close friend of Sir Robert's first wife. He had the Hervey features and attitude of mind and was not fond of his Norfolk country relatives. He confessed: 'I shudder when I see them brandish their knives in act to carve, and look on them as savages that devour one another. I should not stare at all more than I do, if yonder Alderman at the lower end of the table was to stick his fork into his neighbour's jolly cheek and cut a brave slice of brown and fat. Why, I'll swear I see no difference between a country gentleman and a sirloin; whenever the first laughs, or the latter is cut, there run out just the same streams of gravy!'

A description of his own normal diet when at home, as seen by an eyewitness, was as follows: 'His dinner when at home was of chicken, pheasant, or any light food, of which he ate sparingly. Pastry he disliked, as difficult of digestion, though he would taste a morsel of venison pie. Iced water, then a London dislike, was his favourite drink. The scent of dinner was removed by a censer or pot of frankincense. The wine that was drunk was drunk during dinner. After his coffee he would take a pinch of snuff and nothing more that night.'

Another who considered that a special regimen was important was Dr. George Fordyce, whose daily routine is well described by· John Knyveton:

'October 4th 1791: . . . as we strolled down Paternoster Row we were almost bundled into the kennel by a portly red-faced gentleman in a red coat and full wig, making a great play with his long cane, who entered Dolly's Chophouse as if he owned it. . . . This was the celebrated Doctor George Fordyce M.D. of Edinburgh . . . who has come to the profound conclusion that man eats far more than nature intended, thus he takes one meal only in the twenty-four hours, and that always on the stroke of four in the afternoon. As the clock strikes . . . he seats himself at a table reserved for him, on which in readiness for his arrival are placed a bottle of port wine, a quarter of brandy and a silver tankard of strong ale. The moment his loud step and loud voice are heard at the door a solemn and orderly ritual is set in motion. As one drawer hastens to pull out his chair, the cook puts a pound and a half of rump steak on the gridiron and dishes up a trifle of broiled fowl or a dish of fish, which a second drawer lays before the doctor. Of this he disposes whilst the steak is grilling, and caps it with a drink of brandy. He then sets to work on the steak, washing it down with the strong ale, and finally finishes off the brandy and drinks his bottle of port. At exactly one hour and a half to the minute later he rises and returns to his house in Essex Street and makes no other meal till his return to Dolly's at four in the afternoon of the next day. And this he has been doing for upwards of twenty years.'

Dr. Fordyce died in 1802. Not surprisingly, this stout pioneer of dieting in the Georgian manner suffered for some years before his death 'from acute rambling pains in his stomach and bowels.' Even less surprisingly, he suffered from gout.

It might almost have been said that gout was an occupational hazard of life from the point of view of the Georgian gentleman. In

1725 Daniel Defoe, travelling in the West country between Honiton and Exeter while writing his *Tour of England and Wales,* noted disapprovingly: 'They tell us they send 50,000 hogsheads of cyder hence every year to London, and which is still worse, that it is most of it bought there by the merchants to mix with their wines, which if true, is not much to the reputation of the London vintners.'

Due to heavy duties on the import of brandy and wine, also to frequent war with France, smuggling developed into a profitable and almost respectable occupation. The 'Free Traders' and their trains of horses with casks of wine or brandy and packs of silk were common enough spectacles, but they could scarcely supply more than a fraction of the demand.

One result was the increase in port-drinking, for it was imported duty-free under a trade agreement with Portugal. Throughout the Georgian period the taste for port developed and considerable quantities were drunk. Dr. Johnson, for instance, boasted of drinking three bottles and being none the worse and he was by no means exceptional. It must be appreciated, however, that port at this period could not be kept long, and was not 'laid down' in a cellar, but drunk young, tasting something like a Burgundy. The bottles were also smaller. The first effective vintage bottles were laid down in the 1770s, but it was not until after 1812 that the practice of laying down wine and port became common. By that time, the shape and size of the bottles had changed considerably and the wines were more potent.

The disgraceful so-called 'Gin Era' — from around 1725 to 1750 — when the distilling of cheap spirits reached almost epidemic proportions, did not greatly affect the Georgian gentleman of the day, simply because he seldom drank gin; it was essentially a drink of the lower classes. Even at the end of the century, throughout his travels round the country, Colonel John Byng hardly ever drank gin, although he often drank brandy. He also used brandy as a disinfectant, as when he recorded in Rugby in 1789: 'I took off the sheets and employed all the brandy, near a pint, in purifying the room and sprinkling the quilt and blankets.'

Ale, or malt liquor, was still commonly brewed and drunk throughout most of the period, although due to penal taxation the practice of home brewing was virtually discontinued by the end of the century. There were three distinct types of beer; dark, pale and light, and a mixture of all three, known as 'three threads', was the popular drink of the working class. A heavier darker beer, or stout, was also brewed, and became known as porter solely because it was favoured by the porters in London's markets. It soon became an accepted drink among sporting gentlemen. This was demonstrated by Colonel Thomas Thornton, on his tour of the Highlands in 1784, took with him some of 'Calvert's incomparable porter.'

Colonel Thornton's menu of food and wines drunk in the Highlands on this occasion offers some idea of the abundance of food and drink available in the Georgian era for those who could afford it.

Hodge Podge
Pudding   greens
Trout and char
Roast mutton, excellent
Second Course
Brandered Chickens
Cold hams
Snipes
Cheshire cheese, biscuits
Wines
Claret, good – port, ditto,
Limes, Jamaica Rum and,
Incomparable porter from Calverts

Another meal on a later occasion consisted of:

A hodge podge
Remove
A roast pike of seven pounds
Sauces
Greens – reindeers tongue – potatoes
Chickens
Second Course
Loin of Mutton
Black game and partridge
Currant jelly, capsicum, elder, garlick, vinegars
Powerade and char
A carving
Biscuits, Stilton cheese, Cheshire, butter,
Goats milk.

Nor was it necessary to be the equivalent of a millionaire, like Thornton, to feed well in the country. Colonel Byng, despite his many complaints, often fed extremely well and cheaply, as this extract from his account of a tour to the north in 1792 indicates. At Middleham he 'led the horses down the hill into the town to what seem'd to be a sorry inn; however it yielded well (for they spake of their trout and of their cold larder with reason) and I was shown into a clean parlour up one pair of stairs. I not only ordered several trout for dinner, but now dictate their cookery, and to prevent the frying and the parsley and the fennel and the butter and substitute boiling and anchovy sauce; as for cold things they introduce cold ham, cold beef, cold fowl and gooseberry pye. . . . The port wine and the ale seemed equally good. . . . I now felt a haste for dinner and this is a description of it:

A Boiled Fowl
Cold Ham   Yorkshire Pudding   Gooseberry Pye
Loyn of Mutton Roast   Cheesecakes

'A better dinner and better dress'd I never sat down to; but I fear the charge will be *heavy* — 1s 6d at least. We shall see.'
    His bill was as follows:

White Swan, Middleham,
June 9   Dinner   1 3
          Wine   2 6
          Supper   1 0
          Brandy   1 2

His breakfast next morning came to 9d. In a three-day stay, his horses were his most expensive item at 3/4d. for stabling and 4s. for corn in a total bill amounting to £1.0s.10d. Of course, it was cheaper to live in the country than in the town. Those like the Purefoys, who made their own ale and reared or grew much of their food, could live both well and cheaply, but even they had their difficulties.
    In November 1752, we find Henry Purefoy worried about his ale-making and writing to 'Mr. Watts, Junior, a Plummer at Brackley':
    'Mr. Watts/ On enquiry I find the Leaden pipe I brew with to be so foull that wee can't use it unless wee have a forcer to cleanse it with; so desire you will bring over a forcer along with you & send word by the bearer what day you will come on, which I hope will be tomorrow or next day, because wee are full late in brewing our strong beer, & can't brew till the pipe is cleaned. . . . Your humble servt. H.P.'
    The Purefoys, in common with practically every English gentleman of the day, had no objection to smuggling. Nor for that matter did clergymen, as we find from a letter dated 1737: 'To the Rev. Richard Dalby: Sir/ . . . As to good Brandy or good French wine, if it can be got safe to Shalstone, it will be acceptable & wee will pay you for it with thanks. . . . H.P.' Then again, as late as 1777, on 29 March, Parson Woodforde recorded in his diary: 'Andrews the smuggler brought me this night about 11 o'clock a bagg of Hyson Tea 6 pound weight. He frightened us a little by whistling under the parlour window just as we were going to bed. I gave him some Geneva and paid him for the tea at 10/6 per pound.'
    Two final entries on drink from the Purefoy letters bear quotation:

'March 24th 1741: Mr. Stranks/ Some time ago you was kind enough to let mee have a Gallon of your Rumm that was sent you from Jamaica, which has served the family ever since (A Gallon bought on 8th October at 1734 at 10 shillings) I was ye beginning of last week seized with a violent fitt of ye cholick as bad like to have cost mee my life; my Physician tells mee Rumm is proper for my case, so if you could let me have a Gallon of your Jamaica Rumm I should take it extremely kind of you. . . . Your humble servant. H.P.'

'To Peter Moulson: 1735: Sir/ I desire you will send us . . . an hogshead of your best old red Port Wine by Webster the carrier . . . wee still draw the white mountain wine out of the half hogshead & it is brisk enough without bottling.'

Judging by the hogsheads of 'sack', 'port' and 'canary' that the Purefoys disposed of, they can very seldom have drunk water. The 'mountain wine', or malaga, was commonly taken out of the hogshead and then bottled to keep for a longer period. At that time, of course, no wine in a cask kept for more than six months. Thus all wines were drunk young. As the methods of corking and bottle manufacture became more efficient in the seventies and eighties of the eighteenth century, the principle of laying down vintage wines finally began to be accepted.

One practice which prevailed throughout the Georgian period among all classes was the habit of drinking ale or beer to each other from the same glass. De la Rochefoucauld commented on this with distaste.

'There is one thing,' he claimed, 'that must strike everyone and that is the common habit of all drinking beer from the same glass, even if there are twenty at a table. When you ask for a drink some fresh beer is poured into the old at the bottom of the glass and you have to drink or let it pass. Moreover this dirty and revolting habit has become so well established that it has become an act of politeness at a ball for example to drink beer or punch or some other beverage after a lady has drunk from the same glass to show that you do not mind her leavings. This may be all very well on occasions, but there are some ladies with whom I should not care to indulge in this form of politeness.'

In his diaries, Knyveton gives an illuminating description of a literary dinner presided over by Dr. Johnson. Still a medical student in 1751, he and friends unwittingly intruded:

'December 11th . . . We entered the Devils Tavern . . . to find it very crowded. . . . On enquiring the reason of the Host he did inform us that that night one Johnson a famous novelist known to his friends as the Doctor was giving a dinner . . . he and the members of his club coming there from their usual meeting place in Ivy Lane Paternoster Row . . . it seemed likely that there would be no room for us. George Blumenfield however did catch sight of one Doctor Bathurst then entering and he knowing him to introduce us; and as we talked a monstrous fat man afflicted with the dropsy and with a great broad face comes in . . . in a voice sonorous though pleasant and smiling round us did ask whether we were perhaps relations of the Doctor . . . to which George Blumenfield replies that we are Surgeons in Embryo, formed but not Delivered, at which the fat man laughs and . . . does then bid us join his gathering; the which I took kindly of him.'

On going upstairs to a special room reserved for the company, Dr. Johnson was greeted with cheers by those already there. Dr. Bathurst explained that:

'. . . we are fortunate indeed to have been admitted into such a

An early nineteenth-century kitchen scene. The clockwork mechanical spit and the size of the joint are noteworthy. (Radio Times Hulton Picture Library)

company, for Johnson's Club is the most famous in London town and likely long to be remembered, the Doctor now engaged upon a great dictionary and already notable for having published a poem The Vanity of Human Wishes, of which even His Majesty has well-spoken, and a Magazine the Rambler, which is published twice weekly. (Mem. To obtain a copy of same) as well as various other works. . . .

'We four found ourselves chairs at the end of the table, my seat being near the door and thereby intolerably draughty but of satisfaction since it afforded me a good view of the Doctor . . . the waiters did bring in the supper, such a profusion of dishes as I have never seen before, the company being a large one some twenty souls or more and the Occasion an Important One. Amongst those dishes that I remember were:

> A dish of rabbits all smothered with onions
> A leg of mutton boiled with capers and served with walnuts and melted butter
> A side of beef with frizzled potatoes
> A roasted goose with some chickens and other game
> A roasted lobster, served very cunning with all the claws arranged as though alive
> A dish of fish with their bellies stuffed with pudding
> And a currant pudding and a Vast Apple Pie, this last especially ordered by the Doctor . . .

'We did drink Wine and Ale according to our taste with the Meat but the Doctor kept to Lemonade which though a foully sharp beverage did not seem to sharpen his temper. About eleven of the clock the remnants of the food were cleared away and nuts and fruit set out and coffee served; some of the gentlemen being overcome with the Heat of the room and the potency of the Wines. I did feel somewhat foxed myself and on looking round did see that Mr. St. Clair was leaving and that Mr. Pope had already left; but did later find him beneath the table. The Doctor our host had eaten I do believe more than any one else in the room; I did marvel at the way he crammed all manner of meats into his mouth until his face became purple and the veins stood out in his Temples; but he seemed to suffer no inconvenience from it, his face now shining with sweat and merriment until it resembled a Full Moon. Moreover he never ceased talking and the flow of his discourse flowed on like a river the sonorous timbre of his voice drowning all who interrupted him.'

Despite the fact that he was feeling 'somewhat foxed,' Knyveton seems to have managed to pay attention to the conversation, for he quoted:

'In reply to some remark I heard him say "Sir, I have said before and I now repeat, that the Great Chair of a full and pleasant town club is perhaps the Throne of Human Felicity'' the which tolerably explains his tastes. His voice did lull me to sleep . . . and falling beneath the table did there find Mr. Pope sleeping as calm as in his bed at home, in company with sundry other gentlemen. . . . So to my feet again and to take a cup of Coffee which Arabian drink did clear my head so that I could listen with intelligence to a heated argument between the Doctor and Mr. Payne a bookseller . . . about one o'clock they began discussing the Value of Health as an Aid to Morals . . . and so feeling

The alehouse kitchen, after Rowlandson, circa *1790 with turnspit worked by the dog on the treadmill above the fireplace.* (Radio Times Hulton Picture Library)

infernally sleepy and fuddled did awake George Blumenfield who had gone to sleep with his feet on the table and out with him into the Street. The Inn all dark mine host and his servants all gone to bed, and so home to our own beds . . . to slumber till Noon. . . . I heard from Mr. Pope that the supper party lasted until the dawn, when the Doctor was still in Full Cry but the company much diminished and those present with difficulty keeping their feet and their wits . . . it was eight in the morning when the last guest left; at which news I was thankful that I had got me home when I did.'

In all circles, it was an age of deep drinking and the example set by the Prince of Wales was far from good. The monstrous drink named 'Regent's Punch' after its creator was a mirror of the times. It consisted of: 'Three bottles of Champagne, two of Madeira, one of Hock, one of Curacao, one quart of Brandy, one pint of Rum and two bottles of seltzer water, flavoured with four pounds of bloom raisins, Seville oranges, lemons, white sugar candy and diluted with iced green tea instead of brandy.'

Chapter Five
HEALTH, DISEASE AND TREATMENT

'Who can run the race with Death?' — Dr. Samuel Johnson

At the start of the Georgian era the standards of medical knowledge were still extremely low. Anyone who had survived birth, childhood and upbringing was likely to be healthy. It was a case of the survival of the fittest. The old mediaeval idea that disease could be attributed to the different 'humours' in the body still had not been completely exploded. The association between dirt and disease had not been fully established, for the principles of infection and hygiene were not fully understood.

Thus, in the year 1765, when already an established practitioner of some standing, it was possible for Dr. John Knyveton to write on 16 September: 'This year my birthday falls on a Monday . . . must hasten to dress in my new plum-coloured suit — I may even in honour of the occasion take a bath, dangerous though it be at this treacherous season of the year, and I took one as recently as the 8th of June.'

Despite his profession, it seems Knyveton thought a bath once every two or three months excessive. Small wonder that Brummel was looked at askance for his habit of washing daily. Even in the early nineteenth century Byron was unusual in boasting of having a bath installed in his house, for undue washing was not an eighteenth-century weakness.

Only dimly, slowly and painfully, were the surgeons and physicians beginning to associate cause and effect. By the end of the Georgian era medical knowledge had substantially increased in some respects, but until the introduction of anaesthetics and antiseptics it could progress little further. Research was still confused and erratic. Physiology was still in its infancy, yet Knyveton found cause to think deeply in his first year as a medical student in 1751, for he recorded:

'October 22: Was reminded today of my five guineas paid to Mr Kelly for a course in Vegetable and Animal Physiology.

'October 24: Was late to bed last night and so no entry in my journal, my mind moreover being in great confusion . . . did repair in the evening once more to Mr Kelly's chambers. . . . Mr Kelly . . . says he will demonstrate the Circulation of the Globules of the Blood and so to take a frog and spread its toe web out upon the bridge or landing of his microscope and then after much squinting and turning of a great Mirror we all to have a gaze and I for one greatly marvelled to see oval corpuscles tumbling like rocks over a waterfall in channels that try as I might I could not see with the unaided eye. And so to be shown the Animalculae in the Semine Masculino and I for one near foxed to gather reason for these things which must of necessity have a use and yet of which were it not for this Magic Toy we should have no knowledge. . . . Mr Kelly holding that Disease vists from without and is not an expression of Lack or Excess of one of the Vital Humours, as was held I learn by the ancients for example one Tarentius Varro who supposed the air of marshes harmful because of animalculae contained in it. But Lord such matters strike deep.

'October 29: Have led a sober life these two days; my mind still being exercised by what Mr Kelly has shown me. Am half resolved to let my five guineas go; this being a small price to pay if I can preserve my Tranquillity of Spirits.'

For fifty-three years he managed to preserve his tranquillity by resolutely ignoring the subject. Then he bought himself a microscope and commented: 'March 11th, 1804: My new microscope is proving very useful — for reading the small print in the newspaper. I am afraid the use of the instrument in medicine is extremely limited, to measuring the globules in the blood and so forth. A pity —'

The scourge of the eighteenth century undoubtedly was smallpox, which, apart from marking its victims, frequently caused death. Taking every precaution to avoid it, the Purefoys even resorted to making their servants agree to look after themselves if they caught it. In a letter dated 18 April 1742, Henry Purefoy wrote: 'ffor the postmaster at the Post Office Cheltenham in Gloucestershire; I having occasion to drink your waters at Cheltenham am oblidged to write to you, the Postmaster, to let mee know if the small pox be at Cheltenham, if not I shall be there soon after I have your answer, wch I desire you will oblidge me with & am Your unknown humble servant. H.P.'

The Purefoys were not the only ones to dread the disease, but few people did much about it. When Lady Mary Wortley Montagu, the noted letter writer and wife of the ambassador to Turkey, returned to this country in 1718 she did her utmost to stimulate interest in the practice of innoculation. She even set the example by innoculating her own children, but it bore little success at first. Eventually it became fashionable to hold innoculation parties, yet the disease continued to kill around a thirteenth of every generation until Jenner's introduction of vaccination gained general acceptance in 1801.

Another persistent ailment of the times was the common cold. On 29 March 1743, Henry Purefoy wrote to his local practitioner: 'Sir/ My mother has got a very bad cold and so entreat you would send her 12 ounces of Lintseed Oyll cold drawn, pray let it be fresh done; and send an ounce of your best Manna. Should be glad to have your bill as soon as may be . . . Your very hle servt. H.P.'

In the early Georgian era the Company of Barber Surgeons continued to govern both professions. Indeed, it was not until 1745 that the Company of Surgeons was created as a separate body with their own Surgeons' Hall. At that time it was regarded as an extra deterrent if a felon knew that his body would be used for dissection. Hence the bodies of those hanged were passed initially to the Barber Surgeon's Hall and later to the College of Surgeons for anatomising and lecture purposes. An account of 1725 from the old Barber Surgeons' makes interesting reading:

'The charges to be paid to the Masters and Stewards of Anatomy for procuring a Body besides the Dinner at Ye Viscera Lecture:

Horse hire	2	6
For a coach	6	
Expenses in fetching the body	2	6
To the Sheriff's Officers	13	4
To the Beadel's assistant	1	0
For Washing the Body	1	0
For a Coffin	5	
To Parson, Ground Clerk and Sexton	5	10
To the Bearers	2	0
Funeral Expenses	2	6
For a Certificate	0	6
The Clark's Fees	10	0
The 2 Beadle's ffees	10	0
For a link	0	3
To the Chairwoman	5	0
£3	7	5'

Rather more startling is an extract from the Barber Surgeons' records dated 23 November 1740:

'This day Wm Duell (who had been indicted at the Old Bailey for a Rape and had received sentence of death for the same) was carried to Tyburne in order to be executed where having hung some time was cutt down and brought to this Company's Hall in order to be dissected where he had not been five minutes before Life appeared in him and being let blood and other means used for his recovery in less than two hours he sat upright drank some warm wine and look'd often round him. . . . The Sheriffs having ordered him back to Newgate he was carried out in a blankett putt into a Coach and was seemingly much composed. . . . He afterwards obtained a reprieve in order to be transported for life which he was accordingly in the 16th year of his age.

Wardens Accts. re W. Duell:

Paid the Beadles their expences in bringing the body from Tyburne	2	19	0
Paid the Officers of the Two Compters	2	2	0
Paid Joseph Wheeler the Company's Clark his Coach hire and expences in attending the Sheriffs when the Body came to life	0	10	0
Paid the Chairwoman for her trouble and expences abt the Body	5	16	0'

It was not only the barbers and chirurgeons, or surgeons, who were confusingly inter-connected in the early eighteenth century. Overlapping and confusion occurred among all the branches of the medical profession. The apothecaries, for example, who compounded and prepared the medicines prescribed by the physicians, often treated patients on their own account, or after referring their symptoms to a physician. On their part, the surgeons were just as willing to prescribe for diseases as to operate. As for the physicians, they frequently turned surgeon when required, The man-midwife, or obstetrician, was usually prepared to tackle any other aspect of his profession. With a scarcity of doctors available and the difficulties of travel, this was almost inevitable — especially in the country.

Some of this confusion of rôles is apparent in a letter dated 7 July 1736, from Henry Purefoy to Dr. Charles Kimberley of Northampton, whose prescribed treatment for what was probably a chronic varicose ulcer on Mrs. Purefoy's leg was being carried out by a surgeon in Buckingham named Mr. Wallbank. Purefoy wrote:

'Sir/ I had ansered your kind request to know how my mother's leg did before this but she was not willing till she had took all her physick & saw some little alteration in her leg. Mr Wallbank has attended her every day since but one to ffoment & dresse her leg, but yesterday my mother told him that she thought she could dresse it herself so hee sais now hee will come every other day.

'He dressed it for a week & what he put in it that time made very little alteration but my mother told him she imagined that stuff would not do which she supposed to be white Basilicon. Then he put some brown & green stuff in a spoon & did some lint in it & put it as hot as she could bear it into the hole & laid white basilicon upon lint upon that & then a plaister over that & he has swathed her leg pretty tight ever since hee has dressed it. This last stuff he dresses it with torments it much at the first laying on but this day hee sais he has moderated it, but it smarts pretty much still. The wound is now full as broad as a

A dentist at work. The black page appears to be holding two ivory false teeth for the patient. (Radio Times Hulton Picture Library)

shilling, it looks fresh & clean at the bottom & my mother is of the mind it might be healed up. 't would be a favour if you would let mee know, by the return of Palmer the carrier if you can, whether it need be fomented any longer. . . . I am with real esteem Sir! Your very humble servant H.P.'

Presumably because he proved effective, and also because he lived nearer at hand, Mr. Wallbank, the surgeon, became the regular medical adviser to the Purefoy family, as well as their friend. Ten years later in September 1747, Henry Purefoy was writing to him plaintively:

'ffor Mr Wallbank, Surgeon at Buckingham:

Sir/ I took all your Pills about 4 or 5 days ago but not your bitter draft which would not set on my stomach as the first Bottle of Bitters did. I desire no Bitters but being very faint between breakfast and Dinner Time if you could order mee something to help mee, I would take it. My water holds of a good colour. Wee both join you in our service & respect to you & I am Your humble servant. H.P.'

Everything implies that Henry Purefoy was not in robust health in 1747. His increasing bulk — and the fact that he had ruptured himself — may have contributed to this condition. In any case, we find him writing to 'Mr Titchburn at the Golden Ball next door but one to ye Swan in Shoelane near Holborn bridge London,' as follows:

'Mr Titchburn/ Some time ago when I lodged in Cooks Court by Lincolns Inne I had some Dimmothy trusses of you which proved very well & I gave you half a crown a peice for them. Now they have got into another method of making them with Tape to tie about the middle, there may be a small matter more of stuff to make 'em, but not more workmanship, so shall be willing to give you three shillings apeice for them but no more, & if you are willing to take that price I will send you a Truss by ye Buckingham carrier to make them by, & will have half a dozen Trusses of you & if you make them to fit mee shall want more. Your answer by ye Post will oblidge Your friend to serve you. H.P.'

The following year we find that Henry Purefoy was also having trouble with his spectacles. Writing to 'Mr Joseph Hurt at the Archimedes & 3 Golden Spectacles near Ave Mary Lane in Ludgate Street, London,' on 4 March 1748, he complained:

'Mr Hurt/ . . . you have made an ugly mistake in Relation to my Glasses, for I sent to you for six concave glasses number sic for my spectacles, to repair ye same when they chance to break, & you have sent me six Glasses in horn cases which are of no use to mee for I have damaged one of my eyes already by using such as these are & now use only those that are put in spectacles; so must desire you to change these. . . . Your humble servt. H.P.'

Both Mrs. Purefoy and Henry took good care of their teeth, and when tincture for teeth was advertised in several papers, Henry Purefoy wrote in 1751 to Mr. Moulson, his agent in London, in the following terms: 'Sir/ . . . If it would`not be too much trouble I desire you will buy for mee & send three bottles of the Tincture for preserving the Teeth & two Tooth Brushes from Mr. Greenough's near St Sepulchre's Church on Snowhill.'

As early as 1737, Mrs. Purefoy had been corresponding with 'Mr William Coryndon Operator for ye Teeth near the new Church in ye Strand, London' concerning the making of artificial teeth, measuring the length of her gums with tape and biting on a piece of wood to show the position of her molars. On 11 December, she wrote:

'Mr Coryndon/ I have sent you a bit of wood for a pattern the shape of wch I believe will direct you. It must be made a little longer, the length of wch I have sent you on a Bit of Tape.

'If you think you can compleat it by this Direction you may, if you can't I will stay till I come to Town in ye Spring. I do beleive the stick to be too thin at one end & too thick at t'other, but you must manage. I think if you send it down before you make any holes in it I can send it up again for you to finish & am your humble servant E.P.'

It is not clear whether these garbled instructions were successful in providing Mrs. Purefoy with the false teeth she wanted, but toothache and dentistry seem to have been a frequent cause of correspondence throughout the eighteenth century.

Thus in 1768 a lawyer, Mr. William Bray, recorded in his diary on 8 October: 'To Neville Crt & had the nerve in both ears cut for the toothache and received relief in an hour.' Again in 1812 Colonel Peter Hawker, lately returned from the Peninsular Campaign with a severe wound in his hip, noted in his diary for 1 March: 'After being tortured for three days and three nights with the toothache, I had a tooth drawn and driven in again, by which severe operation you effectively remove all pain by destroying the nerve and at the same time restore the tooth for mastication.'

There is no doubt that throughout the eighteenth century quacks without qualifications or any real knowledge abounded in all branches of the medical profession. Added to these, there were plenty with the degrees which qualified them to carry the coveted gold knobbed cane of the physician who were little more than quacks themselves. In contrast, there were others — such as John Knyveton — whose experience and knowledge more than compensated for their lack of a degree. Knyveton served four years' apprenticeship under his uncle, a surgeon in Kent, then received eight months' practical tuition in a London hospital before qualifying as a surgeon's mate in the Navy. After eleven adventurous years, during which time he attained the rank of full surgeon and gained a vast amount of practical experience, he returned to study in London once more, this time as an obstetrician. Finally, deciding that it would be worth while acquiring a degree, he entered in his diary in 1765:

'June 4th: After some discussion with Drs Kelly and Kirkpatrick have decided to apply to the Marischal College, Aberdeen, as an external student for a degree of Doctor of Medicine. . . . This will establish my right to practise; without a degree, however hollow (!) one is dubbed but one more of the quacks, bone-setters, man-midwives without training, and hodge podge oculists, by the public, such rogues swarming in abundance, and making large fortunes; . . . If a degree is required legally to carry the gold-headed cane and kill by blister and purge, how much more is it necessary to those who sincerely wish to serve the public! to aid the sick, to cure their diseases and so to raise our art, by our *own* example, from its present deadly rut and intellectual indolence.'

'July 14th: A large imposing packet all seals and crests by the post boy this morning! — the College express their willingness to enrol me as a graduate and award the degree of Doctor of Medicine! Some further information required from Drs Kelly and Kirkpatrick — and a fee of 20 guineas to pay — little enough for permission *to creep up the backstairs!* . . . shall do no studies today, but to take the precious letter to my friends, and after a reply is writ — hey for a fling!'

Dr. John Knyveton was entitled to his degree and went on to become a well known lecturer, physician and obstetrician. Apart from his wide medical experience in the navy, it must be appreciated that the six months he had served as a medical student was a more intensive experience than can readily be imagined today. When he was studying in London in 1751, his tuition went ahead at a breathtaking pace, for although he only arrived in the capital in September 1751, he was busy assisting at operations by November. He wrote:

'November 25: Assisted Doctor Urquehart with an amputation of the leg . . . taken from an attorney's clerk, who had broken it coming down some dark stairs in the Temple late one night. The tibia whole, but the fibular broken some three or four inches above the ancle joint and protruding through the skin, the ancle itself dislocated. The clerk in great pain and the wound discharging through part of his black stocking having been caught by the bone and drawn into the wound. The wound above the exit of the bone very foul, the flesh about swollen and the skin hard and shiny to half way up the shin; so the Doctor did resolve to remove the leg at the knee. The clerk was taken from his bed in Great Lowness of Spirits, his wife being with him and comforting him and attempting to follow him into the Theatre; from which she was prevented by Doctor Urquehart's man who at a sign from him did pick her up bodily and carry her to the gates, where she was attended by one of the nurses. Then the clerk being bound his leg was held out firmly by the aforesaid servant who wedged it against his belly and Doctor Urquehart with a sharp knife cuts a half circle from below the Tubercle of the Tibia to the middle of the joint behind and repeats same

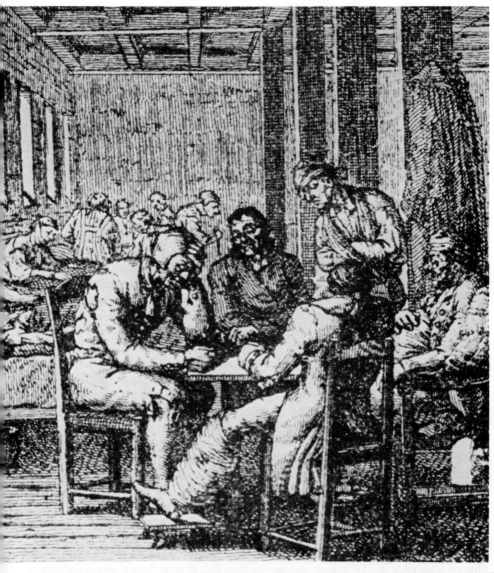

A men's ward in a hospital circa *1740. The overcrowding, lack of hygiene and sanitation, as well as the generally primitive conditions are clearly shown.* (Radio Times Hulton Picture Library)

on the opposing side and I pull these flaps back and get soaked with blood from the great arteries at which the Doctor laughs. Then he severs the Ligamentum Patella and the other ligaments and cuts through the cartilages so that the leg drops to the floor, he leaving the Semilunar Cartilages in place so that they may form a protection for the condyles of the Femur and prevent its retraction and he then ligatures the vessels with cord and sews up the two flaps leaving the end of the ligature cords hanging from the wound. The Doctor a very quick man and the leg off in four minutes, though due to my clumsiness another minute or two elapsed before the wound was secured. I have heard and can well believe that when he amputates with another cunning and experienced surgeon only two or three minutes elapse before it is complete. And so the clerk was removed in all Peace, he having fainted from the Vehemence of his Emotions at the cutting of the second flap and I for one very thankful for his screams at the first nigh deafened mee. So home very sweaty and bloody to change my shirt and cravat. . . .'

Within three months Knyveton was being instructed in midwifery. His reactions were informative. He noted:

'December 6: . . . In the afternoon I and Messrs Blumenfield, Pope and St Clair together with some other young gentlemen of Dr Urquehart's class to Mr Rickard for instruction in the Diseases of Women, especially appertaining to Child-bed and he did show us divers preparations to this end. There is still much prejudice I learn against the Interference of Surgeons in Child Bearing despite the work of that most excellent School of Midwifery founded by the Scots at Glasgow. Women are strange creatures as has been known from the days of the Ancients. They still prefer the ministrations of some Poxy old Harridan and to have their brats in their own homes amongst a mob of squalling sister neighbours, saying that these our Hospitals are as the Jaws of Hell to swallow them up. But Lord how can some dirty fuddled Midwife possess that knowledge of Anatomy without which the Art becomes a mere Empiric? And speaking at least for this my School the patients are well cared for; the sheets on the beds are changed once a fortnight and their night rails once in a week, when there are enough of these for this to be done; and the floors are washed at least once in a month or so. But efforts for the common weal are ever carried out against the Opposition of the Ignorant, who mistake vehement abuse for Reasoned Criticism.'

Throughout the eighteenth century, there were certain standard treatments which the physicians applied almost as a matter of course whatever the patient's complaint. Thus phlebotomy, or bleeding, was almost automatic. In some cases, however, it was more severe than in others, as suggested by this description of the treatment applied to a patient dying of fever after the failure of an operation on his broken jaw:

'. . . he now far gone in a Hectic Fever so that they tied him to the bed and the assistant was applying Hippocrates His Heroic Treatment, the which is bleeding the patient upright till he faints, then laying him down till he recovers, then setting him upright and bleeding him till he faints again, the which desparate course though rigorous is necessitated by the quantity of effete matter rioting in the Sanguinous System and

A view of the peace celebrations in London in 1763 at the end of the seven years war. (Mary Evans)

Hogarth's scene of "The Polling", third in The Election *series demonstrating the 'popular farce' of elections at this time (1758).* (Mary Evans)

An example of the late Georgian coaching services during a stop for breakfast.
(Radio Times Hulton Picture Library)

oppressing the Vital Members.'

A clyster, or enema, was another favourite treatment, generally administered with the aid of a wooden funnel. A blister, or irritant, applied to various parts of the anatomy, was regarded as a useful means of drawing 'evil' humours away from an infected area. Cupping, or applying powerful suction by causing a vacuum inside a bowl, or cup, with a lighted taper, before clapping it to the body was used to remove pressure on various parts of the anatomy, as for instance over the lungs. Apart from these and poultices when required, the use of unguents and herbal treatments — notably 'Peruvian Bark' — or quinine in primitive form, were the principal methods of treatment. When in doubt there was a tendency to use several, or all, of these treatments in turn or together.

Knyveton's description of his routine as a student in his London hospital in December 1751 illustrates the treatments involved and some idea of the intensive work entailed:

'This day at the Infirmary did find my sempstress (whose hand he had amputated) doing well, the wound suppurating healthily and to my joy the Ligatures about the Vessels have sloughed out without Haemoorhage; for which may God be thanked. Her fever within bounds; did bleed her a little and after gave her a Febrifuge Pill to wit:

Powdered Peruvian Bark half an ounce
Oil of cinnamon, two drops
Powdered Red coral, quantity sufficient as excipient.
of this I did make eight pills and give them to the nurse one to be
    given each night and morning in a little Barley water.

'The woman I delivered also doing well, as also her child. Did with Doctor Urquehart and George Blumenfield reduce a Hernia on a coachman with the aid of two Seton Needles, also lanced a Psoas Abcess — this by myself — and reduced a dislocation of a Milk-woman's Arm, she having slipped the Head of the Humerus from its socket in picking up a pail. This a tedious business performed round the bedpost with many ropes, the dislocation proving stubborn: but to reduce it at last. Then Doctor Urquehart did desire to see the stump of my Sempstress; so to unbandage it again, and he well satisfied with my skill, and so away to a fashionable appointment, whilst I and his other young gentlemen with Mr Rickard to the Lying-in Ward. There at his request George Blumenfield and I did deliver a Woman of a fine son and much fatigued ourselves at it; then to turn and find him and the other gentlemen all pressing round a second case where the Child was presented the Breech First: and he using the forceps but even so unable to deliver her. I and my three friends to help him but the other gentlemen growing weary after two hours did go away and we stayed until eight of the clock that night, when Mr Jamie having joined us the child was at last got away; only then we did find that there was a second within, dead. So to administer stimulants to the poor quean — prepared by Mr Rickard and contained Savin Juice, White Wine, Borax and White Sugar — and to burn Shavings of Hartshorn under her nose — and so by infinite trial to remove the second Embryo; and I did think to see her die forthwith from Sheer Languor of Spirits only we rallied her with Powdered Peruvian Bark and Camphor.'

In the circumstances, one would have thought the wretched woman had suffered enough, but with commendable zeal they were determined to do their best for her:

'Then I to the pharmacy and prepared a Dressing or Solution, namely: Borax and Troches of Myrrh, half a dram of each:

> Cinnamon, one scruple'
> Barley Cinnamon Water, two ounces.

'With which at Mr Rickard's direction I did paint the Vulva. Then Mr Jamie to insert a Pessary compounded of Myrrh Powdered, One Dram, Black Ellebor and Staves-acre of each One Dram, Oil of Amber to make the mass; this he rolls in Wool and thrusts within the Pudendum; and Lord Lord it was after ten o'clock when it was all done, and then our labours not finished. For the wench I had delivered very feverish and restless, and so to bleed her and give a Potion containing Powdered Poppy Seeds in Cinnamon Water. I do wonder whether those ministering in such places do ever get any rest.'

This was by no means all. Just as they were leaving, a beggar from the streets — who had had a foot amputated some days previously — suddenly went berserk, attacking a fellow patient:

'. . . a fat nurse comes running, bawling that the beggar is taken with a Frenzy and like to murder them all, at which Mr Jamie swears most furious and sets off at a run with Mr Rickard at his heels and we to follow him; and into the men's wards where we find the beggar out of bed and strangling the old man Ned's friend, shouting that he was a Devil but that he should not drag him down to Hell; and all the other patients screaming too, such a Hubbub as my pen cannot describe. Mr Jamie seizes the beggar and pulls him back and the beggar turns on him and throws him across the bed; and Mr Rickard and I pounce on the beggar and endeavour to loosen his grasp, the which we cannot do he having the Strength of Ten Men in his madness; and so we struggle over the poor old man in bed till Grge Blumenfield snatches up a pot and breaks it over the beggar's head. Then we do discover that the dressing is off his foot and there is blood everywhere; so I tear a strip off the bedclothes and clap on a Tourniquet and so we carry him back to his bed, where the Assistants bind him with ropes and Mr Jamie, having taken a stoup of wine, sets to work to shave his head and then claps on a blister containing Spanish Flies one dram, Leaven half an ounce, Honey two drams, to distract the beggars wits from the Fury at his brain to the skull; then throws up a Mercury Clyster and then the beggar having recovered claps more of the blister in his chest and belly; and so we leave him, and I and Mr Blumenfield to our lodgings, I for one more tired than I have been since I helped our village horse-leech drag the Squire's horse from the river, some three years back.'

In one sphere in particular — the study of anatomy — medical knowledge showed considerable advances. Even if carried on clandestinely on bodies 'snatched' from graveyards, this resulted in the ever-increasing skill of the surgeons throughout the period. Knyveton had some pungent comments to make on the difficulties surgeons faced:

'December 24: My dissection of the trunk now finished and to wonder where the next subject is to come from; can see that we shall perforce have to Raid that Miserable Graveyard again, unless the Doctor can obtain a corpse from the Authorities. It is Intolerable that the progress of our Art should depend upon such uncertain foundations. Have heard that one Professor Rondolet of Montpelier University did for want of subjects dissect the body of his own child before his class, the which I can well believe.'

'January 5: Was up again all last night Corpse Taking. Would have performed the task on the evening of Jan 3 only Mr St Clair had that night to dine with his father, and the new graveyard being a good mile from Doctor Urquehart's we did need all our company. As before the Doctor did lend us his Man, but would know nothing of our doings; and after some discussion we did deem it wise to recruit our numbers, as the streets we were to traverse are roamed at night by Foot-pads, and Bully Boys, the Mohawks and the like. So at the Infirmary that day we did gather the Class together and disclosed to them our plans; at which they did all want to come, but we made them draw lots thus selecting four and by God's grace did get the most lusty of the crew. And so to gather at the Doctors, and at the half after midnight out into the roads and down to the river; catching a glimpse of two lots of Gentlemen of the Road but they not molesting us from the quantity of our numbers. Doctor Urquehart's Servant did take our bringing extra members but ill, asking us why we did not bring also some chairmen with torches and a fife and drum; but to calm him with a guinea and he grumbling to lead the way. The night very dark and bitter cold and the streets thereby empty for which we were duly grateful. The graveyard surrounded by a Very High Wall entered by an Iron Gate, which was locked; at which we were all dismayed, but the Huge Serving Man did produce a Master Key and so we gained entrance.'

The 'Huge Serving Man' lived up to his criminal reputation, but even he — as Knyveton relates — was unprepared for the following shock:

'The graveyard a large one, but we had marked the site of the grave and so found our way to it with tolerable ease, one of the young gentlemen however catching his knee against a Tomb Stone and severely bruising his Patella, or Knee Pan; at which he did swear lustily. Then to dig and by our numbers soon to uncover the coffin; and so to burst it open and drag out the body within, this being a man of some forty years, very well developed, at which we were well pleased. Then to drag off his shroud and the moon comes out faint from behind a cloud and shines on us, at which one young gentleman near took Hystericks; the more so as the Doctor's man drops his spade with a great clatter and cries out with a Fearful Oath that it was his cousin; who had it seems been a Highway Man and but lately caught and hanged; Doctor Urquehart's servant knowing nothing of this. So we to stuff the body in the Sack, he muttering away beneath his breath; and so with some relief of Spirits out into the Lane again. There we did have the Ill Fortune to find some Mohawks awaiting us, they passing and hearing the noise made when the Body was Stripped. They did set upon us with loud cries and I being one of the foremost was straightaway beaten down into the Gutter, where George Blumenfield did in a minute join me; and I very wroth and thankful that we were in force that we might teach these Bullies and Virgin-Breakers a Lesson. So the fight was joined and I to my feet did tug out my Small Sword and to my great satisfaction did receive the rush of one upon its point so his arm was pierced, the which was a lesson to me how soft the flesh be during life, when not stiffened by that Coagulation of the Humours called Rigor Mortis. There were I suppose some half dozen of them and the fight did rage right heartily until Doctor Urquehart's man forced his way into the press and taking two of the young bucks by the throat did knock their heads together with such force that they were stunned, and so the rest to their heels and we in triumph with the corpse to Doctor Urquehart's where as heretofore I did pass the night on a couch.'

Almost inevitably these graveyard outings were full of drama, yet they served a major need. Without the necessary anatomical skill, the surgeons of the day could not operate with the vital speed demanded due to the lack of anaesthetics. Some of the cases which Knyveton cites are impressive by any standards:

'January 15; 1752: Did see today a very pretty example of the dexterity of Doctor Urquehart in Operating. I and my three friends and the other young gentlemen of his class were with him in the Operating Theatre . . . when a man was brought in in haste having a few minutes since fallen from the Bedroom Window of a house adjoining. The reason for the fall was Drink and between that and his Tumble his wits were all abroad; so he was stretched upon the table and his clothes snatched from him, when we saw that the bone of his left thigh was broken but not protruding, but the Patella below it all crushed and the Shin beneath it so that his leg stuck out from the other like the arm of the letter Y. The right leg whole but for sundry abrasions as were his other limbs. The Doctor did take one look at the joint all crushed and bloody with the bones sticking out and then cries for the Amputation Instruments; and these being brought he places his left hand on the man's thigh above where the bone was broken; takes up a sharp pointed knife and drives it through the thigh below the bone; sweeps it outward to the floor; frees the knife and with it transfixes the flesh of the thigh above the bone; then Mr St Clair pulling back these two masses he takes a saw from Mr Jamie and severs the bone, the leg dropping to the floor; then to tie up the Great Artery of the Thigh and the other vessels and to bring across the flaps and trimming them sews them into place making a purse shaped wound. All this under three minutes by Mr Blumenfield's watch, he taking it out the moment the man's injury was laid bare, and I greatly to marvel; hardly more blood than would fill a small bucket being shed, and it over quickly enough no more than to sober the man.'

Another much later incident was possibly even more remarkable:

'April 9th: Returning thro' Holborn, found a crowd gathered round a milk-maid tossed by a bull escaped from Smithfield; her head all bloody, blood and hair on the pavement, and a compound fracture in two places of her right leg; got her with Rogerson's aid to a chair, and to Bartholomew's Hospital, where Mr Percival Pott performed one of the quickest amputations it has been my pleasure to witness; she being laid on a bench, he took one glance at the leg, selected a dismemb'ring knife, whipped up her petticoats and amputated the leg half up the thigh; so swiftly she had time to utter only one scream, and little more blood shed than a pint or so; and so she was got to bed in the Cutting Ward and should do well.'

Bulls running amok and resulting amputations were comparatively straightforward, but Knyveton also recorded the case of a dog running rabid — a not uncommon event in those days. The treatment prescribed underlines how much still had to be learned about disease and the factors causing it. Describing the incident on 28 January 1752, Knyveton recorded:

'Much excitement this morning as I pass to the Infirmary with my friends. Great shouting in the streets and firing off of pistols and blunderbusses and then the Street emptied like magic at a cry of Mad Dog and we to jump hastily into a door as a black cur comes chasing down the road his jaws all frothy snapping and biting at whatever lay in his path. A tall soldier with one eye steps out into the road and as the dog makes for him clubs it over the head with his stick; at which shouts of acclamation from the surrounding houses, and my friends to aid a fat man over whom the dog had jumped he throwing himself into the gutter to avoid it and I to peer curious at the carcase of the dog. This is no more than a pup and as it lay in the road with its mouth open did see that its gums were all swollen; at which I did suspect that it was no Mad Dog, but one driven Hysterick by the Pain of Deliverance of its teeth; as has been told me by the Horse-Leech at home and as I have seen children near distracted from the same cause.

'To join my friends gathered about the fat man, he blubbering and calling on God to aid him, he determined that the Cur's Teeth had met in his flesh, though no signs of this. But we did on searching find a Spot on his Buttock on the Left Side where the cloth was torn; and at this the soldier did run down the Street and fetched a Smith who coming in haste with a hot coal held in his tongs, did clap this to the fat man's seat; and so he leaps to his feet screaming as though the Dog had bitten him in very truth; and so he turning violent the soldier and the smith did lay hands on him and bustled him into the gates of our Infirmary; where Mr Jamie, hearing first their tale, and then ours, did with a faint smile deliver him to the Attendants, who tearing his clothes from him did then hurry him to a large Tub filled with cold water, in which they did submerge him, holding his head beneath water until he was near choked; and then to hustle him all dripping out of the water and to flog him with towels; and so he was put to bed and Mr Jamie did bleed him six ounces.'

In view of drastic treatment, it is not astonishing that the wretched man decided that the cure was worse than the disease; the following day's entry reads:

'January 29: At the Infirmary this day did find the fat man of yesterday gone home, he not thankful for our efforts to relieve him of Fear of becoming Mad, but saying that Mad Dog or No he would rather die in his own bed than be hounded into an Early Grave.'

Major abdominal surgery, of course, was out of the question. Doctors did not understand the need for antiseptics and the fate of patients was inevitably death from gangrene. For the same reason, comparatively minor wounds and broken limbs often ended in amputation, while badly broken limbs were almost invariable amputated. Taking everything into account, the high rate of success was a tribute to the general toughness of the day. Of course, with the best will in the world, the surgeons and physicians often had to watch their patients die, sometimes knowing full well the cause of their trouble, but owing to the limited facilities at their disposal, unable to effect a cure. Knyveton gave an example of a typical case in 1776 while practising in London:

'May 11th: Weary and very sad this morning after a sleepless night spent by the bedside of Mrs Baugh, the young wife of Mr Edward Baugh, glazier and painter, of Orange Street, Red Lion Square. She was pregnant and about five months gone, and I not being satisfied as to the position of the foetus called upon Mr William Osborne seven weeks ago to examine her, when we decided that it was possibly a case of extra uterine pregnancy; but did not inform her, or her husband, of our fears, trusting that we might be mistaken or, if correct, that all might perhaps go well.

'Late last night however was summoned to her bedside and found

The Middlesex Hospital by Rowlandson in 1808. The improved conditions in this female ward compared with the illustration on p. 83 are obvious. (Radio Times Hulton Picture Library)

her complaining of a pain in the iliac region; a short time later she cried out that something had burst within her, and that she felt she was fainting. A little later she began to shiver, and broke into a cold perspiration, and rigors shook her. I at once realised that our fears were only too well founded, that a foetus had formed either within the fallopian tube, or in the mouth of that duct; and that having attained a certain size it had burst its enclosing walls. The case was now one for which no living man could do anything at all; but for form's sake I sent for Mr Osborne.

'Before he arrived, however, the girl had read my eyes, and closed her own, shuddering and shedding a few tears; then sent for her husband and when he came, kissed him lovingly; and as I took her fast sinking pulse, her other hand closed over mine, and she said in a low voice: "Let me hold your hand, Doctor." '

Eventually his friend Mr. Osborne arrived and, although there was nothing to be done, Knyveton recorded this moving scene:

'We kept vigil together in the quiet room, the cry of the watch "Three o'clock — And a Fine Clear Night — And All's Well" and the occasional song of a traveller in the streets without; within, the tinkle of a coal in the grate, the shallow fluttering breath of the sufferer, and poor Mr Baugh sobbing on his knees beside the bed. Towards the end, the vicar of the church hard by softly joined us, and falling to his knees beside Mr Baugh began in a low voice to intone a solemn prayer; and so her life ebbed away in the unseen torrents of blood pouring into her abdomen, and clinging trustfully to my helpless hands, she drifted into eternity.'

Throughout the eighteenth century, many new hospitals were opened and the standards in them were steadily improving, both in hygiene and comfort. A description of Dr. Leake's 'new lying-in Hospital' at Westminster in 1767 indicated a welcome innovation: only one woman to a bed. Furthermore, each bed was to have its own candle and 'thick curtains for privacy.' The windows were 'of good size' to provide light, but 'only opened a little so that draughts and noxious miasmas' were excluded. There were good 'sea-coal' fires and the nurses were 'decent, clean bodies.' It all sounds a considerable improvement on Knyveton's old hospital, but in fact conditions took a long time to change greatly.

One condition which then, as now, was quite common was lunacy. This could take many forms and most families, rather than condemn their relatives to the generally inhumane treatments of the day typified by Bedlam, usually humoured them in their own way. Thus, according to Elizabeth Grant, the successor to the Lord Lovat who was executed for his part in the '45 Rebellion imagined he was a turkey hen, making a nest of straw in his coach and sitting there on a number of eggs. He only left it twice a day to eat. Finally, the hen wife removed the eggs and replaced them with chicks, whereupon he strode around clucking with enormous satisfaction. In the end, apparently considering his duty done, he returned to his normal self.

Dr. Willis, who was in charge of George III during his illness (not lunacy, incidentally, but porphyria — a rare disease producing incoherence, rapid speech and the other excitable symptoms from which he suffered), ran a private asylum in which the inmates were dressed deliberately in a uniform of black knee breeches and coats and white shirts. They were expected to work in the garden, or in similar simple ways, continually occupying themselves. The harmless routine and work therapy were sound practice well ahead of their time.

Knyveton had one startling encounter with insanity, which he recorded in his own racy fashion:

'November 3rd 1795: A very odd experience last night, which has left an unpleasant taste in my mouth. Osborne called about the half after five and hurried me out to the house of a Mr William Purleigh at Barton Street, Westminster, whom he knows slightly by sight, and who, though he studied medicine at Paris, was left a fortune by his father, a soap boiler of Holborn, and so has not engaged in practice. As we bowled along in the coach Osborne explained Mr Purleigh occupies his time in studying zoology and chemistry; on that evening he had sent a white faced footman to the Infirmary asking Osborne to come at once, a woman having been taken very ill at his house; Osborne deciding it sounded a business for two heads rather than one, called for me on his way. We arrived at a tall building where servants ushered us into a gloomy hall hung with gold and black, and retired to watch us from the shadows. A soft footed butler ushered us up into a bedroom on the first floor, where we found Mr Purleigh with Mr Thomas Nelson, a surgeon of Conduit Street, arrived only a few moments before us. The room was in considerable disorder, a chair lay on its back, a mirror was cracked, and a crystal bottle and a severed length of scarlet rope lay on the floor, while on the bed lay the body of a female. Mr Purleigh, whose dropsical figure was eccentrically clad all in black, relieved by a single huge jewel in his black cravat, was in a terrible sweat of anxiety and emotion; he explained he had returned from the city early that afternoon to find the lady his housekeeper, drinking his brandy; he had given her notice of dismissal and then gone to his study, locking himself in, as was his custom, with orders he was not to be disturbed; the housekeeper had thereupon gone up to his bedroom and hanged herself.'

According to Mr. Purleigh, she had been discovered by accident by a footman after some hours, but Knyveton was suspicious, observing:

'On the face of it his story sounded reasonable enough, yet I did not understand why he had sent for medical assistance so far away from his home; and on a quick glance round, I could see nothing to which the woman could have attached herself. Mr Nelson, advancing to the body, laid a hand on its shoulder, and remarked it was still warm; Osborne with a sly wink at me and a whispered "Housekeeper" and a meaning sniff; the housekeeper was a young blonde of about twenty five years of age; drew out his lancet and opened a vein. We all uttered an exclamation as blood ran out of the incision! Mr Nelson hurriedly began putting the female's arms across her breast and forcing them back, to expand the lungs; Osborne called over his shoulder for lights, for the room was very dim; Mr Purleigh slowly approached, a silver candelabra waving in his hand; as I stared into the housekeeper's face I noticed that beside the ugly livid weal round her neck and the purple of asphyxiation her lips were all cut as if a tumbler had been thrust between her teeth and broken; she reeked of brandy, but so did the bedclothes and the bed curtains. I turned to consider Mr Purleigh, whose eyes turned slowly to meet mine; then suddenly he dropped the candelabra and we were plunged into total darkness. There was some fine cursing from Osborne before a light was struck and Mr Nelson held up a flickering candle; we worked till we sweated, but after an hour had had no success, any chance we might have had I am convinced was lost during those precious minutes in the dark.

'When at last we left Mr Nelson was determined not to be left behind alone with his client, but informing him we would report the matter as a case of sudden death, tumbled out with us into the street. We all had our suspicions, but no proof; however Osborne declares the case at least proves his contention that no person can be considered truly dead until they fall apart.'

The answer to their suspicions was provided three weeks later when Knyveton chanced upon some further information concerning Purleigh:

'November 24th: Calling at Child's Coffee House shortly after noon to collect a message, found Doctor Stephen Pellett, up from St Albans and taking some refreshment before his return. Doctor Stephen Pellet who was born in London, was educated under De Saussurre at Geneva, but returned to England to graduate in medicine at Edinburgh. At St Albans he has a house for the reception of lunatics of the upper class and was in London to remove none other than the mysterious Mr Purleigh of Barton Street, Westminster! — who at dead of night had crept into his female domestik's bedroom and slashed at them with a whip — Mr Purleigh, of course, is of the middle class, but very rich — when I told Doctor Pellet of our recent unsavoury adventure with Mr Purleigh and the blonde "housekeeper" he listened attentively, but only smiled drily when I expressed sincere hopes Mr Purleigh would be got safely to St Albans. Later I saw him go away in a large coach with iron frame windows, attended by two enormous broken prize fighters, who had bound and gagged Mr Purleigh and from time to time gave him a

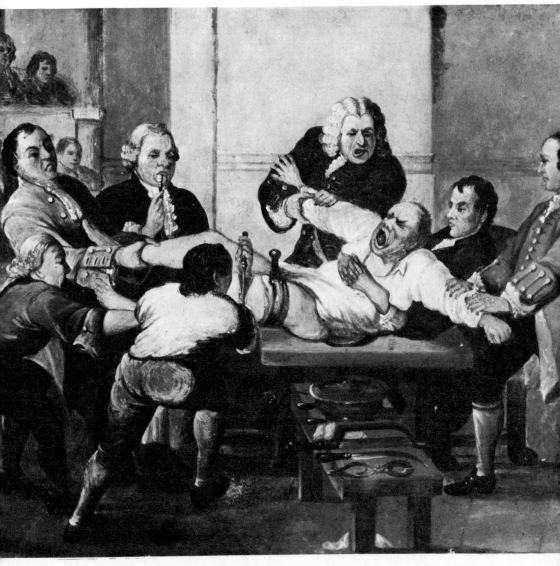

An operation for amputation of a leg above the knee in a teaching hospital circa *1780. Note the tourniquet on the thigh and surgeon's instruments at hand.*

warning rap over the head with the bludgeons they carried.'

Not everyone ended in lunatic asylums or, for that matter, on the operating tables. An amazing number of Georgian gentlemen, and others of the day, seem to have survived to a ripe old age with nothing whatever the matter with them. The principle of the survival of the fittest functioned quite successfully in a number of cases — as, for instance, that of Mr. William Bray, who died within a few days of ninety in 1832. On 15 November 1808, he recorded: 'This day I completed my 72nd year & thanks to God's Mercies I find myself in as perfect health as I ever enjoyed in my life. . . . I read and write as well and as much as ever. My teeth remain perfect in front and without any additional loss to those which decayed some years ago.'

Chapter Six

RELIGION, FEARS AND TRIBULATIONS

'I am afraid he has not been in the inside of a church for many years; but he never passes a church without pulling off his hat; This shews that he has good principles.' (Of Dr. John Campbell)
'I am willing to love all mankind, except an American.' (15th April 1778) — Dr. Samuel Johnson

One of the more remarkable features of the Georgian era was the wealth of genuine religious feeling inherent in the gentlemen of the day. Among the very small minority who were Dissenters, or Non-Conformists, and the hard core of Roman Catholics, this was not hard to understand since the isolation of their faith ensured their devotion. Among the Protestant majority, it was surprising, to say the least, considering the generally bad example set by the clergy, who were often more concerned with their livings, with obtaining preferment, or with extracting the maximum in tithes from their long suffering parishioners, rather than with preaching or attending to the spiritual needs of their flock. Yet, even if in many cases they were empty rituals, daily prayers and regular Bible readings were observed in most households from the humblest to the great. They mirrored a profound and abiding belief in Christianity, reinforced, perhaps, by the uncertainties of the times, which encouraged people to find solace in their religious faith.

The diaries, letters and records of the day are full of pleas from clergymen to potential patrons hoping to obtain livings or preferment. Pluralities were common, with absentee incumbents setting up curates in their stead yet reaping the income. A glimpse of what some clergymen both enjoyed and expected may be obtained from correspondence between the Reverend William Wickham, Rector of several livings, whose home was at Garsington in Oxfordshire, and the Reverend John Warneford, himself Rector of Bassingham in Lincolnshire and resident curate at Wappenham in Northants, who wished to live nearer Oxford where he was also Camden Professor of History. In addition to his other incumbencies, the Reverend Wickham had obtained the living of Stoke Talmage some miles south-east of Garsington, which seemed to Mr. Warneford better suited to him as being closer to Oxford. The resulting correspondence reads more like property dealing between estate agents than clergymen discussing church matters.

On 7 February 1769, Mr. Warneford wrote:

'Revd Sir, I return you many thanks for the obliging intelligence . . . as to the vacancy of your cure at Stoke. I have long wished for . . . a Residence of this kind not so distant from Oxford (whither I have such frequent calls) . . . and on that account I should be glad of an exchange, provided I could find a commodious residence nearer. I presume Stoke to be such, but. . . . I must beg leave to be a little particular in my Enquiries . . .

'I suppose your house fitted for the commodious reception of a Family, which, including 3 servants, consists at present of seven Persons, & may probably ere long be increased to nine. And as I am not without Visitants who at times will make some stay with me, one spare bed however will be necessary. I am persuaded I may reckon upon stable room sufficient for myself & visiting friends, but should be glad to know whether I may be accomodated with Closes for two horses (at least) as well as a couple of cows; for having been used to the comfortable convenience of my own butter, milk & cream, I should be very unwilling to want it. Your mention of Gardens in the plural is a very agreeable circumstance as we deal much in ye production of the Kitchen Garden especially. I take it for granted that you have no thoughts of residing yourself in this Living & that the Curacy is like to be of continuity, so that it would not be necessary for you to come on purpose to do Duty yourself, as you mention your custom has been. I should hope to receive forty pounds per annum (a very usual stipend for a resident Curacy) especially as I have the same at present, & give the same to my own curate in Lincolnshire together with the use of a very good House, excellent and spatious Garden & very pretty home close besides &c. Pray be so good as to favour me with your answer as soon as may be. . . .'

The draft answer to this explicit enquiry reads:

'The house consists of two good parlours and Kitchen, pantry &c, four bed-chambers and Garretts over them, very good Cellars, and a small Brewhouse with good water, stables for seven or eight horses and a large Barn, for what use you think proper. The house is sashed, has not been built above fourteen or 15 years, the Church at the same time, for Wilson's family consisted of himself, Mrs. Wilson, four children and 3 servants. The Church Yard was valued to me as £36 per annum when my predecessor used to turn in his Horses and cow. He also rented another little close near to the House which I imagine may be let again. . . . As to forty pounds a year for serving the Cure — is more than the Living can allow. I shall not reside, nor ever intended it, so that you may be certain of continuing at Stoke. Turnpike from Oxford within a mile and a half; one mile distant from Tetsworth, where the stage coaches and waggons go through every day, & also the posthouse as at Oxford. . . . There is a very good butcher at Tetsworth and more at Watlington about three miles off, who come to the Gentlemen. . . . I don't choose to give more than Thirty pounds. I forgot to mention that you shall have the Church yard. . . .'

That, for one reason or another, Mr. Warneford never resided at Stoke Talmage is beside the point. What the correspondence reveals is a clear picture of the standards of the day as far as many clergymen were concerned. Unquestionably, the Reverend James Woodforde, the diarist, was in many ways a more typical eighteenth-century clergyman, managing in a long life to rear a large family and keep three servants on an income of £300 a year, while at the same time attending more than adequately to the spiritual needs of his parish. His attention to the harvest of his East Anglian glebe farm, a significant part of his income, along with the tithes, no doubt kept him in touch with his agricultural parishioners. Entries on this score for 1776 read:

'Sep 14. Very busy all day with my barley, did not dine till 5 in the afternoon, my harvest men dined here today, gave them some beef and some plumb Pudding and as much liquor as they would drink. This evening finished my harvest and all carried into the Barn — 8 acres.'

'Dec 3. My frolic for my people to pay the tithe to me this day. I gave them a good dinner, surloin of beef roasted, leg of mutton boiled and plumb puddings in plenty.'

Parson Woodforde survived only by stringent economy but he was not ambitious, which was a rarity. Nor was he of a grasping nature. Some of the incumbents made themselves thoroughly unpopular by insisting on full exaction of every tithe payable to them and by demanding exorbitant expenses for burials and similar ceremonies and even, as in an instance given in the Shardeloe Papers, refusing to bury a corpse for two days until payment was made. Yet others were similar to one described by de la Rochefoucauld:

'The clergyman of this parish we were told is the greatest fop imaginable and consequently a very amusing character. His parishioners told us that he always comes to church with his hair beautifully dressed and powdered; but he reads so quickly and preaches so loud that it is impossible for anyone to follow him and people come out of the church they say without knowing anything more than when they went in.'

This was the age of the 'Squarson' — half squire, half parson — often the younger son of a wealthy family able to afford a suitable living. Their interests might centre on hunting, shooting and fishing, but such sporting incumbents were probably more to the taste of the average countryman than some of those described earlier.

When George Elers returned from India in 1808 as a young captain, he was stationed in Ipswich and encountered a fairly typical parson of this kind, whom he described thus:

'There was a clergyman, an old bachelor, a man of good fortune and with a snug living, who was very fond of a game of billiards. One day he came into Ipswich with his servant and saddle horses and after we had done our game he asked me to come home with him and dine; and I rode his servant's horse to his rectory, about four miles from Ipswich at Freston on the banks of the river Orwell, a lovely country all round and full of game which was strictly preserved. Mr. Bond, for that was his name, I found very hospitable; he loved a glass of good port, was well read, fond of music, and strictly preserved a wood of his full of pheasants. His temper was irritable and when excited, I have heard, very violent; but I never through a long acquaintance ever had the slightest difference with him.'

Unlike Mr. Wickham or Mr. Warneford, clergymen such as Parsons Bond and Woodforde were not ambitious for preferment and no doubt their parishioners benefited accordingly. It was not, however, only among the lower ranks of the clergy that preferment was eagerly sought. For instance, the Archbishopric of Canterbury was worth £25,000 a year and the race for this office was sometimes extremely close. In his *Life of George III*, Jesse described one such occasion:

'On the 18th of January, 1805, died, after a protracted illness, Dr. John Moore, Archbishop of Canterbury. As it was more than conjectured by well informed persons that Pitt was bent on elevating to the primacy his old tutor . . . Dr. Tomline, Bishop of Lincoln and Dean of St. Paul's, and on the other hand, as it was whispered that the King was no less anxious for the advancement of Dr. Manners Sutton, Bishop of Norwich and Dean of Windsor, a good deal of interest was excited as to the result. . . .

'The King received a message from Pitt that Archbishop Moore was dead and that he would wait upon His Majesty the next morning. The King, suspecting the cause, ordered his horse and rode over to Bishop Sutton, then residing at Windsor. He found he was at dinner with some friends and sent in the servant to say a gentleman wished to speak with him. The Bishop said immediately he could not go; but something in the servant's manner made him change his determination. When he came out, he found the King standing . . . near the hall door. The King took him by both hands. "My Lord Archbishop of Canterbury (he said) I wish you joy. Not a word; go back to your guests."

'On Pitt's arrival next day . . . Lord Sidmouth told Dean Milman that he believed such strong language had rarely ever passed between a Sovereign and his Minister.'

It is not surprising that the preachings of Wesley and his supporters took a hold on the country as they did. Thus Colonel John Byng, on his tour through the Midlands in 1789, noted: 'About religion I have made some enquiry (having been in many churches) and find it to be lodged in the hands of the Methodists: as the greater clergy do not attend to

The London Auction Mart Coffee Room (circa 1810), an example
of a city coffee room where business was transacted
and news of the day exchanged.
(Radio Times Hulton Picture Library)

Burning and Plundering of Newgate Prison
or to setting the Felons at Liberty by the Mob'
elding 1780). (Mary Evans Picture Library)

their duty and the lesser neglect it; that where the old psalm singing is abolish'd none is established in its place; as the organ is inconvenient and not understood; at most places the curates never attend regularly, or to any effect, or comfort, so no wonder that the people are gone over to Methodism.'

Although undoubtedly a practising Christian, Knyveton was not impressed by the Methodist creed. His Welsh friend Mr. Lloyd, a surgeon on a sister ship in their naval days together and a fellow student of obstetrics, was, however, a keen Methodist both by upbringing and inclination. On one occasion at least this proved extremely fortunate, as Knyveton recorded on 4 November in 1763:

'Up all last night corpse taking, a gentlewoman in distressed circumstances having died of a puerperal fever at noon yesterday and buried at St. Giles in the Fields; raising her for earthly resurrection in Dr. Harvie's anatomy theatre . . . and we lucky not to be lodged in gaol for our night's work; the watch discovering us, only Mr. Lloyd finds he was a Welshman from Carmathen, and moreover, a Methodist convert of Griffith Owen, who converted Mr. Lloyd senior, and so they ran together like two drops of quicksilver, and a guinea passed, and with some sweat we got the lady to a coach and so home. . . .

'The couple at our home are also Evangelicals and we can do little wrong since Mr. Lloyd sings at all their meetings, and 'tis hoped I shall be converted. Sunday last we visited the famous drawing room of the Countess of Huntingdon, a fervent member of the original Methodist sect in Fetter Lane, to hear Mr. Whiteley deliver an impassioned address of near two hours to a mixed congregation of honest tradesfolk and scented beaus hoping to see a young wench in a religious frenzy. Was not, I confess, impressed; I resent all attempts, however honest, to sway reason by passion and naught but lemonade and tea to drink, though the flunkeys were dressed like lords.'

Bearing everything in mind, it is understandable that de la Rochefoucauld, seeing the country from a foreigner's viewpoint, should state categorically: 'As to the way the English practise their religions, it is much more easy-going than ours. . . . They are not under any obligation to go to Church every Sunday, through rain, or fog, or heat — a very slight excuse will keep them away; but they are under an obligation to read the Bible as often as they can. It is in this book that children learn and grown-up people perfect their reading.'

On the subject of 'the English Sunday', he was scathing:

'Is there in the world anything so wearisome as the English Sunday? If working days are gloomy, they are festal days by comparison with Sunday. . . . you are forbidden, on this day, to do anything enjoyable. You may neither sing, nor play upon an instrument, much less dance; every form of card game is forbidden, the lower classes may not play ball games, or skittles, or any game whatsoever. The strictest of those who observe this fantastic regulation . . . stay in their homes to read the Bible, which all of them have in their houses. . . . The Act of Parliament which governs this practice imposes quite heavy fines upon offenders and . . . Magistrates . . . exact the fines from sabbath-breakers. . . .

'But what, you ask, do people do on Sunday? All the men collect together for the whole day in taverns. . . . The women meet after dinner and take tea together. . . . In the evening the family reassembles in time for supper and afterwards for bed. Either the father or the mother reads aloud from the Bible . . . and more often than not, at the end of half an hour everyone is asleep in his chair. All this is strictly true. I have seen it happen many times with my own eyes in the family with whom we spent the whole winter of 1784.'

De la Rochefoucauld does not appear to have encountered the Non-conformist creed of the Methodists. The government attitude to them, however, was perhaps best summed up in the typically robust phraseology of Lord Thurlow, on being confronted by a deputation of Non-conformists when he was Lord Chancellor. 'I'm against you, damme!' he said. 'I am for the established Church, by God! Not that I have any greater regard for the Established Church than for any other Church, except because it is established. If you can get your damned religion established, I'll be for that too!'

Both Knyveton's and Lord Thurlow's offhand contemptuous attitude to Methodism was that commonly held by the average Georgian gentleman. Its appeal, as Knyveton pointed out, was to the emotions, rather than to reason. It thus attracted many of the poorer classes seeking the spiritual comfort denied them all too often by the established church. Yet with the spread of Methodism there also developed the growing prudery of the Georgian era, epitomised by the use of such euphemisms as 'unmentionables' for trousers.

The conversion of William Wilberforce, the Yorkshire M.P. and champion of the anti-slavery campaign, was one of the greatest triumphs for Methodism. He and the blue-stocking Hannah More, another conspicuous convert, waged a powerful campaign in the eighties on many fronts, chiefly aimed at vice. Their Society for the Suppression of Vice attacked such obvious targets as brothels, swearing and Sabbath-breaking.

It was all very well for the Rev. Sydney Smith to term it derisively 'a society for suppressing the vices of persons whose income does not exceed £500 per annum.' For although there was a grain of truth in this, the Methodist creed had a dampening puritanical effect on the Georgian attitudes to life to all levels, attaining full effect in the Victorian era.

Apart from the deplorable state of the established church, another reason for the spread of Methodism was almost certainly the acute tension of the times. Thus with the spread of enclosures, with the uprooting of families from the countryside and the development of the towns — a feature of the later Georgian era — Methodism naturally gained converts. In the mill towns, such as Manchester, Methodism was soon the dominant religion, as Byng observed in 1789.

It is perhaps difficult today to appreciate just how many fears, forebodings and tensions were prevalent in the Georgian age, even among the upper classes. Rumour, lack of reliable information, an absence of quick communications — all these tended to aggravate rather than diminish fears and tensions. Apart from national fears of riot, revolution or invasion, which often seemed real enough at the time, there were many personal fears. Thus there was the ever-present fear of smallpox, of an accident involving the surgeon's knife, and of robbery and assault by footpads or ruffians. With no police force, the government had to rely on the troops in times of civil disturbance and the ordinary Georgian gentleman had to be able to look after himself.

As ever, Knyveton provides us with interesting information on these points. On his arrival in London in September 1751, when he put up at lodgings in Dean Street, Soho, he noted:

'Mr. Hunt warns me that if I am to be much abroad it will be as well to buy myself a cudgel or better small sword, as to the west of us beyond the Marylebone Gardens thieves and gentlemen of the road do swarm in great abundance attracted by the many houses of the rich in that quarter and they do pass even in the day into the streets of the town to the great annoyance of the passers by. He informs me that quite recently some few months back the coach of my Lady Albemarle was robbed in Great Russell Street in broad day by nine men, the King compensating her for her loss the next day by giving her a gold watch and chain, very fine.'

'September 21; Sunday; with Mr. Hunt and his wife to the parish church of Marylebone, it being a fine morning the walk through the fields exceeding pleasant. Mr. Hunt points out to me a portion of the common where last week a gentleman was set upon by thieves and grievously hurt. A wearisome sermon of some hour and a quarter . . . the which I beguiled may Heaven forgive me in quizzing a pretty wench who sat in the musicians gallery and led the singing with a fair sweet voice and she proving demure to sleep. To walk in the Gardens in the afternoon and after supper Mr. Hunt reads prayers and so to bed.'

Gangs of ruffians in the streets could make walking, at night especially, a hazardous business, as Knyveton discovered:

'October 24; 1751: On the road we did meet a gang of Tumblers putting a woman in a barrel and then with great laughter and noise setting her to roll down the street the Watch interfering and being sadly beaten for his pains. So home by another way very tired and muddy from the roads.'

'October 26: This day being Sunday to Church with Mr. Hunt and

'*The New Gallows in the Old Bailey*' (circa *1780*). *The mixed sexes of the felons about to be hanged and their reactions are clearly depicted.* (Radio Times Hulton Picture Library)

wife. Hear that the choir wench has died in child-bed, this greatly astonishing me, till I learn that she was only five months gone but was frighted by a gang of Mohawks a week ago.'

'November 27: Coming home did see a troupe of Sweaters at work these surrounding two poor wights and prodding them with their swords to make them dance, and did halt undecided which way to turn and so they did see me and I to my heels and lose myself in a very ill quarter of the town from which I made equal speed to free myself and so, by asking a Watchman the way, to my lodgings at last very fatigued and muddied from head to toe with dirt from the roads. Will always after this carry my sword.

'November 30; . . . Very wet and foggy but to church by the roads. Mr. Hunt and wife and self joining three neighbours for greater safety.'

Ruffians, footpads, coach accidents and the like were factors which affected everyone, of high or low degree. Fear of the press-gangs, the poorhouse, or the debtor's prison might affect the working man, but the Georgian gentleman had personal worries of a different nature; they concerned his house, property and finances. Banks could, and did, fail ruinously, leaving their clients without a penny and with no redress. A house could burn down and there was no means of insurance against such a loss. Servants and tradesmen could also cause anxiety.

The Purefoy letters mirror the minor worries of this latter kind by Henry Purefoy to his London agent Mr. Moulson in August 1753 indicates an unusually tiresome state of affairs even for them:
an urgent job: 'Master Parker/ This is the third day you have been from my worke, tho you promised faithfully you would never leave it till you had finished it; if you don't come on Monday next I will get somebody else to worke upon it. I think you are a very unworthy man to neglect it so this fine weather & am Your freind to serve you. H.P.'

In November of the following year he is finding a Chimney Sweep troublesome: 'Mr. Hind/ All our Chimneys want sweeping & you promised my mother you would be here at Michaelmas last. Your not coming is a Disappointment to us & if you don't come in a fortnight I must be obliged to send for some other Chimney Sweeper, which that you should prevent by coming over is the Desire of Your freind to serve you H.P.'

The Purefoy servants were a constant problem, but a letter written by Henry Purefoy to his London agent Mr. Moulson in August 1753 indicates an unusually tiresome state of affairs even for them:
'Sir/ I am favoured with yours dated ye 3rd of July last & am much obliged to you for your kind Invitation (to visit London) . . . but at present my coachman is run away from mee for fear of a great Belly a Girl lays to him & our Cookmaid was forced to go to Oxford Assize to be evidence against a felon there & when she came home she said she was married & our Gardiner has married my mother's maid & wee have had a very valuable mare lamed with a fforke, but now in a fair way to recovery; so our little ffamily is in a state of Confusion at present. . . . Your very humble servt. H.P.'

Knyveton also had his servant problems. While still a bachelor, although a rising practitioner in London, he wrote: 'January 4th 1767: My servant girl Sally Moat is cheating me very much. We consumed this last festive season enough vittles for a troop of horse and have apparently drunk enough tea to float a 74, but apparently *not enough to fill the Moat*. The wench is a bottomless well; or else has the worms.'

Later, when he was happily married and at the height of his profession, with coachman, Will Rogerson, footmen, maid and cook among other staff, he recorded a rather different domestic upset, perhaps typical of the times when the French Revolution was causing concern in England:

A doctor of divinity dressed in his scarlet gown (1815) with cassock beneath and bands at the neck. (Radio Times Hulton Picture Library)

'June 26th. 1791: Elizabeth hurried away from the breakfast table this morning when a terrible noise broke out in the kitchen; returning with a heightened colour but a smile round her lips; and slapped down under my nose a pamphlet "The Rights of Man" Part One by Tom Paine; which it appears the second footman was perusing when my worthy Will Rogerson stepped in from the yard; and seeing the obnoxious article twitched it out of the footman's hand, and threw it on the dresser, suggesting that he and the footman should settle the question of man's rights by a set-to outside; the cook and the scullery maid setting up a screaming, and the footman, not liking the glint in Rogerson's eye, threw an iron ladle at him; whereupon Will knocked him down, and dragging him out to the pump, soused his head as he said "to cool it of revolution fever."

'We have dismissed the footman — not for his literary tastes for, even though we do not agree with them, this is a free country — but he was lazy and greedy and was not giving satisfaction; leaving Elizabeth to scold the female domestiks, I sent for Will, gave him a lecture and a guinea for salve for his bruised knuckles — which he accepted with a wooden face — and picking up the offensive tract, retired to peruse it at leisure in my study.'

Such Radical, or Jacobin, sympathies were very prevalent amid the working classes around the time of the French Revolution. Four years later the situation was much worse, as Knyveton noted: 'October 29th 1795: Returned home tonight with my coach windows cracked and a sword cane I have purchased. The streets are grown so dangerous that though swords are now worn only by the services, those whose business takes them about at all hours must have protection. There have been open air meetings of the Jacobin sympathisers and the Corresponding Societies and today on his way to Parliament the King was fired at with a toy gun. It is an intolerable state of affairs.'

The Corresponding Society for the encouragement of discussion of the constitution, formed in 1792, was explosive material, but proved surprisingly ineffectual. It may have inspired some riots, but throughout the entire Georgian era rioting was commonplace, for it required little to raise the indignation of the mob and provoke a full scale disturbance. Nor were they by any means confined to London. There were, for instance, frequent riots at Dissenters' meetings when Wesley was preaching in the West and in the Midlands. A five-day riot broke out over the price of mackerel in Norwich in 1740, and there were riots over turnpikes in Bristol in 1749, over enclosures in Wiltshire in 1752, over the price of goods in Leicester in 1766 and over unemployment by copper miners in Cornwall in 1787, to mention only a few at random.

London, by virtue of its size, had rather more frequent and regular riots, which were virtually treated as a public holiday by the mob on most occasions. The cause of the riot might be innocent enough — a procession of weavers out of work due to the free import of French silks, disaffected sailors demanding more pay, or a political demonstration. In a short time the mob would be streaming through the streets, holding up the traffic, breaking windows, pulling down signs, throwing stones, chasing passers-by, picking their pockets, or rolling them in the gutters, attacking the watch and the beadles and generally putting everyone in fear of their lives. Finally, and usually rather belatedly, the troops would be called in to restore order. The sight of the dragoons jingling up and down the streets, or militia setting up barricades, would generally be enough to cause the rioters to disperse.

On some occasions, however, the mob were completely out of control and appeared to be verging on revolution. With the example of France across the Channel, this was a fear present in many minds at times. The Wilkes riots, in 1763 and subsequently, were an example of mob violence which got out of hand. An M.P. and member of the Hellfire Club, John Wilkes was also the editor of the scurrilous magazine *The North Briton*. In copy No. 45, he attacked the King's Speech to Parliament, but instead of offering him office as the price of his silence, Grenville, the Chief Minister, foolishly arrested him under a General Warrant, a step which Wilkes soon proved illegal in the courts. In so doing, he portrayed himself as the champion of liberty and free speech, obtaining damages from the government. When he was then put on trial for seditious libel, he slipped abroad and in 1764 was duly outlawed, but each stage in his case resulted in popular uprisings which grew beyond control.

There are many records of these riots, but as an eyewitness with a keen pen and ready turn of phrase, Knyveton is hard to beat. His entry for 7 October 1763, when he had just returned to this country from service as a naval surgeon, describes the background of discontent to the Wilkes riots:

'Arrived at the Saracen's Head Inn after a weary dusty journey of two days. . . . Was glad to get here with whole bones and an uncut purse. The roads full of penniless wretches paid off from the fleet and the army, their country's reward for all their heroism and discomfort, the right of a free Englishman to starve neglected in a ditch. The London mob up and pouring now through the streets, in very ugly moods since John Wilkes has been so roughly handled by the Commons. But what have I and those of my comrades fought for if a man may not speak his mind and the freedom of the Press be abolished? Two — three fights in the tap since I arrived and my supper — a fair one of boiled fowls and steaks — near spoilt by a Grub Street hack hurling a tattered copy of the immortal Number 45 of the "North Briton" that great magazine in which Wilkes so boldly and caustically criticizes the King's policy, at a *bagman* aping the airs of a gentleman. A bony Scotchman near drowned in the horse trough in the yard by the

ostlers and grooms as I arrived; Lord Bute, that sly Scots councillor of
the King, has brought too many of his ragged countrymen with him . . .
am weary; shall to bed, to rest if not to sleep, the noise in the streets
very terrible with the rumbling of the market gardeners' carts, the
shouts of the linkmen lighting the quality to masque or club, and the
roar of the crowds.'

These were the typical views of the returned serviceman, disgusted
with the treatment of the discharged sailors and soldiers and politically
unaware of the real course of events. By 25 October, less than three
weeks later, he had begun to change his views. By this time studying as
a physician under Dr. Harvie, he and Mr. David Lloyd, his friend and
fellow naval surgeon, were personally involved. He recorded:

'Great uproar in the streets adjoining Wardour Street and into
Oxford Street this morning a huge crowd carrying in procession a big
dummy boot and a petticoat, on poles, in derision of Lord Bute and the
old scandal of his affair with the King's mother, the petticoat also an
emblem of scorn for the Scotch kilt; the mob intending to hang them at
Tyburn, but turned back by the sheriff's officers and constables, many
heads and windows broken. Seeing two tall Highlanders, twin brothers
by their similarity of feature, hard beset, Mr. David Lloyd sallied out
with a cudgel and I in his support and in that of law and order; and a
brisk little battle ensued, we returning to receive a shrill homily from
Dr. Harvie on the impropriety of conduct both undignified and unwise.
. . . Since John Wilkes won his action for unlawful detention . . . the
mob are in a truculent mood and respectable folk looking nervously to
their shutters.'

Only two years later on 17 May after rioting by unemployed weavers, he wrote that: 'This has indeed been a black week; a terrible fire
. . . in . . . Limehouse, upwards of sixty houses consumed . . . soldiers
clattering up and down the streets and none dared go to bed . . . the
whole city in an uproar; the gaols full, the hangman will be busy.'

All that had gone before, however, was nothing to the riots when in
1765 Wilkes, with powerful support, returned to London in a last
desperate fling, standing once more for Parliament despite having been
declared an outlaw. Amid unprecedented scenes, he was three times
returned as Member for Middlesex by his supporters, despite the results
in each case being declared void. The mob went wild and the citizens of
London locked their doors and dared not stir outside. All the windows
of the Mansion House were broken and society ladies in sedan chairs
were stopped and forced to cry: 'Wilkes and Liberty'. The Austrian
ambassador was turned out of his coach, upended in the gutter, where
he lost his wig, and 45 was scrawled in chalk on the soles of his boots.

John Knyveton wrote simply: 'The world has gone mad.' He even
queried: 'Is this a Revolution? Does John Wilkes intend to topple King
George off his throne? For the riots were not confined to London . . .

'*View of an execution before the Debtor's Door of Newgate*' (*1809*). *The usual crowd of spectators present are shown beginning to disperse now that their entertainment is over.* (Radio Times Hulton Picture Library)

if so, 'tis not to be borne! No true Englishman will ever submit to the Rule of Violence. . . .'

Wilkes organised popular opinion throughout the country by means of meetings and the formation of a supporters' society. By so doing, he introduced a new element into Georgian politics. Perhaps not altogether surprisingly, Wilkes, the reckless libertine, eventually became respectable and a supporter of law and order, but not before he had released the spectre of revolution in the city of London. The riot with a leader was a far more difficult matter to control once out of hand than the normal leaderless mob.

After spasmodic rioting throughout April and May, Wilkes was finally tried and imprisoned for ten months in June 1768 for publishing *The North Briton,* and Knyveton described the resulting riots as follows: 'June 18th . . . the mob have gone crazy again; fighting the Irish White Boys, and the Irish White Boys the sailors, and the sailors the weavers, and all attacking any constable or soldier on sight; the Irish White Boys armed with banners, and pistols and cutlasses, shooting at the soldiers and being shot at in return; scarce a day passes but three or four of them or the mob killed.'

In 1771, there were further riots when the House of Commons tried to assert its rights to secret debate by imprisoning various printers who had offended them in this respect. Once again Knyveton was in the thick of it and wondered whether it would be advisable to move his pregnant wife into the country. Once again the city suffered spasmodic rioting. None of the scenes hitherto, however, was as severe as the notorious 'Gordon Riots' in 1780, led by Lord George Gordon, sometimes charitably termed 'eccentric', but not by Knyveton, who described the events of the week thus:

'June 11th 1780 (Sunday) At divine service today rendered humble and grateful thanks that the horrid mob who for a week past have terrorised the City are now dispersed and I can once more go about my business unhindered; using the cry of "No Popery!" raised by that crazed fanatic Lord George Gordon, as excuse to burn private houses and loot chapels and warehouses; not coming into the fashionable quarters because of chains drawn across the Strand and Holborn and soldiers stationed nearby, but Moorfield, where live many Catholics was wholly given up to their rages, the worst day of all last Wednesday, *Black Wednesday* indeed, when the Fleet and King's Bench prisons, the new Bridewell and several private houses all went up in flames, and an attack on the Pay Office and the Bank was only beaten off by volleys from the Guards. John Wilkes defending the Bank in person; at a Catholic Distiller's . . . on Holborn Hill . . . a very horrid business, crowds rolling out immense casks of impure spirits, which they breached and drank, dozens thereby falling dead or insensible in the gutters, and when the spirits caught fire all were consumed, the quick and the dead together. . . . Night after night we could see from our roof the smoke and flames of burning houses, the weather very dry and hot, fortunately however there was no wind, else it was very likely all the great metropolis would today be ashes. . . .

'On Tuesday and Wednesday came more soldiers . . . and so the city can now breathe again. . . . It is said that nearly two hundred rioters were known to have been killed — and many more doubtless were hid in the stews, or burnt, or thrown into the river — and a hundred and seventy three wounded are prisoners.'

The threat of riots and the fear of Revolution were factors that the Georgian gentleman had to accept as a part of life. In the same way, he also accepted the threat of invasion. This fear was a real one for a great part of the Georgian era. It recurred at intervals from the time of the rebellion of 1715 until Waterloo in 1815 finally ended Napoleon's ambitions.

In 1756, at the start of the Seven Years' War, after a journey from London to Portsmouth in the Guildford coach, Knyveton chronicled on 11 March: '. . . Glad enough to get here after a journey vilely tedious from the bad state of the roads and the incessant challenges of patrols in gutteral German. For so great has this threat of invasion grown that poor King Geordie getting no help from Parliament has had to hire his own countrymen to help him and there are upwards of four thousand Hanoverians and Dutchmen stationed now in Kent.'

Three years later, when ashore at Portsmouth after some well earned leave from his duties as a naval surgeon, Knyveton recorded a conversation with a fellow doctor at Portsmouth: 'March 22nd:1759; . . . Dr. Wilkes to . . . take a glass of wine with me. He is not a navy man and therefore is worried like many of the public at this threat of invasion. It is known of course that King Louis has between ten and twenty thousand men drilling on the Normandy coast and is building a fleet of barges in Le Havre and other ports; but as I pointed out to Doctor Wilkes the Straits have to be crossed and there is the British Navy to see they have a rough crossing.'

In 1778, when France joined America in the War of Independence, there was immediate and widespread fear of invasion once more. Knyveton, who had left the Navy fifteen years previously, no longer seemed so confident of naval power, for he noted: 'June 12th; . . . at this present perilous hour . . . drums rolling in the streets, the militia are drilling in Hyde Park; the only subject now discussed in the coffee houses is whether our regular regiments should be withdrawn from American and if so, whether they can reach home in time to hold Kent at least, if the French Fleet should land an army.'

The attitude of the average Englishman to the Americans and to the War of Independence, is well demonstrated in Knyveton's diaries:

'December 22nd 1770: A young American from New York has joined our classes, Mr. Saunders Stroud, very tall, very thin, very lean and hatchet-faced, and with a distressing tendency to tear off a blood-curdling Indian War whoop in moments of excitement. . . . His yales of the frontiers — for altho' only twenty-two he has fought in numerous skirmishes — and of the Indians, keep us at nights out of bed long after our usual times. . . . But although well disposed towards us, Mr. Stroud has other stories not so sunny, of the misery and distress caused among the colonials by our unsettled policy of government, and of widespread discontent against the attitude of King George towards blood relations treated like unfortunate beggars.'

Two years later came the entry:

'June 3rd 1772: Mr. Saunders Stroud returned to America today on his uncle's packet The Happy Kindred . . . and feel that one of our family circle has gone from among us; we wish him well, tho' the clouds, alas, grow no less in the west; scuffles in the seaboard states between Americans and our lads more common every week. Perhaps it is a pity we conquered Canada; had the French remained on their border, the Americans for safety's sake would have remained close knit to the country from which they sprang. . . .'

A further two years passed and then came his record of the Boston Tea Party, which gave clear warning of what was to come unless there was a sharp change of policy:

'February 12th 1774: The Exchange is in an uproar. India House convulsed — Lord North, to help the East India Company, passed an act importing tea duty free into England and exporting it in America subject to a small duty there; but this monopoly not being at all to the taste of American merchants, comes news now that on December 16th last forty sparks dressed as Mohawk Indians boarded three Indiamen lying in Boston Harbour, threw their cargo of three hundred and forty-two chests of tea overside and burnt the vessels!

'Politics have swamped all scandal at the Literary Club at the "Turk's Head" Gerrard Street and at George's Coffee House in the Strand. . . .'

The next year Dr. Knyveton chronicled events by the following entries in his diaries:

'January 2nd 1775: A long letter this morning from New York from Mr. Saunders Stroud: he writes . . . that an explosion is expected hourly. Worse he writes that he feels he must join the cause of the rebels, yet in the same breath declares that he and they are no traitors but rise in defence of their rights alone, their loyalty to Britain and the Crown as firm as ever. And I must confess I feel some sympathy for him, reminded sadly of our own Civil War, when honest men were finally driven by despair to take up their swords against the ruinations of Charles Stuart. . . .'

'March 22nd: The evening papers are full of Edmund Burke's magnificent oration to the House, calling for repeal of those Acts irritating the Americans, and demanding that the problems of American taxation be left to the American Assemblies.

'Is it too late to hope that the war whoop may yet not echo along the great rivers and through the forest clearings?'

'August 11th: After efforts on both sides to close the gulf rapidly widening between Great Britain and America, blood alas has been shed

An evocative illustration of the Gordon Riots showing the murder of a clergyman and rioters being repelled while attacking a house amid scenes of general chaos. (Mary Evans Picture Library)

. . . at the town of Concord. . . .'

As the War unfolded his further entries mirrored average English opinion:

'February 17th 1776: Lord North the leader of the present ministry has proposed a bill of conciliation with America and 'twould seem the sensible thing. British trade is all out of joint, and tho' the rebel armies are at moment victorious, misery and ruin stalk grisly thro' their states. . . .'

'March 14th: Too late, too late! A pact has been ratified between America and France. Ambassadors in London and Paris have been withdrawn, we are once again at war with France. This is what fifteen years of shilly-shally and the ethics of usury have brought us to. . . .'

'August 14th 1777: The war drags on in America, the American troops commanded by Colonel George Washington outnumbering us twenty to one, but indifferently armed, and so far we have always been victorious in the field . . . but I cannot but feel we are like a child striking with puny fists at a giant as yet only half awake . . . 'Tis a foolish war, with both sides anxious to shake hands, but neither for the sake of honour daring to take the first step towards peace. . . .'

His final entries read:

'January 2nd 1778: There is grave news of a great disaster in America. . . . General Burgoyne . . . was forced . . . to surrender at Saratoga on October 17th last. . . .'

'November 16th 1782: Against the wish of the King, peace has been made with America. Opinion as to the wisdom of this step greatly divided, but the present Government is distracted by the storm over the India Bill and the savage assaults on Gibraltar . . . we have neither the men o' war, or soldiers, to fight in two worlds, and since Holland joined our enemies we are in perilous straits. . . .'

His rancour, in common with most of the country, was not against the Americans, but against the French as his ultimate entry shows:

'January 21st 1783: . . . preliminary articles of peace were signed yesterday with France and the mob are out breaking the windows of Lord North and others to signify their displeasure. For, if we are hard pressed, we have crushed France almost to death. . . . Trust this will be a lesson to that proud tyrant Louis not wantonly again to meddle in our affairs. . . .'

All may have seemed well for once, when in 1792 Pitt stated that 'there never was a time in the history of this country when from the situation of Europe we might more reasonably expect fifteen years of peace than we may at the present moment'. When a titled client endorsed this statement wholeheartedly, Knyveton commented dubiously: 'I trust the noble gentleman's beliefs that it is peace in our time are correct.' The following year England and France were at war again and with the

Napoleonic wars the fear of invasion became more real than ever.

A clear impression of how deep-seated this fear was may be gained from Knyveton's diary in 1797 when the country actually was invaded. Knyveton described the scene in London, obviously quoting rumour that had spread like shockwaves throughout the coffee houses of the capital: 'February 23rd: The French have landed near Fishguard! An infamous Black Legion commanded by a horrid pirate, an American adventurer Colonel Tate is marching inland to burn Liverpool. All the Militia are cramming themselves into their uniforms and the Banks surrounded by angry crowds seeking to withdraw their money. It is fortunate I possess a little landed property, for if the money is all withdrawn from the Banks the country will go bankrupt — which God Forbid!'

He noted another significant reaction to the news on the following Sunday: 'February 27th: . . . This morning St. Georges in Hanover Square was crowded, for society and merchants of the city had come to ask God's assistance in the present ominous fix.'

It is a measure of the slowness of communications at the time that a full week elapsed before news of what had actually happened in the west of the country was finally published. By then everyone doubtless felt a trifle foolish at panicking so unnecessarily, but it is plain that the spirit of unity throughout the country was seldom so great. The threat of invasion undoubtedly strengthened the country internally. Knyveton recorded:

'February 30th: It has been a most horrid scare and the French had all but succeeded in their sly trick; for it is whispered they hoped by the invasion to frighten us into drawing out our capital, thus finally exhausting the Funds and bringing the country to financial ruin. . . .

'As for that bloodthirsty ruffian, that swaggering fire eater Colonel Tate and his band of 1,200 cruel desperadoes, galley slaves and pickpockets for the most part who were landed under the guns of two French frigates, since snapped up by two of our own frigates — why, they appear after all to have been most civilised and gentle folk. For when Lord Cawden of Fishguard called out the Castle Martin Yeomanry and the Fishguard Volunteers and boldly fired on 'em — although Colonel Tate had more than sufficient force to cut their bucolic ranks to pieces — he quietly surrendered "Upon" as he nobly explained "Principles of Humanity!" So his gallant ragged heroes were hustled off and disarmed.'

To counter the threat of invasion, it was decided in the 1790s to build a chain of fortified towers, known as Martello Towers, round the south-eastern coastline. Although the last real possibility of invasion had passed by 1805, their construction was begun in 1808. They were not completed until 1811. No doubt, however, the soldiers who manned them and the militia who drilled nearby were still expecting invasion as long as Napoleon ruled in France. The fear lost none of its potency for being completely unrealistic. It was not appreciated either that the fear of invasion, shared by all and uniting the country against the threat from the Continent, ensured that there would be no revolution while it lasted. It was among the trials and tribulations of the Georgian gentleman that two of his greatest fears were to a large extent imaginary.

Surprisingly enough, another affliction which beset the Georgian gentleman was excessive noise. Complaints, especially in London, were frequent, and Knyveton especially noted one house where he had lodged while setting up in practice:

'January 1st 1766: Have moved . . . I was fairly driven out of Martin's Court — Mr. Miller and his wife are very good civil folk, but although Mr. Miller reads his Bible aloud every evening, never a word was to be heard above the bawling of his family, one or other of whom was always in the fire, or the washing tub, or being scratched by the cat, who average a litter of kittens every week — most remarkable — and drunken brawlers and street walkers in the alley and the iron clanging of St. Thomas' bells. My hours of sleep reckoned up to one night's rest in five — I got scarce any rest.'

A letter to *The Public Advertiser* of 23 October 1783 inveighed against the 'horrid clamour' in the streets caused by 'bell ringers, hawkers of cheap pen knives, ribbons and hot pies, strolling players, Punch and Judy men, ballad singers, milk men and milk maids, butchers, bakers, grocers, vendors of fresh spring water, quack medicines, charms, the beadle, the Town Crier, the scavenger with his cart,' all of whom it was pointed out 'jangled bells of variable hideousness' so that there was no peace to be had 'even at night since the penny post man arrives at any hour up to midnight announcing his arrival with a brazen din to the distress of all those abed.' The writer of the letter suggested having receiving houses for the penny post to be kept open at least till ten at night.

Knyveton, commenting on the letter, added drily that 'he might with profit have offered also some suggestions to mitigate the din at the street markets, which on Sundays, Wednesdays and Fridays throughout the year are declared open at seven in the morning by a bell which rings for half an hour; and at eight o'clock rings on Saturdays; also bells rung whenever a notice is read; church bells too, practicing peels at all hours; a vile clamour which is a disgrace to our city and should be put down as a general nuisance.'

Anyone who has imagined that the Georgian era was one of general quiet, ease and restfulness must surely think again. It was a time of abounding individuality, when curbs on freedom were resented from wherever they might come. That the pace of life may have been slow at times is certainly true, but only in some respects. The Georgian gentleman was subject to different stresses and strains, but the tension was there beneath the surface. While deploring the antics of the rioters, he felt that the mob was something to be repelled by a handful of soldiers. He simply could not envisage the mob getting out of hand in the manner of the French peasantry or the Parisian citizens. Nor, in the last analysis, could the mob. They might pick the Georgian gentleman's pockets, even strip him of his clothes, but they would not hang him. It was un-British.

Throughout the eighteenth century, one public tribulation was heavy taxation. The Georgian gentleman in common with both ancestors and descendants, disliked paying taxes. Taxes on wines, teas, spirits and silks were largely avoided by the comfortable habit of winking at the activities of the free-traders or smugglers, and accepting any contraband offered at a reasonable price. The tax on hair powder resulted in wigs' going out of fashion. A tax imposed on windows resulted in many being blocked up. So it went on.

The end of the eighteenth century, however, saw the ultimate imposition of all. The Napoleonic Wars were responsible for a great deal, but to Knyveton — as to many another Georgian gentleman — the news on 12 January 1799 was almost too much. Indignantly he wrote:

'This is a horrible war — the rapacity and greed of the Government go beyond all limits — Parliament met on 20th November last year to consider the present financial position — not content with squeezing us dry in February, 1798, it is now actually proposed to place A TAX ON INCOMES. No income under £60 p.a. is to pay any duty at all, those from £100–£105 a fortieth part, and above £200 a tenth! It is a vile, Jacobin, jumped-up-jack-in-office piece of impertinence, — is a true Briton to have no privacy? Are the fruits of his labour and toil to be picked over farthing by farthing by the pimply minions of Bureaucracy?'

Chapter Seven
MORALS, DIVERSIONS AND FROLICS

'No man is a hypocrite in his pleasures.' — Dr. Samuel Johnson

Morals might be said to cover a multitude of sins, for what one age regards as moral, or at least acceptable behaviour, another is likely to consider grossly immoral and offensive. It must be admitted that by modern standards, the Georgian age was corrupt at almost all levels — from the highest to the lowest. The political families in power as a matter of course placed their friends and relatives in well-paid government sinecures, even creating such posts for them. Behaviour of that kind was expected and, though increasingly subject to criticism, it continued throughout the Georgian period.

A good example of such patronage, though one of the last, was Charles Greville, the diarist, a grandson of the Duke of Portland, who was Prime Minister for the second time from 1807 to his death in 1809. Due to his grandfather's influence, Greville as a young man was given the sinecure of the Secretaryship of Jamaica. The duties of this post were performed by a deputy, who was paid by the Secretary from the fees he received from the island. In fact Greville never visited Jamaica, but took what was euphemistically termed 'permanent leave of absence'. Another sinecure post as Clerk to the Privy Council provided him with an income of £1,500 a year.

It is significant of the change in mental attitudes by the end of the Georgian era that in 1830, with a reforming government and no grandfather to safeguard his interests, Greville entered in his diary: 'I don't consider myself safe from Parliamentary assaults. In these times it will not do to be idle, and I told Lord Lansdowne that I was anxious to keep my emoluments, but ready to work for them.'

The power of patronage, or control over the choice of applicants for any public office, however humble, was eagerly sought since it was accepted practice to bestow it on the highest bidder when no deserving friend or relative was eligible. This power of patronage extended downwards from the Royal Family to the squire with patronage of a living, or the magistrate with power to appoint beadles and similar minor officials. Even a seat in the House of Commons could be virtually assured by suitable payment to the landlords of 'rotten boroughs'.

In 1790, Palmerston paid £4,200 for the right to represent Newport in the Isle of Wight. The entire electorate was composed of the mayor, eleven aldermen and twelve burgesses. Writing to his wife, he described the farce of his election:

'. . . I arrived at Newport with my companions on Friday at Mr. Holmes's house, from whence we were carried to ask the votes of about half a dozen shopkeepers who looked as if they thought we might as well have saved ourselves the trouble. The evening concluded with a rubber of whist and a supper of which Mrs. Holmes and two other Isle of Wight ladies, tolerably vulgar, did the honours. About eleven on Saturday we were conveyed to the place of election where the ceremony, which was extremely private, took up about an hour, after which we were advised to take a ride to Carisbrook which we did with great pleasure, returned to a dinner of about 80 people.'

Those who had thus gained office expected to make the most out of it, even at the expense of the public whose interests they were nominally intended to protect. To take only one example, those granted contracts as suppliers to the armed forces were famed for cheating them shamefully, but they could not do so without a venal official in their pay. Bureaucracy was rife with bribery and corruption. In the colonies and India especially, it was even worse. There a venal administrator could quickly make his fortune.

During his service in India, George Elers referred to such a situation in 1808: 'There was living at Madras at this time a civilian named James Balfour. . . . The Honourable Basil Cochrane had for many years held the contract for supplying the Navy with meat, provisions, etc., and made a very handsome fortune. . . . James Balfour . . . got Cochrane's situation. He only held it for a very few years (4) and he had made £100,000 and left a Scotchman to act for him at an allowance of £6,000 per annum.'

On a lesser scale, corruption was commonplace throughout Britain. Two extracts from Knyveton's journals illustrate this, the first when he was a naval surgeon in 1758:

'August 14th: The purser is a scoundrel. Did today discover that he had drawn in his expense list moneys for cloathes, hats and food for the men who died in the West Indies and on the Guinea Coast. Reported the matter to Lieutenant Green, who took the matter before the Captain; but little done since the Captain has arranged to take a percentage of the bonus.'

In 1786, Knyveton was well established in practice in London and his journal reveals graft then rampant in a London hospital among minor officials:

'August 12th. The uncle of our cook, a candlemaker, who suffers from dropsy; and to whom I gave a letter to the Governor of Bartholomews Hospital, that he might enter the Cutting Ward to have the

Plate VI from 'The Rake's Progress' by William Hogarth. The scene is White's Chocolate House in St. James's St., on 3rd May 1773 when it was burnt down. Mr. Rakewell is shown in the moment of despair when he realises he has lost his fortune by gambling. (Mansell Collection)

dropsy relieved has returned again, saying he prefers to die in peace rather than be trimmed to death by a pack of b— sharks! But on enquiry I learn that on presenting my letter, it was not considered to cover all expediencies; so that he was requested to pay 19s6d for burial fees (returnable if he lived): and in addition moneys to cover the following items: 1 shilling to the beadle for notifying his friends of his decease; 1 shilling to the porter for taking the certificate of his death to the Parish where he was to be buried; 2 shillings each to the bearers of his corpse for carrying it to the hospital gates and no further; 1 shilling to the Matron for providing an old black cloth as pall; and 1 shilling to the Steward for certifying the death; Nor was this all, for the Sister of the Cutting Ward requested two and sixpence for supplying bandages and her helper 1 shilling; and the beadle wanted sixpence for carrying him into the ward and his helper sixpence also; And so after lengthy argument, and some high words, particularly with the beadle, whom he described as a bloated maw worm and a carrion crow, he returned again home.'

Even an honest country gentleman like Henry Purefoy was not above accepting a guinea in dubious circumstances, although more in the nature of commuting damages than anything else. Mary Davis, a maid of the Purefoys, together with a widow, Hannah Linnee, and others had opened the cellar door and stolen some of the Purefoys' beer. Little real harm was done, but Mrs. Purefoy was incensed and intent on prosecuting them. A warrant was sworn out and Hannah Linnee apprehended, and Henry wrote to his local attorney, Mr. Welchman:

'January 5th, 1736: Sir/ On Monday last Hannah Linnee came over here with Goodman Jones of Wappenham & others. At Jones's intercession I (unknown to my mother) agreed with her to take a guinea, so if Hannah Linnee offers you a guinea, accept it & you may then assure her from mee no further prosecution shall be had against her by reason of taking the strong beer, provided she is secret and sais nothing of it to anyone yet awhile. . . . Your very humble servant. H.P.'

When it came to accepting his turn as High Sheriff of Buckingham, a somewhat onerous duty, Henry Purefoy did not try to evade office by greasing the appropriate palms. He was mainly concerned that he might be in arrears with his annual payment of five guineas paid by those in the county liable to serve, towards 'reducing the expenses attending the office of Sheriff.' In January 1747 he wrote to a friend, who apparently was associated with the fund, inquiring if he was covered by these 'Articles for Regulating the Expences' or not. His letter ran:

'John Pollard, Esquire: Sir/ I have received advice from a ffreind in London that the three Gentlemen who were prickt down for Sherifs for the County of Bucks have all got of(f) and that Mr. Campbell Price of Westbury or myself will certainly be the Pocket Sheriff. . . . If I am within the articles and shall have ye benefit of them I will not endeavour to prevent being prickt down Sheriff; but if you imagine I am not I must write immediately to my ffreinds in Town to use their best Endeavours to get mee of(f). ... I am Sir! Your very humble servant. H.P.'

Henry Purefoy duly served his term and then returned to the quiet life of his manor. But for the administrative work borne by country gentlemen similar to him, who served as Justices of the Peace and attended to parish and county affairs, the country would have suffered. To them, local matters were paramount — far more significant than affairs in London.

They voluntarily undertook various duties, as one instance conveys. A bastard became a burden on the parish in which it was born and a charge on the rates, unless the father from another parish could be apprehended and made to marry the girl or take the responsibility for the child. Hence the following letter from Henry Purefoy, dated 5 May 1739 to 'Mr. John Low at Cold-Harbour in Studham Parish to be left at the Wheatsheaf Inn at Tame':

'Mr. Low/ There is one Catherine Poulton a servant lately delivered of a female Bastard child at my house, and the parish officers have been with you to find the father of it. You were so kind as to proffer your best endeavours to take him. I do believe according to what ye parish officers say it would be as well for your family as our parish if the putative father could be apprehended; so if you should be successfull and get Intelligence of him, if you would let mee have a line or two from you ... our parish officers shall come to you. ... Your unknown freind to serve you. H.P.'

In 1769, Parson Woodforde left on record that he was paid the fee of 10s. 6d. for marrying a couple in similar circumstances: 'I married Tom Bunge of Amsford to Charity Andrews of Castle Cary by License this morning. The Parish of Cary made him marry her, and he came handcuffed to Church for fear of running away.'

Such a marriage would not perhaps bode well for future happiness, but the parish was more concerned with passing the burden on to someone else's rates. In practice, the marriage probably stood as good a chance of succeeding as many of the arranged marriages, then the custom in the early part of the Georgian era. The male attitude to women and marriage was summed up by George Savile, Marquis of Halifax, in his *Advice to a Daughter*. Although written in 1688, his book went through fifteen editions by 1745, being still reprinted as late as 1794. On marriage, he wrote:

'It is one of the disadvantages belong to your Sex that young Women are seldom permitted to make their own Choice. ... There is an Inequality in the Sexes, and ... for the better Oeconomy of the World, the Men, who were to be the Lawgivers, had the larger share of

Reason bestow'd upon them. . . .

'The first part of our Life is a good deal subjected to you in the Nursery, where you Reign without Competition, and by that means have the advantage of giving the first Impressions. . . . Afterwards you have more strength in your Looks, than we have in our Laws, and more power by your Tears than we have by our Arguments.'

He went on to detail the kinds of husband she might expect and their possible vices; also how to counter these. For a faithless husband, he recommended 'An Affected Ignorance'; for a drunken husband, 'be wise and patient'; for a 'cholerick' husband, 'gentleness and a kind smile'; for a sullen husband, 'let the Black humour spend itself'; for a 'Close-handed wretch . . . observe seasonable hours of speaking'; and for a weak and incompetent husband, 'first give him the Orders you afterwards receive from him.' He went on to suggest that she should pray for a 'Wise Husband' and cautioned her to conform with the 'Methods' of 'the Family into which you are grafted,' and look to her husband's 'Friends' for advice and 'gain the Servants you find in a Family' rather than to hold too fast to her own.

This advice was sound enough, especially for the arranged marriage, when it was still considered sensible — indeed, a duty more often than not — to marry an heiress to maintain the family fortunes, or to enlarge the size of an estate.

Encouraged by the example of the aristocracy, for a considerable part of the Georgian period it was considered acceptable either to flaunt a mistress openly or take a lover. These Restoration morals, however, tended to be superseded by the more strait-laced attitudes of the emergent middle class — the merchants and dissenters — towards the end of the Georgian era, for a revulsion of feeling developed at the example set by George IV both as Regent and King. Open immorality gave way to discretion and hypocrisy.

One feature of the Georgian period was the 'ménage à trois', of which there are many examples. The most notorious, perhaps, was that of the 5th Duke of Devonshire, whose first wife, the beautiful Georgiana Spencer, died in 1806. During her lifetime she was devoted to his mistress, the intellectual Lady Elizabeth Foster, who became his second wife on her death. Both were painted by Gainsborough and both were confined at the same time in Paris. Rumour had it that Georgiana delivered a daughter while Elizabeth bore a son and the children were switched, so that the 6th Duke was illegitimate. Many years afterwards, Greville in his diaries contended that the story was a myth, though 'widely believed'.

Another feature of the period was the anomalous figure of the 'Cicisbeo', an Italian term for one privileged to escort a married woman in the evening, paying her assiduous attentions, before returning her to her husband. Several Cicisbei were desirable from the husband's view-

The Union Club carousing, celebrating the Union with Ireland. Amidst the scene of general debauchery is the vast basin of whiskey punch being carried to the table by two boys in the right foreground. (Radio Times Hulton Picture Library)

point in that there was presumably safety in numbers. Doubtless many so called were in fact lovers. A good example of this arrangement was in the household of Colonel John Byng, whose second wife Bridget was one of William Windham's mistresses. In 1775, Windham boasted that 'Mrs Byng was sitting at the door . . . not in expectation of Mr. Byng's return.' Windham, however, was something of a weathercock and had numerous affairs, although Bridget appears to have been his main love, until he married her sister Cecilia — rather to everyone's surprise.

There were, of course, notorious courtesans and outstanding beauties, to whom many Georgian gentlemen paid court. Perhaps the most remarkable courtesan — she can scarcely be termed anything else — was Miss Elizabeth Chudleigh. Celebrated for her ability to drink two bottles of wine, she almost married the Duke of Hamilton before secretly marrying the heir to the Earl of Bristol. Attending George II's Court, she attracted the monarch's attentions, receiving from him a watch worth thirty-five guineas. At the Venetian Ambassador's Masquerade she appeared in the character of Iphegenia, wearing an all-revealing gauze dress in which her portrait was painted. She went on to become the Duke of Kingston's mistress and bigamously married him, thus inheriting his fortune on his early demise. When heirs had her arraigned before the House of Lords, she escaped being branded on the hand on being found guilty, and even managed to retain her fortune and her Earl. Finally, she retired first to Russia and then to France, where she died in 1788 in a palace for which she had paid £50,000.

Perhaps more remarkable still, for the sheer unlikelihood of it, was the romance of the stunning Gunning sisters. Aged about eighteen they arrived in England from Ireland with their father Mr. John Gunning of Castle Coote, in 1751. The younger married first the Duke of Hamilton and on his death in 1758 the Duke of Argyll. The elder daughter married Lord Coventry, but died prematurely young, possibly from using cosmetics with a base of white lead. She seems to have been as simple and stupid as she was beautiful. Typical of her tactlessness was her reply to George II who, towards the end of his reign, commiserated with her because there had been no masquerades or similar spectacles.

'As to that,' she replied, 'there is only one spectacle I wish to see and that is a Coronation.'

Much more typical of the age was Knyveton's marriage in 1770 to Elizabeth Brodie, about which he wrote: 'November 4th: Elizabeth and I are wed, after a quiet ceremony at her father's house. She brought me no money dowry, but the leasehold of two houses in Vine Street, Piccadilly, which produce about eighty pounds a year clear of all deductions. Altho' marriages in church are now more common Mr. Brodie considers it too much trial for a bride to face the gaze of the curious public. Only a few relatives and intimate friends present. ... The Reverend Mr. Ledbury a red-faced benign old buck officiated. After the ceremony Mr. Ledbury offered up a simple prayer and then the wedding gifts were distributed and we all sat down to tea, with cold ham, muffins, and hot pies; later in the evening we slipped away, amongst the good wishes of all.'

An interesting aftermath of the wedding was their first appearance at church when Knyveton observed that: 'Elizabeth had her little feminine triumph on the next Sunday, for fashion and convention, those grim dragons, both decree that a bride if wed at home, must appear with her husband in the neighbouring church on the first Sunday following the ceremony.

'So she put on her yellow stockings and yellow panniered gown, with black lace mittens, a hood and a muff. Kathleen was in blue flowered with little pink rose buds, and as yr, humble devoted wore a new red coat and black breeches we made a brave show, and indeed something of a stir, worthy Parson Ledbury glancing up with a frown and then nodding and smiling a welcome; the verger's mouth fell wide

'*The carousel of Savage and his friends at Lord Tyrconnel's*' *illustrative of a typical eighteenth-century after-dinner scene.* (Radio Times Hulton Picture Library)

open with astonishment and I truly believe never closed again till the benediction.'

As in any age the majority were happily and contentedly married, like Knyveton and his wife, despite the posturings and wild behaviour of those closely associated with the Court. It is noteworthy that de la Rochefoucauld particularly stated this to be the case, for he wrote in 1784: 'Husband and wife are always together and share the same society. It is the rarest thing to meet the one without the other . . . they pay all their visits together. . . . Three marriages out of four are based on affection and one can see by experience that they are perfectly satisfied.'

Another matter on which he commented was the freedom of young girls. Women during the Georgian age appear to have had much greater freedom than during the ensuing Victorian period for they rode astride, followed hounds, and indulged in other outdoor pursuits and were often as accomplished in their studies as their brothers. De la Rochefoucauld noted:

'The English have much more opportunity of getting to know each other before marriage, for young folk are in society from an early age; they go with their parents everywhere. Young girls mix with the company and talk and enjoy themselves with as much freedom as if they were married. . . . The Englishman makes more effort to get to know his bride before marriage; she has a similar desire and I suppose it is on this account that marriage before twenty five or twenty eight is rare.'

On the subject of women, Chesterfield had forceful comments to make. Although he himself had maintained a French mistress, mother of Philip, and although he had married deliberately for advancement, this did not prevent Chesterfield providing sound advice. By his own letters we must assume that the majority of the English did not behave according to this advice, but there must have been some who did. He wrote in 1750:

'I come now to another and very material point: I mean women. . . . I will, by no means, pay for whores, and their never failing consequences, surgeons; nor will I, upon any account, keep singers, dancers, actresses and id genus omne; and, independently of the expense, I must tell you that such connections would give me, and all sensible people, the utmost contempt for your parts and address; a young fellow must have as little sense as address, to venture, or more properly to sacrifice his health, and ruin his fortune, with such sort of creatures; in such a place as Paris especially, where gallantry is both the practice and the profession of every woman of fashion.'

In another letter of the following year Chesterfield, commenting on the activities of a young titled Englishman, wrote: 'I should have thought Lord —, at his age, with his parts and address, need not have

The Great Subscription Room at Brook's Club in St James's (Rowlandson circa 1810), the epitome of the Georgian gentleman's gambling clubs. (Radio Times Hulton Picture Library)

Whist being played in public rooms (C. Hunt circa 1825). Throughout the latter part of the Georgian era whist was the card game most frequently played by both sexes. (J. R. Freeman)

been reduced to keep an opera whore in such a place as Paris, where so many women of fashion generously serve as volunteers. I am still more sorry he is in love with her; for that will take him out of good company and sink him into bad . . . most unbecoming . . . for a man of fashion.'

It was certainly a common practice for elderly noblemen to keep their mistresses in London, as Knyveton described in an evocative record in his diary:

'March 7th 1796: Called into consultation today . . . at the bedside of a lady of fashion but notoriety, residing at Golden Square under the protection of a gentleman of high rank. She had been rescued by her lover, who is elderly and has two married daughters, from the mob who last summer gutted a house of ill-fame at Charing Cross and filled the road in front of Northumberland House with clouds of mattress feathers. . . . But the lady had syphilis, I soon discovered, palpitations and a bad action of the heart; advising Dr. Witherington's new drug digitalis and mercury pills I was glad to escape from the hot, scented candle lit

132

The first Quadrille danced at Almacks, taken from Gronow's **Reminiscences**. *The dancers are, from* left *to* right *Lord Worcester, Lady Jersey, Clanronald Macdonald and Lady Worcester.* (J. R. Freeman)

rooms, negro pages and yapping toy dogs, into the freshness of the open air.'

Other vices were prevalent enough, though seldom alluded to publicly. Thus incest was among the commonest Georgian vices — though neither it nor male homosexuality was often mentioned — while lesbianism was less common and rarely discussed. In his memoirs Elers makes a delicate allusion to one of the first girls with whom he fell in love. Finding himself unable to make any impression despite his ardent protestations of love, he was later assured by mutual female friends that he would never have been likely to do so. He explained:

'After I went abroad she formed a most romantic attachment to a young lady by the name of Arabella Ross. At that time Lady E. Butler and the Hon. Miss Ponsonby lived in Wales together. Their affection, I presume was founded on similar principles . . . poor Sophie . . . died . . . at the early age of twenty five, leaving the whole of her fortune to her friend Miss Ross, for life.'

Despite a minority of unfortunates of this nature, the majority of Georgian gentlemen settled down to a harmonious married life with their wives. As de la Rochefoucauld indicated, they shared their diversions and amusements without feeling the need for extra-marital affairs. Dancing, theatres, dinners, and social evenings among their friends were the normal lot of most married couples.

A typical example of the sort of social evening enjoyed is given by Knyveton for 2 January 1794: 'Elizabeth and I were late home this morning, returning from a most enjoyable and select New Year Fancy Dress ball at the fine Westminster house of the Honourable Jem Rivers . . . an excellent supper at midnight. There was a good orchestra of four violins, a taber, two pipes and a French horn; a master of ceremonies from Vauxhall; the company was most genteel and though there was much laughter and high spirits when the country dances began after supper, no persons left off a dance in the middle, or having gone up the room retired without going up it again and always at the end the lady and gentleman bowed and curtsied to each other. . . . It was a pretty scene, youth and loveliness, courtesy and fine breeding, the gay colourful costumes flashing and the jewels winking, under the scores of wax candles in the cut glass chandeliers.'

The theatre, in both London and the provinces, was a favourite diversion. Although Colonel John Byng claimed that he could not be bothered to go to the theatre in London (where he obviously led a somewhat misanthropic existence, probably as a counter to the activities of his wife), he did occasionally visit a playhouse during his tours of England. He noted that travelling companies of actors were commoner towards the end of the century when travel was becoming simpler. His account of the scene at Ludlow is perhaps typical, although there the town boasted its own theatre and the setting was more sophisticated, unlike the barns around the countryside in which plays were often performed. He recorded:

'June 30th 1784: . . . We had now returned to our inn, but . . . seeing a crowd at a door, and enquiring the cause, were told it was the theatre, and that the play was just begun; in we sallied, took our places in the boxes, amidst a numerous and well dress'd audience, and were sufficiently amused; tho it lasted too late. From a communicative neighbour, I learn'd the history of their playhouse; and particularly that Mrs. Siddons (the celebrated actress of the day) made her first appearance here. . . . Some of the performers play'd with great judgement and spirit; especially Mr. Riley the manager, and Miss Collins, a young, and promising actress: the company consist of twenty eight persons, including the band, and perform 3 times a week; and the gay men of the place subscribe £1.1. for a transferable ticket for 20 nights. This kept us up too late and spoil'd our supper, for we did not get home till $\frac{1}{2}$ past eleven o'clock.'

134

'*Jack just come on shore, with his pockets well lin'd, Was met by fair Kitty, who hailed him thus kind . . . turn in love, turn in.*' (Radio Times Hulton Picture Library)

In his student days Knyveton also went occasionally to the theatre, but he was never an ardent playgoer although he took the trouble to describe a visit in January 1752:

'A very pleasant evening last night. To the Theatre . . . where we did see Mrs. Stanley in the Tyranny of Love . . . Mrs. Stanley a most catching wench. The play a study of Love through the Ages; so that we had Samson and Delilah, with some dancing beauties most diverting; and Good King Hal and his wives; and the Turkish Court with more of the dancing girls, very saucy but scantily clad despite the time of year. . . . The play lasted some two and a half hours with a Pause of fifteen minutes when the Orange Girls did hand round fruit and sweatmeats; these girls being naught but Whores and ogling the Bucks and one saucy quean even inviting yr obt. servant; at which I was mightily perturbed and like to have Gone with her, only by the grace of God she stooping I did see her dugs and one of these Foul with a sore; so that I would have no more of her; and so after leaving the Theatre to a tavern . . . there to sup lightly and take a night cap of mulled wine.'

Twenty-one years later Knyveton, who was by then married and well established in his profession, was persuaded by his friend Dr. John Osborne — an intimate of Garrick the famous actor-manager — to accompany him to a special performance. Finding considerable changes, Knyveton described the evening thus:

'December 30th 1773: At Mr. Osborne's urgent invitation Elizabeth and yr. Obdt. last night attended a performance of Mr. Garrick's new piece "A Christmas Tale" at Drury Lane; a fairy tale likely to set the whole of the town talking. Mr. Philip Loutherbourg astonished and amazed the audience by turning a Summer landscape into an autumn one, so softly, and so naturally, I could scarce believe my eyes; a magical piece of hocus pocus effected by careful lighting in the wings and filtering bright candle light, reflected from tin shield, through silken screens of various colours; Mr. Loutherbourg is indeed a genius and I begin to understand something of the subtle miasma of the stage which has so intoxicated Mr. Osborne.'

Mr. Osborne was a frequent visitor back-stage. The attraction to him was precisely what made Dr. Johnson firmly decide to stay away, saying to his friend Garrick in 1750: 'I'll come no more behind your scenes, David; for the silk stockings and white bosoms of your actresses excite my amorous propensities.'

The theatres were but one of the many attractions of London life, for the capital offered plenty of diversions. The coffee-houses, the taverns and the clubs all provided meeting places for the gentlemen to discuss their various interests or exchange gossip. Almacks, later Brooke's, Boodles, the Cocoa Tree, White's and others like them evolved from coffee-houses and were exclusively male establishments where no woman was admitted. The members could meet, dine, wine,

The Prince of Wales going to Ascot Races circa *1790. The exaggerated equipage was no doubt the height of fashion, but not likely to be comfortable in wet weather.* (Radio Times Hulton Picture Library)

or play other games of hazard as they wished.

In the late morning a gentleman might saunter in the Mall, quizzing the ladies on their way to Betty's fruit shop, or to Gunter's or on other shopping expeditions with their abigails. A stroll in Bond Street or in the park, on horseback along Rotten Row, or in a carriage or chaise was another way of passing the time in casual social routine. There were dances, private social gatherings, more dubious assemblies at Vauxhall Gardens or similar resorts and, of course, dining and wining, gaming and other pastimes to while away the evening as well. London catered for every taste, even then.

As a newcomer to London in his student days in 1751, Knyveton depicted some of the variety of interests and diversions to be found. For instance, he recorded:

'February 4th 1751 . . . to the Museum of the Royal Society in Crane Court, a narrow Court leading off Fleet Street. Vastly interesting. Amongst the exhibits were some most rare and curious brought from the Farthest Corners of the Globe, that I doubt not do not exist elsewhere in England. Quoting from a catalogue for which I paid Two Shillings — this not dear for the pamphlet does contain much rare information — I note these that did catch my Imagination and Amuse and Instruct my Mind:

> A Bone from a Mermaid's Head (This curious like the bone from my Hanged Woman's Head)
> The Leg Bone of an Elephant, till recently supposed the leg of a Giant.
> A Tortoise: his grease good for scurvy; said when turned on his back to sigh and Fetch Abundance of Tears.
> A White Shark, said to swallow men whole, and the harpoon with which such beasts are catched.
> A Humming Bird and his Nest: a lovely beast said to weigh but twelve grains, but more Gorgeous in his Dress than the Sultan I did see at the Theatre.
> The Quill of a Porcupine, which when enraged the creature can shoot at his enemy.
> A large Whale and a picture of one rending a boat.
> The Flying Squirrel, which the Pamphlet informs me, can ford a river on the bark of a Tree erecting his Tail for a Sail.
> Some Petrifactions of Divers Shapes all very curious And many other Rare and Astonishing Things and creatures.'

Admittedly Knyveton was young and unaccustomed to London life at this time. His comments were naïve, but then the average country gentleman was also likely to be overwhelmed in similar ways on his first visits to London. A fortnight or so later he noted while walking in the streets:

'Attracted by the gathering of a crowd; and to join them, to find a Watchmaker who had set up a Booth near Durham Yard in the Strand. There on a trestle he had set out a tiny Chaise with four wheels, this being mighty small; and then he coaxes a Flea out of a box and sets him to draw it; other fleas being taken out which did turn water mills and march in troupes like soldiers; at which I was amazed, never having attributed aught of Intelligence to Fleas but a Malignant Instinct. This London be a marvellous place where one may see more Wonders in ten yards than one would see in Ten Miles at home; the which is no doubt why the inhabitants are more hare-brained, constant Surprises shaking the Wits and enervating the Reason.'

Dr. Johnson phrased this rather differently in his well known dictum: 'No, Sir, when a man is tired of London, he is tired of life; for there is in London all that life can afford.'

It is doubtful whether the average country gentleman who came up to London for the season now and then, or not at all, would have agreed with the famous lexicographer. He probably preferred his hunting and life on his country estate, only reluctantly accompanying his wife to the hurly-burly of the social round in London when he could think of no excuse for staying at home. A season in London to bring out a daughter was the familiar reason for taking a town house for the six months or so from March or April till August.

For the man-about-town such as Horace Walpole or George Selwyn, who were both prominent in London society, it was another matter. Horace Walpole, whose volumes of letters carefully edited by himself have been bequeathed to posterity, was perhaps best known as

Rowlandson's illustration of a scene not uncommon in 'gaming hells' in London during the eighteenth century. (Radio Times Hulton Picture Library)

the creator of Strawberry Hill Gothic. Although acknowledged as the legitimate son of Sir Robert Walpole, the Prime Minister, he was strongly suspected to be the son of Carr, Lord Hervey, who was almost certainly the lover of Catherine Shorter, Robert Walpole's first wife. His behaviour was much more that of an eccentric Hervey than of a stolid Walpole. Selwyn was an altogether different character and famed as a wit. His London life was described thus:

'You get up at nine, sit till twelve in your night-gown; creep down to White's and spend five hours at the table; sleep till you can escape your supper reckoning; and then make two wretches carry you in a chair, with three pints of claret inside you, three miles for a shilling.'

George Selwyn, born in 1719 of a wealthy Gloucestershire family, succeeded in getting himself sent down from Oxford for holding a sacrilegious mock mass. Subsequently he inherited the family estates. These included two 'rotten boroughs' each electing a Member of Parliament and providing several comfortable sinecures. Thereafter, Selwyn up to his death in 1791 did nothing beyond indulging his decidedly peculiar tastes to the full and cultivating the reputation of a wit by his studiedly languid utterances. His delight in hangings was notorious and he seldom missed the chance of seeing one. He was even reputed to attend them dressed in women's clothes. Death, torture and executions were his favourite pleasures.

Horace Walpole was a great friend of his and delighted in recounting stories about his macabre tastes and supposed wit. The best story about him, however, is attributed to Lord Holland who, on his death bed, is said to have told his servant: 'When Mr. Selwyn next calls, show him up. If I am alive I shall be pleased to see him and if I am dead he will be delighted to see me.'

Hangings were intended to be public spectacles to deter the would-be criminal. Dr. Johnson stressed this point, stating firmly: 'Sir, executions are intended to draw spectators. If they do not draw spectators they don't answer their purpose.' In fact the object of all forms of punishment — the pillory, whipping at the cart's tail and the hanging of the felon in chains on the gibbet — was to act as deterrents. The 'anatomising' of those hanged was regarded as a particularly effective deterrent. Yet whereas there had been only thirty-three capital offences under George II, by the end of the Georgian period the figure totalled nearly 200, and by 1795 there were close on a hundred hangings a year in London alone. Nor was George Selwyn on his own in his delight in the spectacle; many Londoners flocked to Tyburn, taking a holiday for the occasion.

Some idea of the summary justice of the day — as well as the attendant circumstances — is to be had from Knyveton's records of such an event:

'February 6 1752: Doctor Urquehart to inform us that he had

'*Rousing the Watch*' *by Cruikshank, a typical eighteenth-century frolic with the watch.* (Radio Times Hulton Picture Library)

bespoke us a New Body that of a Man to be hanged on Monday; he to be tried today having been taken slitting a purse last Saturday, and thereby his conviction a certainty. Doctor Urquehart knowing the Judge and bespeaking his corpse before any other Hospital knoweth of it.

'February 9; This day to another Hanging, thereby as George Blumenfield did put it to see that Our Future Subject was Killed Properly in all Christian Charity. The weather cold, but the day fine with something of a wind; so that a tolerable large crowd was gathered, and a number of the gentry; there being two other men to be Hanged beside Ours, also an Old Woman suspected of poisoning her grandson; and she being very old and destitute the Judges had sentenced her so that she might have an easy Passing. The other two men a Contrast; one poor wight a Grocer, who had given wrong change to a customer and after drawn a knife on him in Wrath; the other a fine sturdy Rogue, a Highway Man who had kept the town in suspense these three months past; robbing the Mails twice, and Lord knows how many private coaches, shooting one coachman dead; and making a fight for it when taken, so that he came to the Gallows with his head bound up and his arm all bloody, but not thereby disturbed, but dressed in a fine bottle-green coat and knee-boots; waving to the crowd and strutting to the last; so that the Mob did cheer him, hissing the poor Grocer, who was in the same cart with him but never ceased to Moan and Cry Aloud. These two and Our Man all turned off at once, the Highway Man taking the rope from the Hangman and bowing adjusted it about his own neck; at which a Fine Lady in a coach nearby cries out despairingly; and he to make her a leg and throw her a Kiss.'

This sort of play-acting was common, for, to the Mob and connoisseurs such as Selwyn, this was a big performance and he was the star attraction. Knyveton casually mentioned learning later that the female admirer had been held up by the highwayman and then gave him 'Great Joy to wit becoming his Mistress.' Thus, altogether, this particular highwayman seems to have been an unusual character. Nevertheless, Knyveton continued:

'. . . so they were turned off; and after some ten minutes the Hangman cuts Our Man and the Grocer down, but leaves the Highway Man swinging; and then Ropes the Old Beldame, she, I do verily believe, having no sense of what they were about to do to her, but chuckling and crowing in the manner of the Very Aged; and so the Hangman cries "Heigh Mother Witch, Up to the Skies With You!" at which the crowd laughs and then she joins the Highway Man; and the Hangman leaves her to twitch and sway in the wind whilst his Assistant stokes the fire beneath a Cauldron of Tar and they prepare their Instruments.

'Then the Assistant cuts down the Highway Man and they lay him on the floor and take off his clothes; at which more screeches from the Lady aforesaid and a gentleman with her to Apply Smelling Salts; and the Hangman shaves the Highway Man's Head and then he and the Assistant disembowel him, and shove him into the Cauldron of tar; then they fix the Irons round him, and so swing him once more to the Gibbet, where they leave him to dry in the wind as a warning to all such Malefactors. The old woman now cut down and she and the Grocer driven off in a cart to Surgeon's Hall; and Our Man put in a cart likewise and driven off by the Doctor's huge serving man to Doctor Urquehart's house; and the Hangman and his Assistant to throw dice for the Highway Man's clothes; and the Lady aforesaid comes up all of a Sweat and a Fluster and gives them a guinea for a lock of the Highway Man's hair. But . . . I did see her and the Gentleman with her drive off in the coach he kissing her neck and she clutching his shoulder with such Passion that you would think she had never loved else but him. And so to dine and later to inspect our body at the Doctor's; it proving to be one of fairish proportions.'

Some notion of the normal man's reactions, rather than those of people such as George Selwyn, can be gained from a further entry in

'Gin Lane'. William Hogarth's famous illustration epitomising the evils of excessive gin drinking at the worst of the Gin Age from 1730 to 1750. (Fitzwilliam Museum, Cambridge)

Knyveton's records for 23 June 1783:

'Alighting from my coach at a booksellers in Fleet Street ran bump against Mr. Boswell, that shadow of the illustrious Doctor Johnson; then returning to call upon the great man after paying a visit to Newgate to see fifteen felons hanged, to wit twelve burglars, two men taken in street robbing, and one rogue found guilty of impersonating another man to obtain his wages; "Quite a fair morning's work," observed the Scot in his high voice; "And excellent pickings for Jack Ketch." With a wink and a knowing grin; and so as he was in a hurry we parted; a very pleasant and kindly gentleman.'

Rowdyism, drunkenness and debauchery combined with the readiness for a frolic were a feature of the age. Much of it was good hearted, good natured and comparatively harmless. The regular baiting of the Watch by young bucks, the wild wagers in the middle of the night to ride a steeplechase by moonlight or have a coach race, all these were in the nature of childish dares to prove that they had courage, or 'bottom', as it was termed. It was an ingenuous age and much of their behaviour showed this clearly. Even Doctor Johnson, woken at three a.m. by his friends Beauclerk and Langton hammering at his door, poked his head out of the window and merely said with a grin, before joining them: 'What is it you dogs! I'll have a frisk with you'.

In his early student days when lodging with Mr. Hunt, a Soho barber, in 1751, Knyveton recorded:

'September 22nd: Was awoke last night by a vile noise of shouting to find two foxed gentlemen endeavouring to make entrance with some idea that it was an Inn. Mrs. Hunt, very courageous, empties slops over them on which they become vehement with rage and were only detained from entrance by Mr. Hunt firing a pistol out of the window at them; the which I took kindly as affording me a case of gunshot wound for treatment only they took fright and retired. So to sleep once more and Mr. Hunt very apologetic at breakfast it seeming that one of the bucks had oft been shaved by him and had returned with his companion to find sport with Mr. Hunt's serving wench; which was sufficient proof of their drunkenness, the wench being undersized, pitted with the Pox and afflicted with Strabismus. So to Doctor Urquehart's . . . Grge Blumenfield being absent for some reason best known to himself. I am afraid he is a sad rogue.

'September 23: . . . at the Doctor's house Mr. Blumenfield still being absent . . .

'September 24th: Arriving at the Doctor's house this morning for my lecture found George Blumenfield there with his arm in a sling and on my enquiring the reason he spoke to me with much choler asking me whether I thought it friendly to fire off powder and ball at my visitors, the which I took exception to the more so as I was hard put to it to imagine of what he spoke. After much talk find that he was one of the

'Richmond Hill' (*Henry Bunbury, 1782*), *illustrating traffic and hazards likely to be encountered on the roads near London at this time.* (Radio Times Hulton Picture Library)

bucks at whom Mr. Hunt fired his pistol the evening of the 21st; that having learnt from me of my lodging at Mr. Hunt's he had thought in all friendliness to call upon me, his friend much liking the idea and assuring him that Mr. Hunt was a worthy man with a serving wench the prettiest doxy in all London; but upon their arrival they were much hurt to find themselves so barbarously treated. I made haste to assure Mr. Blumenfield that he was fortunate to have escaped with a bullet graze only, for the wench aforesaid being I suspect a very repository for all the diseases from the Small to the Great Pox. So to anatomise together with friendliness at last and dined with much liveliness at the Leaping Hart.'

The young bucks had their own ways of indulging in frolics, which may strike us as somewhat odd or excessive today. A habit of imitating a female in distress was regarded as a great amusement throughout the period. Tossing people into horse troughs and similar pastimes were also common enough behaviour since Byng and other writers also mention them, but perhaps Knyveton's description of a Christmas Day party in 1751 is the most graphic of all:

'To supper at an Inn in Fleet Street called the Rainbow Tavern, where we met certain very merry fellows, two of them friends of Mr. St. Clair. We supped off a Roast and some Game and afterwards did gather in an upper room around a fine fire where we did seat ourselves at wine and sundry wights essayed songs. One tall handsome gentleman in a fine scarlet coat and a heavy peruke sang very sweetly a song of Mottreux's:

> Man is for woman made
> And woman made for man
> As the spur is to the jade
> As the scabbard to the blade
> So man's for woman made
> And woman made for man.

To which Mr. St. Clair who had attempted to towsle the serving wench and been scratched for his pains retorted with a satire on marriage:

> Like a dog with a bottle tied close to his tail
> Like a Tory in a bog, or a thief in jail —

at which we did all laugh heartily, the more so as Mr. St. Clair's voice is a doleful bellow peculiar apt for such a Dismal Catch.'

They spent the next hour or so drinking and singing songs with rousing choruses. So far there is little out of the ordinary, but the Georgian element soon showed itself when they had tired of singing. Knyveton continued:

'. . . One gentleman did then jump upon the table and imitate a Female in Distress with sundry shrieks and howls so realistic that Mr. St. Clair still missing his serving wench did in the confusion of his wits pounce upon him and bear him to the ground, where they were with difficulty separated. It was suggested that both should be bled to cool their Ardour, but the gentleman in the Scarlet coat would not agree, saying that the only blood to be shed that night was The Blood of the Grape, at which all did cheer lustily, and so to bear Mr. St. Clair and his friend from the room to find a ewer of water with which to souse them. But this being hard to come by the scarlet coated wight knocks at a door and receiving no answer opens it; at which Terrific Shrieks from within, there being a wench there in her shift. The handsome gentleman

146

makes a leg and asks her pardon and the landlord arrives and we not liking the tone of his converse to bear him down to the street and put him into his own horse-trough; and then missing Mr. Pope upstairs again and find him trying to get into the wench's bed, she squalling and crying on all the saints to deliver her; and a short man bursts out of a door adjoining and nearly knocks down Mr. Blumenfield on which we not liking *his* converse carry *him* downstairs he being in his nightshirt and put him in the horse-trough; and so that he might not catch a distemper to carry him upstairs again and put him to bed with the wench (removing Mr. Pope by vis-a-Tergo) and locking the door on them both in all decency.

'And so back to our room, where we find Mr. St. Clair's friend singing very doleful to himself in front of the fire, but no sign of Mr. St. Clair. So singing until dawn appears, and I to go home, and entering the street take a wrong turning into an Alley where I find Mr. St. Clair leaving a house, the serving wench at the door all Untidy. So home with him in all comfort and friendliness. This morning of the 26th do find my head aches and my stomach recoils from Vittles; shall rest in my lodgings.'

'The Cyprian's Ball at the Argyle Rooms' (*Cruikshank*, circa *1825*). *Such a ball for harlots and mistresses epitomised the licentiousness of the later Georgian era.* (J. R. Freeman)

Such drunken frolics were by no means the prerogative of the young, for in some respects the Georgians as a whole never matured mentally; to say the least, they tended to be late developers. Notably the example set by the Prince of Wales and the Royal Dukes was not conducive to restraint. Knyveton described meeting some late night revellers in 1794:

'Returning home as the clocks in the city were striking the half after midnight, was greeted in the Strand by a wild and dismal shrieking as of females in distress, yells of "Fire!" and a frenzied ringing of a handbell; thrusting my head anxiously out of the coach window espied that rake Jem Rivers staggering up over the cobbles arm-in-arm with that odd creature Thomas Baron Foley of Kidderminster, known to his friends as Number Eleven on account of the shape of his legs; Jem was endeavouring to blow out the street lamps and encouraging his successes by imitating a hysterick female, while Thomas was ringing a huge bell like one demented; with them a certain Mr. John Nash, a stocky, common faced, rather dubious little architect, who had come to town from Wales, resides at No. 28 Dover St. and has built Baron Foley a fine new house at his estate; and who was bawling "Fire!" at the top of his voice; Jem and Thomas returning from St. James, where as Mr. Nash was with them they were not admitted to Almacks. Coming up to the coach hiccoughing and shrieking with laughter Mr. Nash points to the panels and says solemly "Hic! Pure Barroque!" at which sally Baron Foley lets off a piercing yell and jangles his bell hideously under the leader's nose. Whereat the brute reared, then bolted off at a gallop, and the last I saw of Baron Foley his matchstick legs were inverted into the air from the gutter.'

Perhaps it is worth concluding with one final apposite quotation from Knyveton on his cure for such frolics or their inevitable aftermath. He noted: 'On leaving the Mall this morning was stopt by the Honourable Mr. Rowley, who desired my opinion on the best remedies for driving away the effects of over indulgence in wine. But there is of course but one sovereign remedy for all gentlemen of dissipation; rhubarb; it makes them brave next morning.'

Chapter Eight
TRAVEL, INNS AND HAZARDS

'If I had no duties and no reference to futurity, I would spend my life in driving briskly in a post-chaise with a pretty woman.' — Dr. Samuel Johnson

During the latter part of the Georgian age, there were revolutionary changes in modes and speeds of travel which were to affect all aspects of life to a greater or lesser degree. In the early part of the eighteenth century travel was by horse, by coach, or on foot. Goods were transported by slow and cumbersome wagons, or, when speed was required as in the transport of perishables such as fish, by trains of pack-horses. Both coaches and wagons had broad flat wheels to avoid becoming easily stuck in the enormous ruts in the mostly unpaved roads. Where the ruts were too deep or treacherous it was accepted custom to make a detour, thus, frequently and sometimes permanently, altering the line of the road. Flocks of sheep and herds of cattle being driven to market were often encountered, further slowing already painfully slow travel.

The roads themselves were the responsibility of the local parish or county authorities, who delegated the onus of maintaining them to various ratepayers in turn on a rota system. A few half-hearted efforts might be made to repair the worst potholes, but, understandably, in bad weather conditions all but the main roads were virtually impassable to wheeled traffic. Coach travel was slow and uncomfortable.

During the first half of the eighteenth century the road from Aylesbury to London was particularly bad. An analysis of a journey made by Henry Purefoy to London in May 1749, when conditions were considered good, indicates that he took fourteen hours to cover sixty-one miles. He was thus travelling at an average of four-and-a-half miles an hour. Whether he was travelling by coach or on horseback is not clear, but he broke the journey overnight. The probability is that he was travelling by coach as, even though he was an indifferent horseman, he would surely have made better time on horseback.

With the improvements in the roads in the second half of the century, the coach and horse were to become the symbols of Georgian travel. It was the last age when the horse remained undisputedly supreme as a means of land transport. As a result the Georgian gentleman, willy-nilly, was compelled to ride a horse and drive (or at the very least travel in) a coach. A further result was almost inevitably that he smelt of horse. The smell in the towns was of horse manure, horse sweat and coal fires.

When Georgian gentlemen met, a favourite topic of conversation — apart from the weather — was horses. Whenever one gentleman visited another the first enquiry was as to his requirements for stabling, oats, hay and water for his horse or horses. In almost every gentleman's household of any size there were a coachman, grooms and stableboys. Even where the gentleman did not like horses, or understand them, he had perforce to buy and sell them, ride them and drive them or else employ someone else to do so for him.

The man who was prepared to admit that he disliked and did not understand horses in the Georgian age was an exception to the rule. Unless he lived in London or some other large town and always travelled on foot or in a sedan chair, he was not likely to avoid horses. In this respect, poor Henry Purefoy seems to have been something of a misfit. It is clear that he did not particularly like horses largely because he did not understand them. For a country gentleman to write to his farrier as he did was indeed an admission of weakness:

'ffor Mr. Pratt a ffarier at Helmdon: May 29th, 1739: Mr. Pratt/ I shall go to Banbury ffair on Thursday morning next & shall be at the 3 Tunns Inne there at eleven o'clock at the farthest. I desire you will not faill either to call here to go along with mee to the fair at 8 a clock or else meet mee at the Three Tunnes Inne at eleven a clock, for I shall depend upon your judgement in what horses I buy . . . Your freind to serve you H.P.'

In the circumstances it is scarcely surprising that he ended up with a bad bargain. On 20 June we find him writing as follows to an old schoolfellow, Mr. William Holloway, who seems to have been a party to the deal:

'William/ I received a letter without a name to it but suppose it came from you because it was about the new mare. I much wonder you should advise me to buy a surfeited mare wch I mistrusted & questioned in the yard of the 3 Tunns at Banbury; but you and Pratt & the owner of the mare said she was not surfeited but entirely sound. Now it proves to the contrary for at the return of Thomas Esom I had the judgement of 2 ffarriers & they both agreed the mare was surfeited before she came home to my mother. Upon bleeding in the Tail her eye was well, but now the Humour comes into it again and the ffarrier's opinion is she will be blind & the grease runs out of one Heell. The mare has never been used above 4 or 5 days here & that only to walk to plough, & has had great care taken of her in every respect, & had you not said your brother knew the mare to be sound, my mother would not have bought her for she saw her eye amiss the day you brought her over, so pray tell Mr. Ward if hee don't come & take the mare again & refund the money, my mother will lay an action against him and pray show him this letter that if occasion be you may be a witnesse of it. I am your freind to serve you. H.P.'

One feels sorry for Henry Purefoy, for the same sort of experience was repeated time and again. Even when he found a reliable horse-dealer who supplied him with suitable mounts, he still encountered trouble. Apparently in December 1749 he suffered a bad fright, as the letter to his long-suffering dealer friend, Mr. Gibbs, reveals:

'Changing Horses for the Royal Mail' circa 1780. The change here is leisurely compared with the speed evolved at the height of the stage coach era. (Radio Times Hulton Picture Library)

'Mr. Gibbs/ The Bay Mare you sold mee last as I was riding her to Brackley Market last Wensday started with mee & threw mee in the fford of the River at Westbury Town's End. I fell from off her farther side on my head in the River & received no other Damage (thro God's Mercy) but a Bruise on the muscle of my right arm which pains mee very much. Had not the Water saved my ffall it would undoubtedly have been worse with mee; after so bad an accident I don't intend to get on her back any more, but must desire you to dispose of her for mee. I don't know but what you might sell her at next Banbury twelfth ffair. The next I have I resolve shall be a Gelding not above fourteen hands high or thereabouts; I have a notion that mares when they go to horse are Resty & gamesome & not fit for mee. This mare's cold is quite gone & sound in all respects as far as I know. . . . Your humble servant. H.P.'

Soon after this accident the roads around Aylesbury seem to have improved greatly. By 1753 there was a regular coach service between London and Birmingham which ran through Buckingham. In a letter to his London agent in August of that year Purefoy wrote: 'I hope wee shall see you . . . here. The Birmingham Coach runs thro' in a day from London to Birmingham & the fair is Ten Shillings each passenger & if you let us know when you will come our Charriott shall meet you at Buckingham.'

The Purefoys seem to have bought their 'Charriott' and their coaches from a coach-builder in London, and if he was a poor judge of a horse, Henry was particular about his coaches, demanding 'a coach pretty near the fashion they make them now.' A reference in a letter of February 1745 to the 'chariott', when the Purefoys were considering swapping their large coach for another, reads: 'ffor Mr. Henry Lake, London: Mr. Lake/ My mother would exchange a large sized coach wch she now has (that is little ye worse for wearing) for a second hand light coach that will follow ye horses well; if you have, or hear of any such thing let mee know, which will oblidge your humble servant. H.P. P.S. The chariott wee bought of you gives great content.'

The introduction of private turnpike companies, deputed by Act of Parliament to maintain the roads in return for the right to install toll bars and gates and charge a fee to users of their stretch of turnpike, brought about a dramatic improvement in travel in the second half of the eighteenth century. During the first half of the century there were only some four hundred Road Acts of this kind, but in the second half there were four times as many. As a result, the roads improved greatly and the lightness and speed of the coaches improved with them. Coach travel, instead of being a penance, began to be quite exhilarating.

The youthful Knyveton gives two excellent descriptions of coach journeys around the middle of the century before the turnpike roads had begun to make much impression. The first of these was on 22

'*Toll gate scene*' (*D. J. Egerton*, circa *1760*). *The flock of sheep, the gig, the horseman and the coach to Oxford make up the typical traffic of the times.* (Radio Times Hulton Picture Library)

September 1751, when he left his uncle's house at Hestley in Kent and travelled to London to take up lodgings in Soho prior to studying at medical school. He does not give the time of the start, but the journey seems to have taken somewhere around fourteen hours for about seventy miles, thus averaging about five or six miles an hour allowing for stops. He wrote:

'Up betimes to catch the coach, on which my uncle had taken me an outside seat. . . . A fine morning, and the company on the coach very agreeable, passing tales and one gentleman a flask of Eau-de-Vie, of which the guard partook heartily, so that his tunes on his horn became ever more frequent and lusty. Dined off a leg of mutton at a tolerable Inn whose name I have forgot though it had a Crown in it.

The plump gentleman with the flask very hearty and playful with the serving wench. To coach once more and so to London, which we approached in a smother of rain about nine o'clock, the city very fine as it grew before us a great dark mass all twinkling with lights. Was 'mazed to find the streets thronged with folk and all lit up despite the lateness of the hour; they were as bright as noon-day with the horn lanterns in the shops and Inns, and with the flambeaux carried by the chairmen; these worthies swearing and crying out in a manner that would have earned them the stocks at home. My journey was not finished even when we arrived at the posting house, but to hackney coach and so to Mr. Hunt's, the barber, of Dean Street, Soho. . . . The room to which they showed me tolerable comfortable. . . . Unpacked and so to bed, scratching at a flea contracted from that jail of a coach.'

His experiences on leaving London to join the Navy as a surgeon's mate on 7 April the following year indicate the hazards of coach travel. With his ready observation of the behaviour of his fellow passengers as well as his descriptions of the events, it is easy to visualise the scene. He recorded:

'To the Coaching House . . . and the Coach waiting in the Yard, I did climb to the outside seat I had taken, and the Guard blew his horn and we drove off. . . . The day fine and I rather glad thereat, for I was somewhat downcast in my spirits. But I took pleasure after a while in the ride and could look about me with enjoyment, the country just commencing Spring Time and the buds showing on the trees. But when we had covered scarce half of our journey, and were out on the first marshes, the Off Leader shies at a hen flying across the road, and before we had scarce time to think what was afoot, the Coach lurches, and then tumbles over into a ditch, the road being soft with mud at that point. The ditch was deep so none was hurt bad; but two women inside began to scream most piercing, being badly shook in their wits; and one gentleman was thrown clean off the roof into the hedge and was hauled out by Yr. Obdt. Servant and the Guard all abroad in his Wits.

'The horses were in an aweful Tangle, kicking and struggling so that it was as much as the Coachman could do to calm them; the Guard and a Gentleman in a bottle green coat went to aid him, and after some twenty minutes and much hard swearing of Oaths the horses were got free of their harness and taken up on to the road; when it was found that the bay leader was lame in the near fore, and I to bathe the swelling then coming up with water from the ditch and at the Guard's suggestion to bleed the beast also in the neck.'

Unfortunately for the travellers the coach proved to be firmly wedged in the ditch, and no amount of effort would move it. They then turned to pacifying the still hysterical females and Knyveton improved the shining hour by bleeding the man with concussion, who had been thrown from the coach top; 'he becoming quite sane thereby and thank-

A highwayman arrested by the Watch in Covent Garden in the early eighteenth century. Armed with staves and lanterns the Watch was the forerunner of the police. (Radio Times Hulton Picture Library)

ing me for my Timely Aid.' Then an argument arose between the Guard, who insisted on staying with his mails, and the Coachman, who wished to remain with his horses, as to who should go for aid. Neither would give way and finally a farmer who was among the passengers took one of the horses and went off for help. By this time it was drizzling and they were all somewhat miserable.

'After nigh two hours the Farmer returns with fresh horses and Assistance, and the coach was dragged out of the ditch and the team harnessed afresh; only, that the wheel which had hung in the ditch being thought insecure, it was decided that only the ladies should ride within, and the team proceed at a walk. . . . It took us an hour more to reach the Posting House, and we were glad enough when we reached it to find Mine Host had prepared a meal both of hot and cold meats, with Tea for the Ladies and Wine and Ale for the gentlemen. There were sausages and eggs and ham, with pork pies and brawn, and a side of beef, with a crusty new loaf, and salt and fresh butter, and as there was moreover a roaring fire we were all greatly comforted. There was another coach in the yard, but this had to be prepared and it was past dusk when we once more took our seats and gone seven before I alighted.'

In September 1758, when Knyveton returned after six years at sea, he met by chance in London his old friend from his medical student days, Mr. Pope. Inviting him to stay at home in the West Country, Knyveton explained that on their journey from London '. . . we rolled away and had so much to discuss that though the roads were bad we scarce noticed the passage of time. The journey took two days, we sleeping at Newbury and Warminster, and the roads growing worse as we drew away from the coast and very empty also, not many going abroad because of the time of year, and also this threat of invasion.'

By 1782, the roads had improved considerably, as may be noted from Parson James Woodforde's diary entries on a trip from Norfolk to Somerset in May of that year. His journey, though mainly at night, took only a day from London to beyond Salisbury. The details of the costs and general conditions are interesting. Clearly he regarded a journey of this distance as a major expedition, although bugs seem to have been the sole hazard:

'29. May . . . about five o'clock this evening . . . Nancy and myself went in the Lenwade Bridge chaise . . . for Norwich and there we drank tea at the "Angel" where the London coach puts up and in which we are to go tonight. To the driver of the Lenwaide chaise gave £0.1.6. Paid and gave at the "Angel" for eating, etc., £0.2.6. My servant, Will Coleman, went with us. . . . For 2 inside places in the London coach pd. at Norwich £1.16s. For one outside place in do. pd. £0.10.6. To extraordinary weight of luggage at 1½d per pound pd. £0.8.6.

A night scene near Charing Cross (*William Hogarth* circa *1750*). (Radio Times Hulton Picture Library)

At 9 o'clock this evening we all set off for London.

'30. May: We travelled all night long and I thank God safe and well. We breakfasted at Sudbury — and I paid there £0.2.6. Our coach was quite full having six in it — 4 gentlemen and 2 young ladies. We got to London about 2 o'clock in the afternoon. . . . To coachmen from Norwich gave £0.4.0. . . . We got into a Hackney coach and drove to the "Bell Savage" on Ludgate Hill and there dined, supped and slept. . . . We were all very glad to get to bed tonight being tired.

'31 May: We breakfasted, dined and spent the afternoon at our inn. . . . For 2 inside places in the Salisbury coach pd £2.2.0. For 1 outside place do. pd. £0.10.6. Paid and gave at the "Bell Savage" for all of us abt. £1.15.0 . . . a very good house it is. About 10 o'clock at night we set off in the Salisbury coach . . . and the coach guarded. I was bit terribly by bugs last night, but did not wake me.

'1 June: We travelled again all night long . . . got safe and well to Salisbury between 2 and 3 in the afternoon. The coach was full also. Gave the coachmen that drove us £0.4.0. We breakfasted at Whitchurch for which I paid £0.2.6. Paid at Salisbury for extraordinary luggage £0.6.6. . . . between 3 and 4 in the afternoon we got into a post-chaise for Hindon — and Will went on a hired horse thither. Pd. . . . at Salisbury for chaise, horse, etc., abt. £1.1.0. We got to Hindon abt. 6 o'clock — then took a fresh chaise and set off for Stourton and Will on a fresh horse. Pd. and gave at Hindon for chaise etc., abt. £0.12.6. We got to Cole about 10 o'clock . . . safe and well. . . . I was terribly swelled in the face and hands by the bugs. Mr. Pounsett . . . very glad to see us.'

Another clerical traveller in 1782 was the German Pastor Karl Philipp Moritz, who journeyed through England mainly on foot. He did, however, take the stage coach from Leicester to London, and he recorded his ride on the outside of the coach from Leicester to Northampton as follows:

'This ride from Leicester to Northampton I shall remember as long as I live. The coach drove from the yard through a part of the house. The inside passengers got in, in the yard; but we on the outside were obliged to clamber up in the public street, because we should have had no room for our heads to pass under the gateway.

'My companions on the top of the coach were a farmer, a young man very decently dressed, and a blackamoor. The getting up alone was at the risk of one's life; and when I was up, I was obliged to sit just at the corner of the coach, with nothing to hold by, but a sort of little handle, fastened at the side. I sat nearest the wheel; and at the moment we set off, I fancied that I saw a certain death await me. All I could do was to take still faster hold of the handle and to be more and more careful to preserve my balance.

'The machine now rolled with prodigious rapidity, over the stones through the town, and every moment we seemed to fly into the air; so that it was almost a miracle that we still stuck to the coach and did not fall. We seemed to be thus on the wing, and to fly, as often as we passed through a village, or went down a hill.'

At this point in his journey, Moritz, by now growing quite desperate, seized his opportunity and crept into the basket behind, where all the luggage was carried. The negro warned him that this was dangerous, but while going uphill it seemed quite comfortable. Then, on the downhill slope, he discovered the snag; the luggage all jolted round him, bruising him black and blue. The coachman, however, paid no attention to his moans and he was unable to get back to the comparative safety of his old seat until the next uphill slope, after nearly an hour of purgatory. Even then his trials were by no means over. He continued:

'About midnight we arrived at Harborough, where I could only rest myself a moment, before we were again called to set off, full drive, through a number of villages, so that a few hours before daybreak we had reached Northampton, which is, however, thirty-three miles from Leicester.

'From Harborough to Northampton I had a most dreadful journey; it rained incessantly, and as before we had been covered with dust, we now were soaked with rain. My neighbour, the young man who sat next me in the middle, that my inconveniences might be complete, every now and then fell asleep; and as, when asleep, he perpetually rolled against me, with the whole weight of his body, more than once he was very near pushing me entirely off my seat.

'We at last reached Northampton, where I immediately went to bed and have slept almost till noon.'

Another foreign observer of the English scene in 1784 was François de la Rochefoucauld, whose interest in the English way of life extended to almost every aspect of living. He was particularly impressed by the high standard of the horses he saw in England and with the amount of traffic on the roads. This obviously struck him as far greater than he was accustomed to in France, for he wrote:

'It is impossible to give any idea of the number of travellers who are always to be met on the English roads. You cannot go from one post to another without meeting two or three post-chaises, quite apart from the regular diligences. . . . When you hire a post-chaise to go out to dinner, or to visit someone in the country five or six or even ten miles away, you pay something between five and eight shillings according to the distance.'

Although not given to obvious exaggeration, he was clearly impressed with the speed of the racehorses he saw at Newmarket when he recorded: 'When you are close to them you can hardly follow them with the eye — they travel more swiftly than a flash of lightning. The jockeys are obliged to keep their heads low in order to breathe. Their passage through the air is so swift that otherwise they would be choked.'

The pace of the regular stage coach services was speeding up considerably by this time, and the fact that many of them carried mail, although illegally, inspired the introduction in 1784 of the mail coach. The combination of good turnpike roads, good horses, lighter coaches and good organisation had the effect of speeding these mail coaches to an unprecedented level. Whereas eight or ten miles an hour had been considered fast, the new mail coaches carried passengers and mail for the Post Office at speeds in excess of twelve and fourteen miles an hour.

Knyveton remarked of a young medical friend in 1784: 'By the aid of the novel fast mail coaches now introduced — which are said to travel at twelve miles an hour — and what I will not believe — even at fifteen — ! — that young man now flits about the country like a Will o' the Wisp.'

On occasions, however, when not carrying mail and therefore not bound to a rigid schedule, the mail coach journey could be a comfortable and jolly affair. Colonel Peter Hawker, retired from the Army, after being wounded in the Peninsular Campaign only two years previously, recorded a mail coach journey from Longparish in Hampshire to Exeter in 1811:

'January 7th: At four in the morning got into the mail, and at eleven at night reached Exeter. Had a delightfully jolly party, and, not being post day, the mail stopped whenever we saw game, and during the journey I killed 4 partridges. When it was too dark to shoot, our party mounted the roof, and sang choruses (while I joined in them and drove) and in which the guard and coachman took a very able part.'

With the development of coach travel, the elegance of the coach or carriage, the matching of the team of horses, the appearance of the footmen behind the coachman, and particularly the turn-out of the coachman himself began to have immense social significance. From Samuel and Sarah Adams' manual *The Complete Servant,* printed in 1825, some estimate of the coachman's place in the servants' hierarchy below-stairs may be readily obtained: 'On the sobriety, steady conduct, and respectable appearance of this important servant depends the exterior appearance of the family with which he resides. Every genuine Coachman has his characteristic costume. His flaxen curls or wig, his low cocked hat, his plush breeches and his benjamin surtout, his clothes also being well brushed and the lace and buttons in a state of high polish.'

Towards the end of the Georgian era, the importance of the coach and its general turn-out had attained high social significance, and the opportunities for sheer ostentatious display reached ridiculous levels. Creevey, in his records, noted an absurd occasion at the Doncaster

An inn yard scene (Hogarth circa 1750), showing the preparations for the departure of the coach. The galleried courtyard of the 'Old Angle Inn' is visible in the background. (Radio Times Hulton Picture Library)

races in 1827 when the Duke of Devonshire was eclipsed by the 4th Earl of Fitzwilliam:

'You must know our steward, the Duke of Devonshire, started the first day with his coach and six and *twelve* outriders, and old Billy Fitzwilliam had just the same; but the next day old Billy appeared with *two* coaches and six, and *sixteen* outriders, and has kept the thing up ever since.'

As the standards of roads, coaches and travel improved, so the standards of the inns improved as well. When travelling, inns were available where a gentleman could find comfort and good standards, but there were other inns where the standards were low. John Byng acquired expert knowledge of English inns after touring the country several times between 1781 and 1794. He concluded after his first journey to the West in 1781 that:

'The imposition in travelling is abominable; the innkeepers are insolent, the hostlers are sulky, the chambermaids are pert, and the waiters are impertinent; the meat is tough, the wine is foul, the beer is hard, the sheets are wet, the linen is dirty, and the knives are never clean'd!! Every home is better than this.'

In 1787 he was, for once, forced to take a coach, which he loathed, and he wrote: 'Walking; — or riding, on a tolerable horse, are delights to me; but boxed up in a stinking coach, dependant on the hours and guidance of others, submitting to miserable associates, and obliged to hear their nonsense is great wretchedness! However, the vulgarity of women is at all times better than the brutality of men; two women were my companions and harmless enough — the one eternally threaten'd to be sick.'

His normal custom was to travel with a servant, whom he sent ahead of him to find a comfortable inn for the night and prepare the way for his arrival and that of his horses. He observed: 'This is the true use of servants on the road, tho but seldom what their masters require of them; trusting to the waiter and the chambermaid for dirty glasses and ill made beds, and confiding the care of their horses to drunken, roguish, hostlers; & whilst their own genteel followers are regaling themselves in a genteel parlour, the horses are neither clean'd, nor fed. As for my sheets, I always take them with me, knowing that next to a certainty five sheets must be dirty and three damp out of number ten; these with a very few other necessities travel behind my servant; as for my night cap, great coat and such other etceteras, they travel behind my own person in and upon a small cloakbag.'

Although Byng was somewhat misanthropic and a reactionary, ready to find fault with much of the contemporary scene, even he had to admit that he occasionally found an excellent inn. To do him justice, he was generally ready to acknowledge the fact. The Sun at Biggleswade was an inn he thoroughly approved of, and on a tour to the north in 1792 on 28 May he wrote:

'The country look'd gay from the red cloaks flocking to the fair. My dinner (I love to repeat good ones) consisted of spitchcock'd eel, roasted pigeons, a loyn of pork roasted with tarts, jellies and custards. . . . In the evening the weather, after much wind, turn'd into heavy rain; so I had only to write, to tea and to stable and to wish for some quiet society; wondering where I saw chaise travellers, masters of their time, not put up in such weather & be comfortable, instead of forcing thro the storm and seeing poor post boys wet to the skin! Why there is a good inn, with good coffee and good wine? Stay then, and play at cards and backgammon; and depart when the wind does not blow an hurricane and the rain fall a deluge.'

It was particularly in areas such as Manchester, where industry was beginning to leave its mark (even as early as the turn of the eighteenth century), that he noted some of the worst inns he visited. The reason for this, was that 'the upstart man of riches knows no better; the inns therefore are bad, dear, and presumptuous; but on roads where gentlemen travel, and scold, there will be *a reform.*'

In this he was correct enough. As the standard of stage coach travel improved towards the end of the Georgian era, so the standards of the inns rose correspondingly. In 1827 W. Kitchiner, author of *The Traveller's Oracle,* acknowledged the high standard of many inns, but added a cautionary note, which in view of Byng's comments is not altogether surprising. 'The elegance and magnificence of some English inns and taverns,' he wrote, 'are equal to those of many noblemen's houses . . . but the generality of taverns, in our opinion, are rather to be endured than enjoyed.'

As well as bad inns, Byng noted various other hazards on his journeys. In 1789 he mentioned an accident that had occurred to an old acquaintance of his while travelling in a stage coach. Byng unfeelingly found it somewhat funny, for he described it thus: 'Going to town some days since, in a Stage Coach, the coach was broken down near this Inn-door, and Mr. T— fell under 5 female Passengers with not much damage; (The Horses running off with the fore-wheels) When the Roof breaking inn, sent an upper Cargo upon him, which added to his former Load, bruis'd him and cut his Head so much as to confine him here for several days.'

Byng was not so amused by an accident which happened to him in 1794 while driving a fresh young horse in a one-horse phaeton through London at the start of a tour. 'I had passed Cavendish Square,' he recorded, 'when the shaft breaking away from the chaise, the horse could do no less than follow the example. The reins were wrench'd from my hands, and I sat (safely indeed) in my triumphal car, observing the outrageous kicking of my new horse, running to ruin, follow'd by a crowd, as highly diverted as I was chagrined!'

On this occasion all was well for no-one was hurt, and the horse was none the worse either. On an earlier journey into Kent in 1790, Byng recorded a much more unpleasant scene, which unfortunately in the Georgian age must have been quite common: 'In our Road of last night, all the way from London, a man often gallop'd by us, often stop'd; and at last upon his very Jaded Horse, Reach'd this Inn. It then appear'd to be an hired Horse from this Inn, which his drunken Rider had so abused in the course of this day, that the animal, soon after coming in, Expired of a Broken Heart; — Surely such Barbarity should come under the Law's Notice and the Perpetrator be amply punished!'

There were many facets to Byng's character. This was Byng the humanitarian. A few paragraphs later, Byng the reactionary would be deploring the turnpike roads and the speedier travel of his day. 'How different are these Roads and the mode of Travelling to . . . 40 years ago. . . . Instead of the cool overshaded Lanes there now runs a wide exposed Road over the Hill and dale; which, no doubt, meets universal approbation; but I look back with Pleasure to the shaded Lanes, twining round the Cherry Gardens. . . .' He was also cautious. He made a point of never travelling at night if he could avoid it and openly scorned those of his friends, or acquaintances, who were assaulted by highwaymen or footpads through not following his example.

Throughout the Georgian period footpads and highwaymen were frequently encountered on the roads. As late as 1794 Knyveton, on being called to Portsmouth to visit an old and valued patient, noted that it was a bad time to travel, and that with 'fogs and cold rain the roads will be all clotted with mud.' On his return he wrote: 'Safe home again seated in comfort in my favourite chair, and vastly glad to be off the lanes and highways, such a dismal, jolting and soaking as I have seldom suffered of late years, but thank God no robbers, though Rogerson and the coachman and I were all armed to the teeth, with a blunderbuss and a bludgeon and a pocket pistol apiece; perils all the way over the dismal wastes of Surrey and many rogues lurking of course in the ditches near the great and busy port.'

No doubt Knyveton would have given a good account of himself had he been stopped by a highwayman. As a rule, however, most people were prepared to let the highwayman have his way. This was certainly the case with Horace Walpole, when he was waylaid, as he himself recounted:

'. . . I heard a voice cry "Stop!" and the figure came back to the chaise. I had the presence of mind, before I let down the glass, to take out my watch and stuff it within my waistcoat under my arm. He said, "Your purses and watches!" I replied, "I have no watch," "Then your purse!" I gave it to him; it had nine guineas. It was so dark that I could not see his hand, but felt him take it. He then asked for Lady Browne's purse, and said "Don't be frightened I will not hurt you." I said, "No, you won't frighten the lady?" He replied; "No. I give you my word I will do you no hurt." Lady Browne gave him her purse and was going to add her watch, but he said: "I am much obliged to you! I wish you good night!" pulled off his hat and rode away. "Well," said I, "Lady Browne, you will not be afraid of being robbed another time, for you see there is nothing to it."

This sort of reaction was quite a common one. Often the mere

A highwayman robbing the Oxford Wagon showing the slowness of transport at the start of the Georgian era. (Radio Times Hulton Picture Library)

presence of a highwayman caused the occupants of a coach to start concealing their valuables rather than resorting to counter-measures. The cramped interior of a coach, of course, was no place in which to start reaching for pistols. The Georgian tendency to protect and reassure females, as typified by Walpole in this instance, may also have been partly responsible.

In 1758, on his way to spend Christmas with his friend Mr. Pope at Glastonbury, Knyveton described an attempted robbery of the coach he was travelling in: 'December 26 . . . I came here (Glastonbury) by stage from London on December 10 and a weary voyage it was, with snow drifts piling thick on the road sides, and a stiff head wind sharp with cold and hail. Outside Guildford the off-leader went into a ditch and we were delayed two hours; and hardly had got on our course again when a rascally footpad attempted to rob the mails; only being confused by the gale, the guard fires off his blunderbuss at him, and he galloped away, pursued by scornful shouts from the coachman and the execrations of the passengers, who had been busy secreting their watches and purses in their boots and coats, and now had to drag 'em out again.'

On a subsequent occasion in 1766, while Knyveton was still a young practitioner in London, he was himself taken for a highwayman. Later involved in the detention of the real robber as a material witness for the prosecution, he wrote: 'January 6th: Taking a long tramp over Hampstead fields — was strolling up the Swans Lane to Highgate Village, when suddenly a horseman burst away like a startled partridge — and rounding a corner, I came on a poor robbed man, his head all bloody, groaning in the mud — When I shouted for assistance, after some time a silly Chawbacon appeared, very nervous, who seeing yr. obdt. bending over a prostrate man, runs away, bawling and returns with more folks from his farm, all brandishing pitchforks and rakes; and I was arrested, the farm folk very threatening . . . the injured gentleman recovering his wits and after much noisy talk it was made clear I was not the robber; but perforce had to go into the village to give evidence before the Justice. The robber being, it became clear, a light horseman discharged from the army, one William Barlow, a warrant out for his arrest.'

Barlow managed to keep out of the hands of the Justices for a mere three weeks, for as Knyveton's diary relates:

'February 2nd: A thief catcher called early this morning. . . . William Barlow taken in his cups a week ago at the Bald Faced Stag at Finchley, and now securely lodged in Newgate; and would I come at once and identify the wretch? . . . So with very little stomach for my errand, into a waiting coach, and to the gaol; the thief-catcher saying never a word all the way, but whistling blithe as a bird. The gaol crowded as usual, the stone passages echoing to the defiant shouts of the prisoners and the clanking of their chains; a most horrible stench of foul humanity and rotting straw; and so came to the hold where Barlow sat with two-three others in his rags and shame, shackled with heavy links, wrist to wrist and his ancles to the wall, throwing dice rudely carved from soup bones in the sopping straw; the best part of his cloathes and those of his mates, gone, stolen from them by the turn-keys, or to pay for their food, so that on a cold day he was three parts naked; no bed but a worn clammy stone bench; the smell of them and

'The Cock Tavern interior in 1750'. Note the clay churchwardens and the wigs, also the tricorn hats hanging in the background. (Radio Times Hulton Picture Library)

their prison worse than the bilges of a ship; no lord would tolerate it for a moment in his stables. "Stir about, Villum" said the thief-catcher. "Here's a gentleman come to take your likeness" and the robber got slowly up, not badly formed, but his rags revealing ribs like a washer-woman's basket. Meeting my eye, he recognised yr. obdt, and turned away, half sullenly, half in despair; and so, pinching my nose, I left, and took deep breaths of the cold air in the street. How awful is the felon's doom!'

Knyveton went, perforce, to give evidence at the trial which took place on 24 February. He noted that 'forty two felons were sentenced to be transported for seven years, four to fourteen years, two persons to branding as irrevocable vagabonds, and two poor women to be whipped for begging.' William Barlów, as expected, was sentenced to be hanged along with two others. On 19 March Knyveton noting that the three hanged, and recorded: 'to help John Hunter I attended the turning off, hoping to secure one at least of the bodies.'

Not all highwaymen, however, ended on the gallows. Nor were all travellers in coaches ready to pass over their valuables without resistance. In many cases, highwaymen were forced to shoot guards or passengers or were themselves shot. In his *Annals of an East Anglian Bank*, W. H. Bidwell mentioned the case of a Mr. Mottram, an employee of Gurney's Bank of Norwich, who was known at times to carry as much as £80,000 by the coach which travelled over Thetford Heath, a regular haunt of highwaymen in the early nineteenth century. Once, in 1812, he was fortunate indeed. Bidwell wrote:

'When starting from London he found the other seat of the coach occupied by a gentleman of his acquaintance who said to him, "This coach has been stopped several times lately, but I don't intend to be robbed. I have arms and if necessary I shall use them."

'All went well until Thetford Heath was reached when a man rode up to the window of the coach and the travellers thought they could see a pistol in his hands, and Mottram's friend, on whose side he made his appearance, warned him to fall back. A second time the highwayman rode up to the window, and was told in sterner tones that if he showed himself again he would be shot. Not daunted he tried a third time to overawe the occupants of the coach when a gleam of light was glinted from the bright metal in his hand and he was fired at and killed. On arriving at Thetford the encounter was reported and on a search being made, and his body found, it was discovered that his only weapon was a brass candlestick, and with this make-believe pistol, he had, acting in collusion with the driver, on previous occasions robbed the coach.'

Despite their hazards — whether breakdowns, floods, horses shying or bolting, overturning in ditches, or highwaymen armed with real or make-believe weapons — the coach and horses epitomised the Georgian age. Telford and Macadam's improvements to the surfaces of the roads

Watchmen in the time of George II equipped with staves and lanterns. (Radio Times Hulton Picture Library)

in the early nineteenth century increased the speed of the coaches even more. By the 1820s and up to the mid-1830s the stage coaches had begun to achieve perfection in the short-lived coaching hey-day.

The opening of Brindley's Manchester canal in 1761 had led to a brief and hectic period of canal building and development, but it had little effect on road traffic. The canals were effective largely for the bulk transport of grains, coals and similar materials for industry, rather than for travellers. It was the opening of the Stockton to Darlington Railway in 1825 that spelled the end of the Georgian Age.

In 1829, Creevey observed: 'Today we had a *lark* of a very high order. Lady Wilton sent over yesterday from Knowsley to say that the Loco Motive machine was to be upon the railway at such a place at 12 o'clock for the Knowsley party to ride in if they liked, and inviting this house to be of the party. So of course we were at our post in three carriages and some horsemen at the hour appointed. I had the satisfaction, for I can't call it *pleasure,* of taking a trip of five miles in it, which we did in just a quarter of an hour — that is, twenty miles an hour. As accuracy upon this subject was my great object, I held my watch in my hand at starting, and all the time; and as it has a second hand, I knew I could not be deceived. . . . But observe, during these five miles, the machine occasionally made to put itself out or *go it;* and then we went at the rate of 23 miles an hour, and just with the same ease as to motion or absence of friction as the other reduced pace; But the quickest motion is to me *frightful;* it is really flying, and it is impossible to divest yourself of the notion of instant death to all upon the least accident happening. It gave me a headache which has not left me yet. Sefton is convinced that some damnable thing must come of it.'

By 1830 the Manchester to Liverpool railway line had been opened, and the Georgian era drew to a close in the hiss of steam. The rule of the horse was almost ended, though it was to be a long time a-dying.

Chapter Nine
SPORT, WAGERS AND DUELS

'Most vices may be committed genteelly; a man may debauch his friend's wife genteelly; he may cheat at cards genteelly.' — *Dr. Samuel Johnson*

In sport, as in many other aspects of life, the eighteenth century was a transitional age between the primitive methods and ideas of the previous centuries and the more sophisticated methods and ideas of the nineteenth century. It was an age when courage, or 'bottom' as it was termed, was esteemed above almost all other virtues. The man who followed hounds across country regardless of his own life and limb was admired for his 'bottom', despite the fact that he might often kill his horse under him. Horses were plentiful and horseflesh was a secondary consideration to showing 'bottom.' The pugilists who fought with their bare fists were also admired for this quality. Men such as Broughton, Belcher, and 'Gentleman' Jackson — each champions in their turn — were praised and sought after as much for this as for their skill. The fighting qualities of a champion fighting cock were valued for the same reason, as much as for the wagers won. It was a virile age when the weakest went to the wall and 'bottom' was an essential quality in survival.

The standard of 'bottom' displayed by such men as Jackson was shown in his fight with George Inglestone, the Brewer, at Ingatestone in Essex on 12 March 1789. The odds were even to start with, but Jackson knocked down the Brewer in the first round and soon showed his superior skill and science so that they rose to two to one by the start of the fourth round. Unfortunately the stage was slippery from the rain that had fallen and Jackson slipped and dislocated his ankle as well as breaking a bone in his leg. Unable to stand he could not continue, but 'to prevent disappointment to the numerous spectators, Jackson . . . offered to be fastened down in a chair, if Inglestone would adopt the like manner, and to fight it out — but . . . the Brewer positively refused.'

Gentlemen greatly admired the spectacle of bare-fisted pugilists pounding away at each other for as many as thirty rounds, with their faces bloody masks and their bodies like sides of beef, for the sheer endurance they displayed. It was admiration for this quality that encouraged hard riding in the hunting field. Thus in the *Sporting Magazine* for 1783 there was an account which reads:

'Upon the 19th of February 1783 a Fox was unkennelled near Boroughbridge, Yorkshire at twenty minutes past *nine* and except half an hour taken up in bolting him from a rabbit burrow the hounds had a continued run until fourteen minutes past five in the evening, when they killed. During the space of nearly *eight* hours hard running several horses died in the field and many others were hurt as never to be perfectly recovered.'

This performance was the result of a wager made by Colonel Thomas Thornton, a Yorkshire squire and leading all-round field sportsman of his day, who had. '. . . proposed an annual match of twenty guineas that he would find a fox which should run twenty miles in the month of February in eleven successive years. A day was accordingly appointed, the fox was viewed off, ran twenty three miles in a most glorious style before he was killed. The first essay put an end to the engagement.'

In the latter half of the century foxhunting came to be regarded as the foremost form of hunting, but there were still those who agreed with Mr. Smallman Gardiner, who wrote in 1740 in his book *The Art and Pleasures of Hare Hunting:*

'A lover of hunting almost every man is, or would be thought; but twenty in the field after a hare find more delight and sincere enjoyment than one in twenty in a fox-chase, the former consisting of an endless variety of accidental delights, the latter little more than hard riding, the pleasure of clearing some dangerous leap, the pride of bestriding the best nag, and showing somewhat of a bold horseman; and (equal to anything) of being first in at the death, after a chase frequently from county to county, and perhaps above half the way out of sight or hearing of the hounds. So that, but for the name of fox-hunting, a man might as well mount at his stable door and determine to gallop twenty miles on end into another county.'

Thornton simply enjoyed hunting and did not mind what he hunted. He brought back two wolves from France after a visit during the Peace of Amiens in 1802 and caused consternation by proposing to loose them in the Yorkshire countryside so that he could hunt them. He was prevented from doing so by a public outcry, but not before he had issued his programme for a week's mixed sport as follows: 'Monday, Stag-hunting, followed by Coursing. Tuesday, Wolf, Stag and Fox-hunting and Beagling. Wednesday, Stag-hunting and Coursing. Thursday, Wolf, Stag and Fox-hunting, Beagling and Coursing, to meet every day at Falconer's Hall, where there will be a sportsman's breakfast provided for all the company.'

The sort of life Thornton led may be obtained from a description of him by George Elers who, in 1808, visited Falconer's Hall:

'It was the middle of March and bitterly cold, but we had magnificent fires, the finest hare soup I have ever tasted, and dinners *tolerably* good, for the Colonel was never famous for his dinners. He ate little himself, all he thought of was giving his friends lots of wine. He was a very extraordinary man; he could sit up drinking night after night and sleep in his chair instead of going to bed, and then get on his horse and hunt all day. At this time he was over sixty, and I, who was only twenty eight, could hardly stand this.

'He had no less than sixty couple of beagles, and one day we took the whole pack out together. As they galloped down the hills their white and yellow backs close together, they looked like a sheet of water.'

In the latter half of the eighteenth century, there was bitter feeling against those landowners who killed their foxes and the antipathy between hunting and shooting men was at times very strong. In a letter to his father Lord Pembroke, a noted roué, Lord Herbert, who was then managing his estates in 1787, wrote on 10 January: '. . . Mr. Grove has complained of your keeper killing the foxes. I have given strict orders that none should be destroyed. Seagrim says you ordered them to be killed secretly; if you did, I must say you did very wrong, & your character will suffer for so doing. A pretty free conversation about you at one of the hunting dinners, I was told of. Grove himself, I believe to be a gentleman like man, & if you counteract them in their pleasures you cannot but expect them to do the same by you & secret orders about anything I have an antipathy to. I wish you would give me leave to order them not to be destroyed in future.'

His father wrote back from Paris, where he was living with his current mistress, on 1 February 1787: 'Dear George . . . Do as ye please about the foxes at Fovant, tho' where they are there can never be anything else; but pray keep Barford Heath & the Warren, at least, clear of them. The keeper at Fovant certainly costs more than he is worth & had better be discharged; the sooner the better.'

Even in the eighteenth century there was a tendency for some of those who did not hunt to regard hunting men as necessarily coarse and uncouth. The normally mild-mannered Byng, who was a keen hunting man when opportunity offered, was annoyed by this to the extent of writing: 'I do experience (with peevishness sometimes) the plumpest opposition on the subjects of hunting, wine, &c., from those who never sported and only drank water.'

Chesterfield was a good example of this type of critic and wrote to his godson in the following terms: 'Eat as much game as you please, but I hope you will never kill any yourself; and, indeed, I think you are above any of these rustick, illiberal sports of guns, dogs and horses, which characterise our English Bumpkin Country Gentlemen.'

His moral stand might have carried a great deal more conviction if this polished frequenter of courts and salons had possessed the ability either to ride to hounds or shoot game flying. Despite an obvious ignorance of the subject, he was as ready to pontificate on it as on manners and graces. It was unfortunate that he never encountered Peter Beckford, the author of the classic *Thoughts on Hunting,* of whom Laurence Sterne wrote: 'Never had a fox the honour of being chased to death by so accomplished a huntsman; never was a huntsman's dinner graced by such urbanity and wit. He would bag a fox in Greek, find a hare in Latin, inspect his kennels in Italian, and direct the economy of his stables in exquisite French.'

Hunting in one form or another was the principal rural sport in which almost everyone took an interest. Henry Purefoy's was exceptional in preferring coursing and shooting. In a letter to the Reverend Dalby in August 1737 he added an interesting postscript:

'P.S. I had almost forgot to tell you here is the greatest scarcity of hares that has been known. Wee have got a new sort of wild Cats, almost the colour of a polecat, which haunt all the gentleman's woods hearabouts & have destroyed most of the young Leveretts already. I have killed one of them with some difficulty in my Cow pasture; when the Dogs pressed her hard she ran up a tree, but wee got her down agen & then the dogs demolished her tho' she fought well for her Life & tore the dogs greivously. Mr. Price of Westbury his huntsman has killed about half a dozen of these new sort of cats, but I don't hear any of the other gentlemen have as yet taken it into their heads & go about to suppresse them. Wee have pretty plenty of Partridge & Pheasants.'

Shooting was never as keenly favoured as hunting during the eighteenth century owing to the iniquitous and complex Game Laws. By an Act of 1671, no-one was allowed to kill game except owners of land worth £100 a year, the eldest sons of esquires, or persons of higher degree, and lessees of land worth £150 a year. The Game Laws were full of anomalies, but remained unaltered throughout the Georgian era.

An effect of the Game Laws was that gentlemen permitted to shoot were able to sport anywhere, unless officially warned off by a gamekeeper or landowner for trespass. That notable shooting figure of the early nineteenth century, Colonel Peter Hawker, took full advantage of this. As a young ensign newly joined, he was stationed at Ipswich in 1808 and the well-stocked coverts of that sporting Parson Bond (mentioned by Elers) proved too great an attraction for him. He played the leading part in a foray upon them described in his diaries thus:

'Oct. 3rd 1808: Went with a party amounting to near twenty (besides markers and beaters) to storm a preserved cover belonging to a Parson Bond, who never allowed anyone a day's shooting and had man traps and dog gins all over his wood. I had made out a regular plan of attack and line of march, but our precision was frustrated by the first

The Hon. John Corbett and his foxhounds. (*Thomas Weaver of Shropshire, 1812*). *Accompanied by his whippers-in he is encouraging his hounds at a check*. (Mansell Collection)

man we saw on reaching the ground being the keeper. We had therefore no time to hold a council of war and rush'd into cover like a pack of foxhounds before his face. Away he went, picking up everyone he could, who joined him in the hue and cry of "Where is Parson Bond?"

'In the meantime our *feu de joie* was going on most rapidly. At last up came the parson, almost choked with rage. The two first people he warned off were Colonel Hawker [his namesake] and myself. Having been served with notices, we kept him in tow while the others rallied his covers and serenaded him with an incessant bombardment in every direction. The confused rector did not know which way to run: the scene of confusion was ridiculous beyond anything, and the invasion of an army could scarcely exceed the noise. Not a word could be heard for the cries of "Mark!" "Dead" and "Well done!" interspersed every moment with bang, bang, and the yelping of barrack curs. The parson at last mustered his whole establishment, to act as patriots against the marauders; foot-boys running one way, ploughmen mounted on cart-horses galloping the other, and everyone from the village that could be mustered was collected to repel the mighty shock. At last we retreated, and about half past four those who had escaped being entered in his doomsday book, renewed the attack. The parson having eased himself by a vomit, began to speak more coherently, and addressed himself to those who being liable to an action for trespass, were obliged to stand on the footpath and take the birds as they flew over. At last so many were caught that the battle ceased. Tho' an immense number of pheasants were destroyed the *chasse* did not end in such aggregate slaughter as we expected, and not more than a third of those brought down were bagged in consequence of our being afraid to turn off our best dogs.

'We brought away some of his traps, one of which was a most terrific engine, and now hangs in the mess room for public exhibition. Only one dog was caught in the whole day, and whose should that be but . . . Parson Bond's.'

Land guarded by spring guns or mantraps or where poison was laid for dogs had officially to be signposted. That redoubtable sportsman Colonel George Hanger objected to the laying of poison and in his book *To All Sportsmen* (published in 1814) also wrote forcibly on the subject of keepers shooting dogs:

'I have heard that sportsmen have had their dogs shot. There is a very heavy penalty for shooting a qualified man's dog. But I swear, by heaven, that however heavy the penalty may be, that would not satisfy me; for that, I would instantly shoot his horse, and stand prepared with the other barrel to defend my own person. (And there is a far more heavy action against the master of that keeper provided he sanctions that unwarrantable act; this action is called The Statute of Powder and Ball at about twelve paces!)'

Colonel Hanger had a good deal to say on the subject of shooting. During the entire course of the eighteenth century, all shooting was with flintlock guns, for the percussion cap was not introduced until 1807. The quality of the flint was all important and the best flints were acknowledged to come from Brandon in Norfolk where they had been found since prehistoric days. Even so, Colonel Thornton found when on tour in the Highlands of Scotland in 1784 that 'at eight good shots my guns mist fire, though I put in five different flints.'

Loading was a lengthy and sometimes dangerous procedure as Colonel Hawker and others described: '. . . to load a single gun, of six, or double gun or seven, eight, or nine pounds weight, take a steel charger which holds precisely one ounce and a half of shot, fill it brim full of powder, from which first prime (i.e. fill the pan), and then put the remainder into the barrel; to this add the same measure *bumper* full of shot, and then regulate the tops of your belts and flasks accordingly.' It was recommended not to ram the wadding down too tightly and to hold the ramrod loosely between thumb and forefinger, in case a spark remained from the previous charge and ignited the powder.

Hawker added a final caution: 'If you should have fired one barrel and, while in the act of re-loading it, other game should be sprung, *beware* of firing the other barrel until you have *either put the flask in your pocket,* or *thrown it on the ground.* I could name several who, through neglect of doing this, have been severely wounded by blowing up their flasks.'

It was perhaps due to this sort of hazard that in 1784 Colonel Thornton stated that in his view double-barrelled guns were mere 'trifles, rather nick-knacks than useful.' In common with most sportsmen at that time, he preferred single barrels, but was generally accompanied by a servant with a spare gun. Almost all game was shot by

The Oaklands Sweepstake. The fastest race at Ascot during the eighteenth century. 40,000 spectators saw the Prince of Wales's horse Barnet win over £17,000 for his royal owner. (Radio Times Hulton Picture Library)

sportsmen sallying forth, either singly or in pairs, with pointers or spaniels which bustled the game up underfoot. As late as 1789, the method practised in Italy of posting guns round a covert was regarded as 'in general a very murderous practice.'

Large bags were deplored and, because of the necessary limitations of muzzle-loading flintlocks, were nearly impossible to achieve. It was not until the widespread use of the percussion cap, long after its invention, that driven shooting developed. Shooting in company — or 'battue' shooting as it was termed — did, however, become popular in East Anglia early in the nineteenth century. Colonel Peter Hawker, on a visit to Horsey in East Norfolk in 1816, wrote:

'July 15th. Came up to Norwich by way of Newmarket (110 miles) within 13 hours ! ! by the Light Telegraph morning coach which beat the mail by nearly five hours.

'N.B. Our object in going to Norfolk was to shoot young wildfowl and catch pike, perch, tench, bream, etc., but as the custom of the country is to sport in large *battue* parties, I at last gave up attempting to reckon what I killed myself, though I had far more sport than the others. The fish were a size greatly beyond any I had before seen, but the wildfowl shooting was most capital. We killed immense numbers of almost every kind of sea and marsh birds, interspersed with occasional good shooting at leverets and rabbits, young snipes, plovers, etc. The only birds however that I had not killed before were the crested grebes and shoveller ducks, with which I had (one day in particular) most excellent sport. The circumstances that makes the birds so plentiful here cancels all the pleasure of shooting, which is — that the fear of death deters strangers from hazarding their constitution in such a pestilential climate! I came home unwell, but was happy to escape as well as I did.'

The developments in sport during the Georgian era, though far reaching and even revolutionary, were gradual. Thus the slow, deep-chested Spanish Pointer — introduced by officers returned from the War of the Spanish Succession in 1714 — developed into the faster breed of English Pointer as the century progressed, in the same way that foxhounds also developed in pace from the old slow scenting hounds of the previous century. The single barrel gradually gave way to the double barrel from the 1780s onwards and the use of the percussion cap revolutionised the sport of shooting, ultimately replacing the uncertain flintlock although by no means popular with all even by the end of the Georgian period.

To a large extent, Colonel Thomas Thornton was responsible for popularising the splendid sport to be had in the Highlands of Scotland, both in shooting and fishing. His *Sporting Tour of the Highlands of Scotland*, printed in 1804, but recounting journeys made in the 1780s, was the first book on the subject. Elizabeth Grant noted in 1804 that there were many English 'making hotels of the houses of the Highland proprietors' during the shooting season. By 1808, the approach of the shooting season meant a visit to the Edinburgh dressmakers, 'silk mercers, linen-drapers and haberdashers, etc.' By 1816, the English were renting farmhouses and in 1826 the Grants themselves moved out 'because the house was to be left in a proper state to be let furnished with the shootings, a new and profitable scheme for making money out of the bare moors in the Highlands.'

It was not only the shooting which Thornton had praised that attracted visitors. He also encouraged the fishermen with accounts of the tremendous catches he made. Although these sound today like fabrications they were by no means impossible in the almost unfished waters of the times. Thus the following account of fishing just south of Loch Lomond is almost certainly quite accurate:

'June 30. Recollecting the salmon I had observed to leap yesterday, though I prefer trout fishing, I was inclined to see what might be done and accordingly rose by five and rode sharply on to the Moss of Balloch. . . . I . . . began my operations, and, before eight o'clock killed five, to the no small surprise of my friend Mr. Garrard. One of them weighed forty-one pounds; the others from twenty-two to nine pounds. Having put up my tackle, and perfectly satisfied with my success, I returned home as expeditiously as possible.'

He also claimed that he caught a perch of seven pounds in Loch Lomond itself and a pike of forty eight pounds in Loch Alvie. The former exceeds the present record, but the latter though a near record has now been exceeded. His greenheart rods, his 'multiplying reel' and the rest of his tackle were much the same as those at the end of the following century. Most of his fishing was with a rod and flies, though he sometimes also trolled. He also set 'trimmers', or floats baited and left to drift about the water, a method now strictly illegal. He further indicated that netting was considered an amusing pastime for ladies and gentlemen. On his return via the Lake District he noted: 'We came to Rydal Water . . . Sir Michael was gone to fish for char. . . . We joined the party, all busy in drawing a pool in the river; it consisted of ladies and gentlemen.'

There were other less civilised pastimes in Georgian days. There was the unsporting practice of setting dogs onto a pinioned duck released in a pond, with the owner of the dog which seized it the winner. Bull-baiting, or baiting of other animals, was another unsavoury and gory pastime, while dog-fighting was yet one more. By far the most popular pastime of this kind, however, was cock-fighting. The considerable support this received from gentlemen throughout the country was surprising to foreigners, but not to anyone who appreciated the tremendous admiration the Georgian gentlemen had for 'bottom'. None of these undoubtedly cruel pastimes were suppressed prior to the death of

George IV, although all, with the exception of cockfighting, were very much on the decline by the end of the Georgian age.

De la Rochefoucauld described cockfighting he witnessed as follows:

'One of the games . . . at which the English play a great deal and lose a lot of money is cockfighting. It is conducted in this way; they have a large round table covered with a carpet, and two cocks of a particular breed with a lust for battle, are set upon it. Their wings and tails are clipped; their beaks are filed down a little and to each of their legs a strong steel spur is firmly fixed. This is the weapon with which they fight. The spectators . . . make enormous bets and have the keenest interest in the cock on which they have put their money. After they have fought a number of rounds and have freely used their spurs, it nearly always happens that both cocks are almost equally exhausted and both covered with blood. At length one of them, with a supreme effort, overpowers and kills his adversary. The whole fight sometimes lasts three or four hours. All fighting cocks have names which are known throughout the country; their breeds are most carefully preserved and they are fed and trained with a view to getting them into as vigorous a condition as possible. They fight with an incredible ferocity and never flag until one of them is killed. Sometimes the victor dies soon after his defeated rival. . . . It is a cruel sport, a relic of barbarism, which one cannot forgive in a nation like the English.'

Other more polished and gentlemanly pastimes were games such as cricket. This gained in popularity as the eighteenth century progressed. As early as 1711, Kent was challenging All-England. In 1744, Kent was again challenging the rest of England — and winning. Five years later, Horace Walpole wrote of 'Lord Montford's making cricket matches and fetching up persons from different parts of England to play on Richmond Green.'

The early curved bat and the two wickets of the early days gave way gradually to a more modern form in the 1770s. In 1787, Lord's cricket ground was opened. In 1805, the first of the Eton and Harrow matches was played. Teams might consist of the squire captained by his own gardener and considerable sums were sometimes wagered on the issue. It was a game popular among gentlemen and working class alike where all rubbed shoulders in a spirit of equality. Only skill counted in the game. Foreigners could not understand it.

Cricket or cockfighting, bull-baiting or shooting, pugilism or anything else, it made no difference to the Georgian gentlemen when laying a wager. The English obsession for placing bets at the slightest pretext was another source of perpetual wonder to foreigners. It was directly connected with their deep-rooted admiration for 'bottom'; for it required a special brand of courage to wager vast sums on the turn of the cards or other whims. Fortunes were made and lost in an evening

The fight between Gully and Gregson at Greenwich, a typical bare-fist encounter during the eighteenth century. (Mansell Collection)

on the spin of the dice or other games of skill or chance. In 1770, Horace Walpole wrote admiringly:

'The gaming is worthy the decline of an Empire. The young men lose five, ten, fifteen thousand pounds in an evening. Lord Stavordale, not one-and-twenty, lost eleven thousand last Tuesday, but recovered it by one great hand at hazard. He swore a great oath — "Now, if I had been playing deep, I might have won millions!" '

Vast sums were also wagered on horse racing — itself taking many forms on the flat or, latterly in the century, over hurdles, across country from point to point, or in the chaises or coaches. Racing of any kind attracted wagers and some whimsical bets were made, including the following reported by Walpole: 'My Lord Rockingham and my nephew, Lord Orford, have made a match for five hundred pounds between five turkies and five geese to run from Norwich to London.'

Anything might be made an excuse for a bet. The gentlemen in Brooks Club, seeing a passer-by fall down on the pavement apparently lifeless, promptly laid wagers on whether he was dead or not, and those who maintained he was objected strongly to the attempts to revive him as affecting the wager. Or they might — and frequently did — bet on their physical prowess or ability in some sport. Thus Colonel Thomas Thornton bet that he could jump his own height, five feet nine inches, and 'in another match he leapt over six five-barred gates in six minutes and then performed the same feat on horseback.' He also backed his mistress in a horse race at York against the champion jockey of the day and won.

Lord Kennedy of Cassilis, another of the same kidney, was prepared to wager considerable sums on his personal prowess, though often more rashly than Thornton. A description of his physical fitness reads:

'On one occasion Lord Kennedy backed himself for 1,000 guineas to shoot forty brace of grouse and ride from his shooting quarters at Feloar in Perthshire, to his house Dunnottar near Stonehaven and back to Feloar in a day. He started very early, rain falling all the time. He killed forty brace by 9 a.m., changed his dress on the hillside and mounted a very clever hack on which he rode the first seven or eight miles. There was no road for that distance; but thence there was a very tolerable road to Dunnottar, along which he had relays of horses. From Feloar to Dunnotar is about eighty miles. He got back to Feloar at 8 p.m. having shot forty brace of grouse and ridden 160 miles in less than 15 hours and was not in the least knocked up.'

Lord Kennedy was even prepared to lay a wager on a game of golf, but no ordinary game by any standards: 'Lord Kennedy and Mr. Cruikshank of Langley Park got up a match of three holes for £500 each hole and agreed to play there and then. It was half past ten and quite dark. No light was allowed except one lantern placed on the hole and another

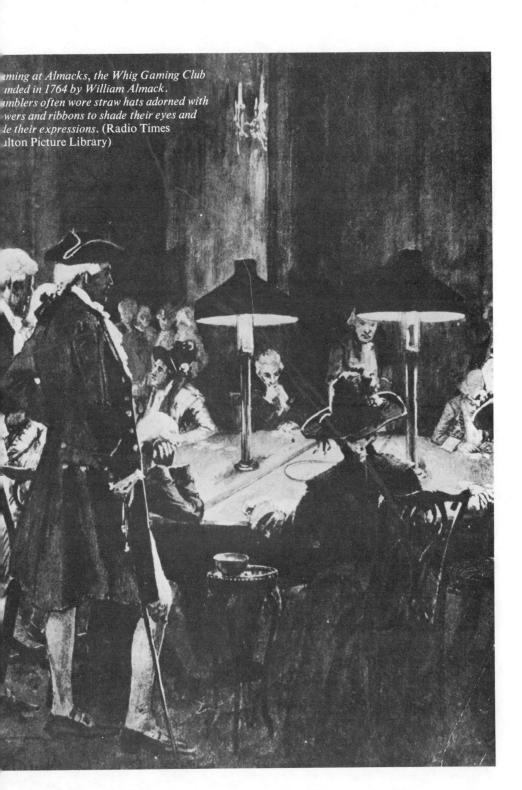

...ming at Almacks, the Whig Gaming Club ...nded in 1764 by William Almack. ...mblers often wore straw hats adorned with ...wers and ribbons to shade their eyes and ...le their expressions. (Radio Times ...lton Picture Library)

carried by the attendant of the player that they might be certain to whom the ball struck belonged. Boys were placed to listen to the flight of the balls and run to the spot when a ball fell. Lord Kennedy won by the odd hole . . . in the same number of strokes in which he usually did it by daylight.'

On another occasion Lord Kennedy bet Captain Horatio Ross, one of the crack shots of the age, that he could not kill twenty brace of swallows on the wing in a day. Ross accepted, and boasted: 'I sent him the twenty brace in a box and they arrived while he and a party were at dinner and were brought into the dining room. He sent me the twenty pounds and said in his note that it was "the most expensive entrée ever handed to him.'

This somewhat eccentric Kennedy also challenged a friend to a midnight coach race, only winning because his rival took the wrong turning and nearly ended in the sea. Then there was the dinner dispute as to whether one route to Inverness was quicker than another. Kennedy backed himself for £2,500, along with sundry side bets of similar amounts, and set off straight across the Grampian mountains dressed in silk evening clothes and stockings accompanied by Ross as umpire. They walked throughout the night and all the next day, then on into the next night, in tight Wellington boots, losing the sole of one some twenty-five miles from Inverness and finishing barefoot. They reached Inverness after some ninety miles across rugged country — four hours ahead of their rival who had taken the coach road.

By wagering and gaming with such fantastic sums, financial ruin was the fate of many. Charles James Fox, for instance, lost over a hundred and forty thousand pounds in the course of three years. Sometimes, like Brummel, they fled the country to avoid the debtors' prison. In other cases they found a simpler solution. Knyveton records one such instance:

'January 1st 1787: Summoned early this morning to the house of a lady of rank, whom I was to attend in her second pregnancy. Her pains had come on in the early hours, and the midwife was sent for. About an hour later the lady's husband returned home in company with her brother; both were intoxicated, and the husband particularly had plunged very heavily at the Cocoa Tree, losing, it is said, upwards of eleven thousand pounds at the faro tables between eight and one o'clock; and so rose and came home, where making an excuse to his brother-in-law stepped aside into the library and blew out his brains.

'The poor lady hearing the shot and feet running up and down, asked what had occurred, to which the midwife very sensibly replied that the butler had accidentally fired off a pistol. A little later however the lady's brother burst into her bedroom, and foolishly acquainted her of the tragedy; whereupon she uttered a loud shriek and fell back insensible.

'It was in vain I was summoned. The lady was quite dead when I arrived, and there is no doubt the sudden shock of the terrible news thus rudely broken to her was responsible. Ladies at such times are always in a highly emotional state, but it is sad to reflect that this vice of heavy gambling has at a stroke claimed three victims.'

Confirmed gamblers were incorrigible and, short of complete ruin, nothing could stop them. Their pleasure in life was gaming at their clubs which they attended every evening, sometimes playing the night through. An account of their ritual approach to the tables at Almack's runs "They began by pulling off their embroidered clothes, and put on frieze great-coats, or turned their coats inside outwards for luck. They put on pieces of leather such as are worn by footmen when they clean the knives, to save their laced ruffles; and to guard their eyes from the light, and to prevent tumbling their hair, wore high crowned hats with broad brims, and adorned with flowers and ribbons.'

They may have appeared comic spectacles but it was unwise to laugh or to pass any derogatory remarks. The Georgian age has been rightly termed the age of politeness for the good reason that it seldom paid to be rude when the result might be a quarrel leading to a duel.

A gaming session in progress at a St. James's Club circa *1820*. (Radio Times Hulton Picture Library)

Failing to offer satisfaction when challenged was to become an object of public infamy and disgrace.

Horace Walpole recorded such an instance when George, Lord Hervey, a rather effeminate looking member of the remarkable Hervey family, was grossly insulted and took full revenge. 'About ten days ago, at the new Lady Cobham's assembly,' he wrote, 'Lord Hervey was leaning over a chair talking to some women and holding his hat in his hand. Lord Cobham came up and spit in it — yes, spit in it! — and then with a loud laugh, turned to Nugent, and said, "Pay me my wager." In short he had laid a guinea that he committed this absurd brutality, and that it was not resented. Lord Hervey, with great temper and sensibility, asked if he had any further occasion for his hat? — "Oh! I see you are angry!" — "Not very well pleased." Lord Cobham took the fatal hat, and wiped it, made a thousand apologies, and wanted to pass it off for a joke. Next morning he rose with the sun, and went to visit Lord Hervey; so did Nugent; he would not see them, but wrote to the Spitter (or, as he is now called, Lord Gob'em), to say, that he had affronted him very grossly before company, but having involved Nugent in it, he desired to know to which he was to address himself for satisfaction. Lord Cobham wrote him a most submissive answer, and begged pardon both in his own and Nugent's name. Here it rested for a few days; till getting wind, Lord Hervey wrote again to insist on an explicit apology under Lord Cobham's own hand, with a rehearsal of the excuses that had been made to him. This too was complied with, and the *fair conqueror* shews all the letters.'

Duels were fought on much less provocation than Lord Hervey suffered. Indeed, although as a rule some slight to honour was conceived, at times challenges were issued for the flimsiest of reasons. George Elers recorded one such instance in a regimental mess concerning a raw Irish subaltern named Derby, aged about nineteen:

'(He) very gravely addressed the mess one evening after dinner: "By Jasus, gentlemen, I am conscious you must have the meanest opinion of my courage. Here have I been no less than six weeks with the regiment and the divil of a duel have I fought yet. Now, Captain Craigie, you are the senior Captain of the regiment and if you plase I will begin with you first; so name your time and place." . . . a man could not be too guarded in his conduct with such heroes.'

Duels were fought all the time with or without provocation. Even the Prime Minister fought a duel, as described by Knyveton: 'May 27th. 1798: Whitsunday . . . Mr. Pitt has had to drive down to Putney Common to exchange shots with Mr. Tierney. High words arose between them at a recent debate in the House. Mr. Pitt accusing Mr. Tierney of raising objections to his proposals of manning the fleet, in order to wreck the Government; and refusing to retract his words — 'tis said he was drunk at the time — this silly duel was arranged. But in the heat of

their emotions, both fortunately missed and their seconds hastily separated them, declaring honour satisfied.'

When the Prime Minister and the highest in the land could and frequently did fight duels, it is not surprising to find that students did likewise. After the fracas with the rival hospital, which was described earlier, Knyveton, recounting the consequences, wrote:

'The other letter more serious, though not more Impudent, being of all things a challenge to George Blumenfield from the tall youth with the pimples "He Being Wounded in That Tenderest Portion of A Man's Conscience His Honour; and Trusting that His Aggressor of Yesterday at least Understood What was Due to a Gentleman would Afford him the Satisfaction of Personally Avenging the Slight put upon him" at which George Blumenfield smiles crookedly and turning to me asks "May he borrow my Small Sword?" and then requesting leave to quit the class from the Doctor, goes out to the messenger, and to send by him an answer to the pimply gentleman that he was At His Service; that as the Challenged Party he had chosen Swords; and that he would be with his seconds at the Leaping Hart that afternoon and trusted that he would find the pimply gentleman's friends there to arrange the Meeting Place; and so returns; and we settle down again, and to Anatomise.

'When we adjourned to the Tavern aforesaid we did find two gentlemen there very cold and haughty; and it was arranged that the Meeting was to take place at six o'clock the next morning, at my suggestion in a secluded Walk that I knew of behind Marylebone Church; so that tomorrow, despite it being Sunday, I am to see my first affair of honour and do pray that all will go well.'

Students they might have been, but in Georgian terms they were also gentlemen. In an age when midshipmen might be fighting at the age of twelve or fourteen, the tendency was to be adult early. That the behaviour of the adults was often childish was by the way. The duel was the ultimate proof of 'bottom.' Knyveton described the duel itself in the following terms:

'March 22: Up betimes this morning and to the Meeting place appointed for the duel; took a stoup of milk and a piece of bread in the kitchen before setting forth, being most Confoundedly Low in my spirits; though this I could not understand, as it was not I who was to face Cold Steel. The morning perfect for the time of year; clear and sunny, with a frosty sparkle on the grass; few souls about save labourers and such going to work; found George Blumenfield and Mr. Pope there when I did arrive; Mr. St. Clair joined us after a few minutes; our adversaries already present, the pimply youth very Pale, but striving to Preserve a Composed Exterior; marred somewhat by a chattering of teeth that he did not seem able quite to control; Mr. Blumenfield almost indecently cheerful; whistling, and after my sword has been measured with that of the pimply youth's, suppling it in his fingers and making it whistle through the air, at which the chattering of the teeth of the Pimply Youth broke out afresh; and I to have a strange, sudden notion that he was a Coward, and had been forced into this Rencontre by his friends. But Mr. St. Clair and one of the opposing seconds paced out a Stretch; and then the second cries out "Salute! Present!" and the two Duellists stood up on Guard with their weapons crossed, that of the Pimply Youth's waving like an aspen, with the Vehemence of his Emotions. And then St. Clair calls out "Onset!" whipping out a sword of his own to strike up the blades when blood was shed.'

So far the entire meeting had gone more or less according to the customary code for such affairs of honour. Countless such meetings must have taken place, many with needlessly tragic effects. On this occasion the end was rather different. Knyveton continued:

'Despite the freshness of the morning I did find my hands clammy as the blades flashed and twinkled in the sun; the pimply youth had found Courage from his Despair and was using the length of his arm to hold off my friend. But this soon evaporated before the rapid lunges

Bear baiting at Westminster in Charley's Theatre (*Alken*, circa *1820*). *Despite enlightened protests such scenes continued through the entire Georgian era.* (Radio Times Hulton Picture Library)

and thrusts of Mr. Blumenfield, and I to wonder where friend George had gained his knowledge of fencing; and in that second he darted in under the pimply youth's arm, swung his blade up and round, dashing aside his adversary's weapon, and brings his own home in the pimply youth's shoulder; at which that worthy squeals like a stuck pig. But George's foot slips, and the pimply youth with another squeal, snarls and tries to slash open Mr. Blumenfield's head; prevented from this by Mr. St. Clair's blade, which by the Mercy of God caught it as the youth's sword descended; so that Mr. Pope and I cried ''A Hit! A Hit!'' and the tall youth's seconds ''A Foul! Let them fight on!'' which the Principals did, though not in the manner expected. For George Blumenfield grunts, drops his own blade, and wrests that of his opponent from his hand; and with a Dex'trous twist jerks the pimply youth's head beneath his arm, and falls to belabouring him with the flat of his own sword. The youth's seconds rush to aid him, and we to prevent them; and we grappled and smote until suddenly George's instrument of Chastisement breaks, and he flings the pimply youth away from him; at which his seconds break off their fight with us and rush to succour him. Mr. Blumenfield very cool puts on his hat, cleans and sheathes his weapon, and hands it back to me; then walks over to the pimply youth, we following, to find his injury no more than a scratch that had scarce pierced the cloth of his coat. So George speaks to him kindly and the youth Blubs a bit with Pain and Mortification; and then we all shake hands and to breakfast in all Kindliness at the Leaping Hart; the pimply youth calling for wine and then asking friend George if he would take a glass with him, which George does in all Friendliness; and so we sit down to beef and eggs, new bread and tea, the jolliest souls in the City; Afterwards, feeling that a day so begun should not be allowed to pass without mark, we did hire a coach and drove down to Richmond; so that I have but lately returned; tired and very thankful that a day with such Ominous Beginnings had ended so happily.'

An early eighteenth-century cricket scene. The widely spaced wicket with only two stumps bears a resemblance to trap ball, an earlier allied game. (Mansell Collection)

Chapter Ten

ROYAL GENTLEMEN, ROGUES & OTHERS

'George the First knew nothing, and desired to know nothing; did nothing and desired to do nothing; and the only good thing that is told of him is, that he wished to restore the crown to its hereditary successor.' — Dr. Samuel Johnson

In the life of the Georgian age, the example set by the throne and by the Court cannot be wholly ignored. It was an enclosed circle of courtiers, aristocracy and politicians, but the peripheral fringes included many comparatively ordinary gentlemen and a number of ordinary and some quite extraordinary ladies. Younger sons of aristocratic politicians like Horace Walpole, or more distant connections like Greville, or simply hangers-on like Creevey, had, or claimed to have, an intimate acquaintance with life behind the scenes in royal circles. Such figures were a source of endless gossip, rumour and scandal with which the coffee-houses and taverns were always rife. Discussion of the latest tit-bits of gossip or scandal was of continual interest to the society of the day. Inevitably the examples set, whether good or bad, were emulated.

Lord Chesterfield's description of George I is not a very flattering one, for he wrote: 'George the First was an honest, dull, German gentleman . . . lazy and inactive even in his pleasures, which were therefore lowly sensual. . . . He was diffident of his own parts, which made him speak little in public, and prefer in his social, which were his favourite, hours the company of wags and buffoons. Even his mistress, the dutchess of Kendal, with whom he passes most of his time, and who had all influence over him, was very little above an idiot.'

Horace Walpole gleefully recounted the story of how George I, with a premonition of his approaching death, had attempted to reassure the Duchess with unexpected consequences: '. . . in a tender mood he promised the Duchess of Kendal, that if she survived him, and it were possible for the departed to return to this world, he would make her a visit. The Duchess, on his death (in 1727), so much expected the accomplishment of that engagement, that a large raven, or some black fowl, flying into one of the windows of her villa at Isleworth, she was persuaded it was the soul of her departed monarch so accoutred, and received and treated it with all the respect and tenderness of duty, till the royal bird or she took their last flight.'

Chesterfield's conclusions regarding the King were perhaps not wholly damning, but they were certainly faint praise indeed: 'His views and affections were singly confined to the narrow compass of electorate; England was too big for him. If he had nothing great as a King, he had nothing bad as man; and if he does not adorn, at least he will not stain the annals of this country. In private life he would have been loved and esteemed as a good citizen, a good friend and a good neighbour.'

Lord Hervey referred to life at Court in 1728 in anything but complimentary terms: 'I am just come from Court, where I saw nothing but blue noses, pale faces, gauze heads and toupets, among the younger gentry; lying smiles, forced compliments, careful brows, and made laughs amongst the elders.'

His description of George II, though vivid, is hardly complimentary either. He was a small, obstinate quick-tempered man, who kept a number of mistresses in Hanover and suffered from piles. 'His Majesty,' explained Lord Hervey, 'stayed about five minutes in the gallery, snubbed the Queen, who was drinking chocolate, for being always stuffing; the Princess Emily for not hearing him; the Princess Caroline for standing awkwardly; Lord Hervey for not knowing what relation the Prince of Sultzbach was to the Elector Palatine; and then carried the Queen to walk, and be resnubbed, in the garden.'

Small wonder that when the Duchess of Queensberry was forbidden the Court by the King for rather tactlessly having attempted to obtain subscriptions there for an opera which was strongly anti-government in tenor, she wrote to the King in high dudgeon: 'The Duchess of Queensberry is surprised and well pleased that the King hath given her so agreeable a command as to stay from Court, where she never came for diversion, but to bestow a great civility on the King and Queen.'

No doubt this story went the rounds of the coffee-houses and taverns, just as another repeated by Hervey about the Duke of Newcastle almost certainly did. According to Hervey, writing in 1731, the Duke of Newcastle: 'was t'other night most excessively drunk, and the next morning fearing he might have said or done something improper to the Princess Royal with whom he had a great deal of conversation, he came to her making a thousand excuses for his conduct, to which she graciously answered: "Mon Dieu, vous etiez charmant; vous ne m'avais jamais diverti de votre vie. Je voudrais vous voir toujours ivre." '

Of George II's heir, Frederick Prince of Wales, Hervey was even less flattering than he was about his father. He described him with penetrating candour and contempt, but also indicated the drawbacks of his circumstances in this revealing sentence: 'His carriage, whilst it seemed engaging to those who did not examine it, appeared mean to those who did. . . . he had a father that abhorred him, a mother that despised and neglected him, a sister that betrayed him, a brother set to pique him, and a set of servants that neither were of use to him nor desirous of being so.'

On Frederick's early death in 1751, at the age of forty-eight, George, his son, was created Prince of Wales. Reared by his domineering mother and the Earl of Bute, reputedly her lover, when George III came to the throne in 1760 aged 22 on the sudden death of his grandfather, he was very much under their influence. The general impression, however, was favourable.

Even Horace Walpole, generally a waspish critic of royalty, wrote: 'His person is tall and full of dignity, his countenance florid and good-natured, his manner graceful and obliging. . . . I saw him yesterday and was surprised to find the levee had lost so entirely the air of a lion's den. The Sovereign does not stand in one spot with his eyes fixed royally on the ground, and dropping bits of German news. He walks about and speaks freely to everybody. I saw him afterwards on the throne, where he is graceful, sits with dignity and reads his answers to addresses very well.'

'Farmer' George, as he came to be known, had many drawbacks as a monarch, but his outlook, his prejudices and his temperament were very similar to those of the country gentlemen over whom he ruled. He was obstinate, honourable, high-minded and rigid in outlook on some subjects, and unfortunately his relationship with his sons followed the familiar catastrophic Hanoverian pattern. Hanoverians were not good parents.

At the age of eight the young Prince George August Frederick was entrusted to the ministrations of Dr. Markham and Cyril Jackson, 'with the injunction to treat him as they would any private gentleman's son, and to flog him whenever he deserved it. . . .' Not surprisingly the young Prince 'took the earliest opportunity of showing his antagonism to his father.'

In 1776, the prince's tutors were changed to Bishop Hurd and the Rev. Mr. Arnold, who '. . . adopted the old plan of severity; but on endeavouring to carry it into effect, when the high spirited boys were considerably advanced in their teens, one or both of the royal pupils turned on their preceptor, Arnold, who was about to most grossly castigate them, tore the weapon from his hand, and roughly administered to him the punishment with which they themselves had been threatened.'

At the age of seventeen, in 1779, the floridly handsome young Prince fell in love with an actress, Mrs. Mary Robertson, then playing Perdita in Garrick's production of *The Winter's Tale*. The outcome was a familiar one. Eighteen months later 'Florizel', as he signed himself, had tired of his 'Perdita', but unfortunately by now a bundle of compromising letters existed. Eventually it proved to be an expensive escapade and the first of many causes of contention between father and son.

It was not long before the attentions and personality of the dissolute Charles James Fox proved attractive to the young Prince, despite, or because of, his opposition to the government and hence the King. The dissipated company and way of life which resulted from this friendship were a further source of rupture between the royal father and son. Inspired by Fox and Sheridan, the young Prince — still only nineteen in 1781 — found himself adopted as the patron of the Whigs when they challenged the Tories over the loss of America. For the first time in many years, a political opposition party was in the process of formation and the Prince willingly gave them support.

One derives a good impression of political events from various entries in Knyveton's diaries:

'April 30th 1783: Court circles, dear Lord, are playing at politics now, the Ministry has finally foundered on the reefs of the India Bill, the Prince of Wales has joined the new Coalition and society and all its courtiers are to wear white rosettes and blue ribbons and similar nonsense — including yr. obdt., who must watch his tongue when attending the great, the ladies of course all supporting the Prince because he is a rake. . . .'

'January 12th 1784: William Pitt the Younger has been elected Prime Minister at the age of 26 — surely one of the youngest the country has known — and the Prince of Wales is playing the fool again, setting up a hustings booth ornamented with ostrich feathers in the Mall to sell favours and the beautiful Duchess of Devonshire and her sister Viscountess Duncannon to inspire his pranks.'

While the Prince dabbled in politics, gambled heavily at the card tables, at dice, or at the races, or dined and drank too much with his profligate friends Fox and Sheridan, on the whole he was just considered young, wild and foolish. It was not long before the 'pranks' took a more serious form in the shape of his morganatic marriage to Mrs. Fitzherbert. Knyveton's diaries are revealing on this score and obviously mirror informed feeling on the subject:

'August 26th 1784: All the town is whispering and sniggering over the Prince of Wales' latest escapade. He has fallen violently in love with a pretty widow, a Catholic, a Mrs. Fitzherbert, who with modesty and decorum has hitherto repelled all his advances. But a few days since a message was brought her he had for love of her tried to commit suicide — !!! and though she would not enter his doors without feminine escort, the Duchess of Devonshire was prevailed upon to act as abigail, and so she and Mrs. Fitzherbert and Keith the Prince's surgeon

George III as a young man. (National Portrait Gallery)

(a coarse fellow) my Lords Onslow, Lord Southampton, and Mr. Edward Bouverie, came to the Prince, who was discovered sitting in a chair dabbled with blood; but who at the sight of his beloved leapt up and threw himself at her feet, moaning and kissing the hem of her gown; and in her confusion the poor little widow was prevailed upon to accept a ring from her *Royal*(!)suitor — and 'tis rumoured they are to elope; a pretty piece of scandal, and what the King will have to say of it I know not.

'December 21st: Mrs. Fitzherbert has consented to marry the Prince of Wales!!! Now there will be a rumpus!'

A further three years elapsed before Knyveton wrote again on the subject, but in 1787 there were two more entries — a month apart — which indicate public reaction to the scandal:

'April 20th: There has been an enquiry into the debts of the Prince of Wales — he has been scattering guineas like pennies, and foolishly plunging deeper and deeper, till now his creditors are pressing for payment, over £300,000 debts and the rebuilding of Carlton House stopped; and the King it is said requires assurance that this marriage with Mrs. Fitzherbert is a lie, before he approaches Parliament for assistance on behalf of the Prince.

'May 20th: Those of us who hear the whispers of society scandal consider the conduct of the Prince of Wales very extraordinary, if not dishonourable. In order to obtain a grant of money from Parliament, he has, it is said, *authorised* Fox to declare in public that there is no truth in the "wicked rumour" he married Mrs. Fitzherbert!

'But if he has so authorised Fox — and Fox has always declared the story false, we thought from ignorance — then it is most shocking and villainous behaviour.'

By this time public opinion had hardened. The young Prince was charged with villainous behaviour in the public mind. These were no longer youthful pranks, having passed the bounds of decency. The public's sense of honour was outraged, but by the end of the year it had even more reason for revulsion. Knyveton continued:

'November 11th: The King is gravely ill in his mind, taken first with mental seizures and hallucinations last month when he attempted to shake hands with an oak tree in Windsor Park, declaring it to be his kinsman Frederick of Prussia. Opinions in the faculty as to his chances of recovering are divided.'

The disease known as porphyria from which he was suffering was due to faulty metabolism resulting in poisoning of the nervous system, including the brain. It was not diagnosed, being unrecognised at that time, and the drastic treatment of straitjackets and blisters which the King was forced to undergo was about the worst possible for it. There was considerable public fear as to his sanity ever being recovered and Knyveton, recording the events faithfully, commented:

Colonel George Hanger about to be floored by a fat fishwife known as Big Bess in 1788. Behind are (from left to right) the Duke of York, the Prince of Wales and Prince William. (Radio Times Hulton Picture Library)

'December 10th: The King's physicians have been examined before a Parliamentary Commission and since an early recovery of his Majesty is doubtful, Fox has proposed the Prince of Wales as Regent until that happy event; but the Prince is not in good odour — his behaviour since his father's illness has been outrageous — drinking and gambling, openly boasting of what he will do if the King should die — and driving down for a drunken frolic with his boon companions, notably that rogue Lord Lothian, to Windsor to hear the King raving.

'March 10th 1789: The streets are all illuminated, the bells are ringing, special thanksgiving services are to be held — the King has regained sanity again, and the country very delighted with the decorum and sensible behaviour of the Queen, to whom his care was committed.

'But the Prince of Wales is not asked to Court, his father having heard something of his coarse and brutal attitude of mind while he was sick; not that the Prince, one imagines, greatly cares, for since he was disappointed of the Regency, he has turned more and more to his cards and horses and wine.'

It was, however, an immensely thwarting situation for the Prince of Wales. He could and did play at politics as head of the Whig party, although his friendship with Fox cooled over the years. He could play at soldiers as Colonel of the 10th Light Dragoons (The Prince of Wales's Own), for the regiment had, in effect, been a twenty-first birthday present to him from his father in an unsuccessful bid to divert him from his friendship with Fox. He could also play at being a leader of fashion with his friend and protégé Beau Brummel, or he could play at being an architect and interior designer, making grandiose schemes for his beloved Brighton Pavilion with his friend and adviser John Nash. He could play at almost anything he wished, but his real power was negligible and he was surrounded by toadies and sycophants.

By 1795, his debts amounted to over £650,000 and he was forced to consent to an arranged marriage with Princess Caroline of Brunswick, hoping that Parliament would agree to settlement of his financial affairs. The Princess was stout, coarse and dowdy with a strong body odour and the Earl of Malmesbury (previously Sir James Harris), who introduced them, wrote:

'I according to the established etiquette introduced (no-one else being in the room) the Princess Caroline to him. She very properly, in consequence of my saying to her it was the right mode of proceeding, attempted to kneel to him. He raised her (gracefully enough) and embraced her, said barely one word, turned round, retired to a distant part of the apartment and calling me to him, said: "Harris, I am not well; pray, get me a glass of brandy." '

Notwithstanding his revulsion to the sight and smell of his future wife, the marriage went ahead but on his wedding night the groom was dead drunk on the floor. Parliament did not live up to his expectations and most of his married life was spent in devising ways of getting rid of his wife. His affairs continued with Lady Jersey, then Lady Seymour, and finally, at the turn of the century, he returned to his morganatic wife, Mrs. Fitzherbert, for some years. Society was titillated by the spectacle of the corpulent lover apparently settling down to connubial bliss, but inevitably even this did not last.

While Mrs. Fitzherbert was still in favour in 1805, Mrs. Creevey described life at the Pavilion in Brighton in the following letter to her husband:

'Brighton Oct. 29th 1805. . . . Oh, this wicked Pavillion! We were there till half past one this morning and it has kept me in bed with the headache till 12 today . . . the Prince did not come out of the dining room till after 11. . . . I instantly saw he had got more wine than usual, and it was still more evident that the German Baron was extremely drunk. . . . Afterwards the Prince led all the party to the table where the maps lie, to see him shoot with an air-gun at a target placed at the end of the room. He did it very skilfully, and wanted all the ladies to attempt it. The girls and I excused ourselves on account of our short sight; but Lady Downshire hit a fiddler in the dining room, Miss Johnstone a door and Bloomfield the ceiling. . . . At last a waltz was played by the band and the Prince offered to waltz with Miss Johnstone, but very quietly, and once round the table made him giddy, so of course it was proper for his partner to be giddy too; but he cruelly only thought of supporting himself, so she reclined on the Baron.'

When, eventually, the Prince of Wales was finally appointed Regent in 1811 at the start of George III's prolonged decline into total insanity and blindness, he was forty-nine and had attained a degree of maturity at last. He might continue to have mistresses, themselves grandmothers, and he might continue to indulge himself grossly in many ways. His political views, however, were basically akin to those of George III and once in power he maintained a similar status quo to the best of his ability. Trusted by no one and widely disliked, he had no chance of exercising the very real control over Parliament that his father had attained.

In January 1820, George III — a tragic, wasted, senile figure — died at last aged eighty-one and three months. George IV was promptly proclaimed King, but immediately fell sick with an attack of pleurisy and for a while seemed himself in danger of dying. He was too ill to attend his father's funeral and during his recuperation was plagued by Caroline's return from Italy, where she had been behaving with a gross indecency almost worthy of her husband. The attempt to obtain a subsequent divorce was hopelessly mismanaged. The so-called 'Queen's Trial' before the House of Lords led to six months of sordid revelations and violent partisan support for a female who seemed to the mob to have been greatly 'wronged.' By the end of the year it was obvious that Caroline had still to be treated as his wife, but the King determined to exclude her from the coronation.

With his flair for showmanship, he stage managed this ceremonial successfully and, surprisingly, Caroline, who a few months earlier had been the centre of public sympathy, was booed when she tried to obtain entrance to Westminster Abbey. A five-hour ceremony in the abbey itself was followed by a further ceremonial dinner in Westminster Hall. When the King finally returned to Carlton House amid scenes of wild enthusiasm from the mob, for once he was the object of popular adulation. To complete his general well-being, Caroline was seized with a stomach disorder less than a fortnight later and within three weeks lay dead.

In 1822, at a month's notice, George IV decided to visit Scotland and arrangements were placed in the capable hands of Sir Walter Scott, a showman and promoter after the King's heart. Elizabeth Grant described the scene in these terms:

'This autumn King George the Fourth visited Scotland. The whole country went mad. Everyone strained every point to get to Edinburgh to receive him. Sir Walter Scott and the Town Council were over-whelming themselves with the preparations. . . . There were processions, a review, a levee, a drawing-room and a ball . . . A great mistake was made by the stage managers — one that offended all the southern Scots; the King wore at the levee the Highland dress. I daresay he thought the country all Highland, expected no fertile plains, did not know the difference between the Saxon and the Celt. However . . . it gave occasion for one of Lady Saltoun's witty speeches. Someone objecting to this dress, particularly on so large a man, "Nay," said she, "we should take it very kind of him; since his stay will be so short, the more we see of him the better."

'Sir William Curtis was kilted too and standing near the King, many persons mistook them, amongst others John Hamilton Dundas, who kneeled to kiss the fat Alderman's hand, when, finding out his mistake, he called "Wrong, by Jove!" and rising moved on undaunted to the larger presence.'

It is difficult not to feel a certain pity for George IV. He so badly wanted to be liked and admired yet somehow farce so often resulted. The butt of cartoons and wits for most of his life, he both loathed and feared ridicule, and his pose as the 'First Gentleman of Europe' was a pathetic one. Corsetted and creaking, dressed in full Highland regalia, with pink silk tights beneath the kilt to preserve the decencies, he must have been a remarkable spectacle indeed, though no doubt convinced that he was the epitome of a Highland chieftain.

The last years of his life were full of illusion and indolence, as was conveyed by Greville who reported a conversation with the King told to him by Wellington:

'One day he was talking of the late King, and asserted that George III had said to him, "Of all the men I have ever known you are the one on whom I have the greatest dependence, and you are the most perfect gentleman." Another day he said that he recollected the old Lord Chesterfield who once said to him, "Sir, you are the fourth Prince of Wales I have known, and I must give your Royal Highness one piece of advice; stick to your father; as long as you adhere to your father you will be a great and happy man, but if you separate yourself from him you will be nothing and an unhappy one;" and, "by God" (added the King) "I never forgot that advice and acted upon it all my life." "We

A fencing match between M. de St. George (left) *and the Chevalier D'Eon* (right) *at Carlton House in 1787 before the Prince of Wales. Large wagers concerning the sex of the extraordinary Chevalier D'Eon were only decided after his death when he proved to be male.* (Radio Times Hulton Picture Library)

all,'' said the Duke, "looked at one another with astonishment . . ." '

Greville, of course, did not like George IV and minced no words in saying so in his diaries. He noted:

'The King's indolence is so great that it is next to impossible to get him to do even the most ordinary business, and Knighton (Sir William, his personal physician) is still the only man who can get him to sign papers, &c. His greatest delight is to make those who have business to transact with him, or to lay papers before him, wait in his ante-room while he is lounging with Mount Charles or anybody, talking of horses or any trivial matter; and when he is told, "Sir, there is Watson waiting" &c., he replies "Damn Watson; let him wait". He does it on purpose and likes it. This account corresponds with all I have before heard, and confirms the opinion I have long had that a more contemptible, cowardly, selfish, unfeeling dog does not exist than this King, on whom such flattery is constantly lavished. He has a sort of capricious good-nature.'

Much of the responsibility for his sons' imperfections must lie with George III himself. On the credit side, George IV was a patron of the arts and on occasions a master stage-manager. Despite his failings and weaknesses, which admittedly were considerable, he was by no means the worst of the royal brothers. The best was probably William, Duke of Clarence, who succeeded him as William IV. Having joined the navy in his youth, William was totally lacking in education and in Brummel's biting description he was 'only fit to walk about on a quarter deck and cry "Luff!" ' Yet he lived in happy but penurious circumstances with Mrs. Jordan, the actress, and his ten children.

Perhaps typical of his behaviour was the scene after dinner on 4 June 1791 with Madame Schwellenberg, Queen Charlotte's lady-in-waiting, who was commonly regarded as a dragon. Celebrating his father's birthday and his recent promotion to rear-admiral, the Duke was due at a royal ball, but meanwhile drank with Madame Schwellenberg and her friends, proposing toast after toast.

Fanny Burney, describing the scene in her diary, wrote: '. . . Mrs Schwellenberg, who had sat laughing and happy all this time, now grew alarmed and said; "Your Royal Highness, I am afraid of the ball!"

' "Hold your potato-jaw, my dear," cried the Duke, patting her; but, recollecting himself, he took her hand and pretty abruptly kissed it and then, flinging it hastily away, laughed aloud, and called out; "There! that will make amends for anything, so now I may say what I will. So here! a glass of champagne for the Queen's Philosopher and the Queen's gentleman usher! Hang me if it will not do them a monstrous deal of good!"

Next day he recollected his actions with amazement and confessed to his sister, Princess Mary: "You may think how far I was gone, for I kissed the Schwellenberger's hand." She, however, seems to have been delighted. Though not exactly ducal behaviour, by the standards of the royal brothers this was positively saintly.'

The Duke of York, George III's favourite son, came to grief over the selling of Army commissions by his mistress, Mrs. Clarke. Between 1803 and 1806, this designing female had the Duke of York so much under her influence that she was able to do whatever she liked with his papers and proceeded to offer for sale commissions in the army, of which he was at the time Commander-in-Chief. In 1809, the affair was exposed in Parliament by a Colonel Wardle, and an inquiry found the case proved, but exonerated the Duke, although he was forced to resign.

Greville, perhaps because he was frequently invited to Oatlands, the Duke of York's residence, considered him the best of the royal dukes. Conveniently overlooking the scandal of the commissions, he wrote in 1818: 'The Duke of York is not clever, but he has a justness of understanding, which enables him to avoid the errors into which most of his brothers have fallen and which have made them so contemptible and unpopular. Although his talents are not rated high, and in public life he has never been honourably distinguished, the Duke of York is loved and respected. He is the only one of the Princes who has the feelings of an English gentleman.'

Greville also ignored the fact that the Duke was perennially bankrupt and that he and his wife went their separate ways, although he generally found it convenient to live with her, despite her tight hold on her purse strings. In his diary, however, Greville recorded: '. . . the Duke . . . desired he would take the curricle and two Spanish horses. . . . The Duchess, however, chose to call these horses hers. . . . The curricle came to the door . . . a servant came from the Duchess . . . and told the coachman . . . that the curricle must go home, which it accordingly did.'

The Duke of Kent, who was universally loathed, was forced to retire from the army after his brutal behaviour at Gibraltar had provoked a mutiny. Even worse, however, was the Duke of Cumberland, who by all accounts was an incestuous pervert with alarmingly violent tendencies. In 1810, he claimed to have been attacked in the middle of the night by a would-be murderer armed with a sword. His page, named Sellis, was then discovered with his throat cut. Although it was proved that the wound could have been made only with the right hand and the page was known to be left handed, the inquest jury brought in a verdict of suicide after an attack on the Duke. Rumour hinted at homosexual practices and murder to keep it quiet.

In 1829, Greville jotted in his diaries about Cumberland, 'It is notorious that the old Queen forbade the Duke access to the apartments of the Princesses.'

His diaries for 1830 also recorded:

'January 22 . . . The King is horribly annoyed about the story which has come out of the Duke of Cumberland and Lady Graves, they had been detected by Graves in an amour at the house of old Lady Lansdowne at Hampton Court. Graves went to the King and laid the matter before him, it was going on last year, but now the story is all over town.

'February 10 . . . The day before yesterday it was known that Lord Graves had cut his throat the night before, a catastrophe which excited universal horror, after all that has passed. The Coroner's inquest was hurried over with almost indecent haste, hardly any witnesses examined and a verdict of insanity of course. There is a violent paragraph in the *Times* yesterday about the Duke of Cumberland . . . it has done for him.'

It is hardly surprising that many dubious characters were included among the companions of the royal dukes. Notorious was Baron de Ros, who was at last detected using packs of marked cards at his club. Even after his flagrant behaviour had been proved in open court, he was unable to understand what all the fuss was about. Greville regarded him as a close friend, but even he was shocked at his blatant cheating.

There was also the Earl of Sandwich, who gave his name to the meal he devised for his own convenience at the gaming tables. Knyveton, referring to him in scathing terms in 1783, observed: 'April 30th: . . . My Lord Sandwich has been rewarded for his scandalous neglect of the Navy — thereby nigh losing us the war — by receiving in this ministry, no monied sinecure, but only the hollow title of Ranger of St. James' Park; tho' a forester's of course is a more wholesome occupation than his latest amusement of dressing himself up in a surplice and delivering blasphemous travesties of a religious service to a church filled with squalling cats to which diversion he turned when his old sport of hunting dairymaids grew stale.'

Typical of the Prince of Wales's confidants were such men as Brummel, Lord Alvanley, Fox and Sheridan, but these were perhaps the most outstanding. Each had the seeds of his own destruction in him. Brummel was forced to flee to the Continent because of debt. Alvanley also ended his days in poverty. Fox was perennially short of money due to colossal gambling losses and Sheridan seldom had enough. Their spendthrift attitude was perhaps all that they had in common with the Prince, but without the public purse to dip into their eventual ruin was almost inevitable. They all drank and gambled inveterately.

Describing Sheridan in 1805, Creevy wrote: 'Sheridan entered into whatever fun was going on at the Pavilion as if he had been a boy, tho' he was then 55 years of age. Upon one occasion he came into the drawing room disguised as a police officer to take up the Dowager Lady Sefton for playing at some unlawful game; and at another time, when we had a Phantasmagoria at the Pavilion and were all shut up in perfect darkness, he continued to sit upon the lap of Madame Gerobtzoff (?) a haughty Russian dame, who made row enough for the whole town to hear her.'

Not long afterwards he referred to an incident in different terms: 'Sheridan made himself so ill with drinking, that he came to see us soon after breakfast one day, saying that he was in a perfect fever, desiring that he might have some table beer, and declaring that he would spend the day with us, and send his excuses . . . for not dining at the Pavilion. I felt his pulse and found it going tremendously, but instead of beer we gave him some hot white wine, of which he drank a bottle, I remember, and his pulse subsided almost instantly. . . . After dinner that day he must have drunk at least a bottle and a half of wine. In the evening we were all going to the Pavilion, where there was to be a ball, and Sheridan said he would go home, i.e. to the Pavilion (where he slept) and would go quietly to bed. He desired me to tell the Prince if he asked me after him, that he was far from well and had gone to bed.

'So when the supper was served at the Pavilion about 12 o'clock the Prince came up to me and said: "What the devil have you done with Sheridan today, Creevey?"

'I said he was by no means well and had gone to bed; upon which the Prince laughed heartily as he thought it all fudge, and, then, taking a bottle of claret and a glass, put them both in my hands and said: "Now, Creevey, go to his bedside and tell him I'll drink a glass of wine with him, and if he refuses, I admit he must be damned bad indeed."

'. . . When I entered Sheridan's bedroom, he was in bed, and . . . said: "Come, I see this is some joke of the Prince, and I am not in a state for it."

'I excused myself as well as I could and as he would not touch the

Pitt the Younger addressing the House of Commons in 1793. (Radio Times Hulton Picture Library)

wine . . . the Prince seemed satisfied he must be ill.

'About two o'clock, however, the supper having been long over, and everybody engaged in dancing, who should I see standing at the door, but Sheridan, powdered as white as snow, as smartly dressed as ever he could be from top to toe. . . . He ate away and drank a bottle of claret in a minute, returned to the ballroom and when I left at between three and four he was dancing.'

Yet among the same circles were men like Colonel Henry Mellish of the Tenth Hussars, who was Assistant Adjutant General on Wellington's staff in the Peninsular Campaign. He was reported among the prisoners on one occasion, but Wellington was not impressed. 'They won't keep him long,' he prophesied.

The next day he returned, having made good his escape, mounted on a decrepit Iberian donkey. There was some laughter at the spectacle and a brother officer was unwise enough to state that it was not worth £5. 'I'll make it worth £35 in a short while,' he retorted and made a considerable wager to this effect.

Charging the donkey straight at the enemy lines until it was shot from beneath him, he came back and claimed the £35 government compensation awarded for the loss of an officer's charger. It is possible that he later found his duties as Equerry to the Prince of Wales — from 1812 onwards — a somewhat more onerous task.

Some of Knyveton's sketches of naval captains under whom he served also reveal the wide variety and individuality to be found afloat as well as ashore. He recorded:

'March 8th 1757: My new Captain, Captain Appollo Dare, a thin man with a stoop and a narrow forehead and of peculiar temperament. When I went to his state-room to report, there was a great noise of dogges barking in the alley, and in the cabbinn were five spanells, a poodle, and a pugge dogge, and one hideous cross-eyes mastiff with a bark like a thirty two pounder; and among 'em sat the captain with his wig off, reading aloud the Odes of Horace to 'em. But he is a disappointed man, being the only son of a rich widow, who hoped to make him an Admiral by buying him a commission; but after nineteen years he still has not received promotion, so comforts himself with the company of his pack.

'November 9th 1762: The Oxford fired a gun and brought to, and her captain Elias Hackbut came aboard . . . a devotee to John Wesley's creed, but a good sailor . . . a very tall thin man with a small head and an embarrassing habit of not taking meat till he had stood in a corner with his back turned and sung two verses of a hymn, but a pleasant well informed fellow for all his oddities.'

Irrespective of the sphere of life, individuality was the keynote of the age. Soldiers, sailors, country gentlemen, town gentlemen, even among the gentlemen in royal circles from the 'First Gentleman' downwards, there was an infinite variety. With so many individuals to choose from, surely there must have been some who deserved the title — at that time if at no other — of a truly representative 'Georgian Gentleman'.

CHRONOLOGICAL APPENDIX:

1714   Accession of George I on death of Queen Anne.

1715   Jacobite Rebellion in Scotland to restore the 'Old Pretender'. Suppressed.

1717   Horace Walpole born. M.P. for Chesterfield when aged 21.

1718   A Spanish Fleet defeated off Cape Passaro by the British.

1720   The South Sea Bubble resulted in ruin for many speculators.

1721   Sir Robert Walpole appointed Prime Minister (until 1742).

1727   George II succeeded to the throne on the death of George I.
      Lord John Hervey began his Memoirs.

1729   The Methodist Society was founded by John and Charles Wesley.
      John Knyveton was born in Kent.

1732   The colony of Georgia was founded.

1737   Lord John Hervey's Memoirs ended.

1738   George, eldest son of Frederick Prince of Wales, was born (the future George III).

1739   War with Spain resulted from the incident of Jenkin's Ear.

1740   The War of the Austrian Succession begun in Europe.

1742   Sir Robert Walpole resigned and was created Earl of Orford. The Duke of Newcastle and his brother, Henry Pelham, formed the dominating political clique.

1743   France allied with Spain against England, attacking British forces in both India and America.
      Lord John Hervey died.
      John Byng born.

1745   Prince Charles Edward Stuart (the 'Young Pretender') raised his standard in Scotland and defeated General Cope at Prestonpans.

1746   The 'Forty-five' rebellion was ended at Culloden.

1748   The War of the Austrian Succession was concluded by the Treaty of Aix-la-Chapelle.

1749   Thomas Thornton born.

1751   Clive successfully seized Arcot in India.
      John Knyveton enrolled in London as a medical student.

1753 The French forced English traders out of the Ohio Valley.
1755 The French defeated an attack by General Braddock in Pennsylvania.
1756 England and France began the Seven Years' War.
      Power in the ruling clique passed to Pitt the Elder, later Earl of Chatham.
1757 Clive defeated the French at the Battle of Plassey in India.
1758 The English captured Fort Louisburg and Cape Breton.
1759 On the Continent the English defeated the French at the Battle of Minden. In Canada, Wolfe captured Quebec and Hawke defeated a French fleet in Wuiberon Bay. In America, Fort Dusquene was captured from the French and renamed Pittsburg.
1760 George III succeeded to the throne on the death of his grandfather, George II.
1761 Pitt (the Elder) resigned and Newcastle regained control, favouring peace.
      George III married Charlotte and showed his intention of governing through his supporters and advisers, prominent among whom were his ex-tutor Lord Bute — his mother Augusta's lover.
1762 George Frederick Augustus, Prince of Wales, was born. Newcastle resigned and was succeeded by the highly unpopular Bute.
      William Cobbett was born.
      Henry Purefoy died, aged 65.
1763 The Seven Years' War ended with the Peace of Paris.
      Bute resigned and was succeeded by Grenville.
      John Wilkes, editor of the *North Briton,* challenged the King's speech. Grenville applied a General Warrant for his arrest, but was ruled as acting illegally. Riots.
1764 Literary Club formed by Dr. Samuel Johnson.
1765 George III had his first mild attack of porphyria.
      Mob rule in London.
      Mrs. Elizabeth Purefoy died aged 93.
1766 The Earl of Chatham (Pitt the Elder) formed a ministry.
1767 Townshend introduced a tax on glass, paper and tea imported to the colonies.
1768 Sir Joshua Reynolds became President of the newly founded Royal Academy.
      Captain Cook voyaged to Australia and New Zealand.
      Wilkes returned to London and stood as M.P. for Middlesex.
      Thomas Creevey was born.
1769 Wilkes was expelled from the House of Commons, tried and sent to the King's Bench prison.
      Richard Arkwright's 'water frame' patented.
      The Duke of Grafton succeeded Pitt.
1770 Lord North became Prime Minister (until 1782) backed by

George III and his 'friends'. The American duties, except on tea, were repealed.

1772   Coke of Holkham began his famous 'Shearings', gathering those interested in advanced methods of agriculture.
Lord Chesterfield died.

1773   The Boston Tea Party.
The Earl of Chesterfield's *Letters to His Son* were published.
Johnson and Boswell toured the Highlands of Scotland.

1774   Penal measures instituted against Massachusetts by Lord North.
Burke spoke against American taxation in the House of Commons.

1775   The Battle of Bunker Hill.

1776   The American Declaration of Independence.

1777   George Brummel was born.
George Elers born.

1778   The Earl of Chatham died after addressing the House of Lords.
The French declared war against Britain and allied with America.

1779   Spain also allied herself against Britain.

1780   Burke attacked the influence of the Crown.
Lord George Gordon encouraged riots against Popery.
William Pitt (the Younger) became an M.P., aged 21.

1781   Cornwallis surrendered to Washington at Yorktown.
Pitt attacked North's Government in a brilliant speech.
Colonel John Byng made his first tour.

1782   North resigned and was succeeded by Rockingham. On his death Shelburne succeeded him. Pitt became Chancellor of the Exchequer.

1783   American Independence was recognised and the Treaties of Paris and Versailles ended the war.
Portland became Prime Minister with North and Fox as Secretaries of State.
George III opposed their proposed India Bill and Pitt became Prime Minister at the age of 26.

1784   The Board of Agriculture was formed under Sir John Sinclair with Arthur Young as Secretary.
Thomas Thornton toured the Highlands, shooting and fishing.

1785   The Prince of Wales secretly married Mrs. Fitzherbert.
Cartwright invented the power loom.

1786   Peter Hawker was born.

1787   The Society for the Abolition of the Slave Trade was formed.

1789   George III had a serious attack of porphyria and a Regency was proposed by Fox with the Prince of Wales as Regent.
The French Revolution began.

1791   Tom Paine's Rights of Man was published.

1792   France declared war against Austria and Prussia.

1793   Louis XVI was guillotined and war was declared against France.
1794   Colonel John Byng's last tour.
       Charles Greville was born.
1795   The Prince of Wales went through a marriage ceremony with Princess Caroline of Brunswick.
       Brummel obtained a cornetcy in the 10th Light Dragoons.
1797   Horace Walpole, the diarist, died.
1798   Nelson defeated the French Fleet at the Battle of the Nile.
       Brummel resigned his commission on being posted to Manchester.
1801   Pitt resigned on the question of Catholic emancipation. Addington succeeded him.
1802   The Peace of Amiens temporarily ended war with France.
1803   War with France was renewed.
1804   Pitt returned to office.
       Hawker started his diaries. Thornton's *Tour* was published.
1805   Nelson defeated the French fleet at Trafalgar and was killed.
1806   Pitt died and a 'Ministry of All the Talents' was formed.
       Fox died.
1807   The Abolition of the Slave Trade was decreed.
1808   The Peninsular War in Spain was begun.
1809   John Knyveton died aged eighty.
1811   The Prince of Wales became Regent for George III.
1812   Napoleon's Russian campaign was decisively repulsed.
       The United States declared war against Britain because of the effects of the blockade.
1814   Wellington finally invaded France across the Pyrenees. Napoleon surrendered and was sent to exile in Elba.
       The war with the United States ended after the defeat of the British at New Orleans.
1815   Napoleon returned to France and was defeated by Wellington at Waterloo.
1818   Greville began his diaries.
1820   George III died, aged 81, and was succeeded by George IV, aged 58.
       The Cato Street conspiracy to murder the Cabinet was revealed.
1821   George IV's Coronation.
       Queen Caroline died.
       William Cobbett began his rides.
1822   Geoorge IV visited Scotland.
1825   The Stockton to Darlington Railway was opened.
1826   Peel, the Home Secretary, reformed the penal code.
1829   Peel introduced the first police force in London, known as Peelers or Bobbies after him.
1830   George IV died and was succeeded by William IV.

BIBLIOGRAPHY
(Contemporary)

Adams, Samuel and Sarah. **The Complete Servant.** London 1825.

Annals of the Barber Surgeons, ed. by S. Young. London 1890.

Boswell, James. **Life of Dr. Johnson.** 3rd edn. ed. by Malone. London 1795.

    The Grand Tour, ed. by F. Brady and F. Pottle. London 1955.

Bray, William. **Diary, 1756–1800.** London 1876.

Burney, Fanny. **Diary, 1768–1778.** London 1907.

Byrom, John. **Letters, Journals, etc,** ed. by J. Bailey. London 1882.

Chesterfield, Lord. **Letters,** ed. by Phyllis Jones. London 1929.

Cobbett, William. **Rural Rides,** 2 vols. London 1912.

Creevey, Thomas. **Papers,** 2 vols. ed. by Sir Herbert Maxwell. London 1903.

    Life and Times, ed. by John Gore. London 1934.

Defoe, Daniel. **A Tour thro' Great Britain,** 4 vols. London 1742.

Egan, Pierce. **Boxiana.** London 1812.

Elers, George. **Memoirs,** ed. by Lord Monson and G. L. Gower. London 1903.

Glenbervie, Lord Sylvester. **Diaries,** 2 vols. ed. F. Bickley. London 1928.

Grant, Elizabeth. **Memoirs of a Highland Lady: 1797–1827.** Edinburgh 1898.

Greville, C. F. **Memoirs,** 8 vols., ed. by H. Reed. London 1904.

Gronow, Captain. **Reminiscences and Recollections,** 2 vols. London 1900.

Hanger, Colonel George. **To All Sportsmen.** London 1814.

Hawker, Colonel Peter. **Diaries,** ed. by Sir R. P. Gallwey. London 1893.

Hervey, Lord John. **Memoirs,** ed. by Romney Sedgwick. London 1952.

Howitt, William. **The Rural Life of England,** 2 vols. London 1838.

Jesse, J. H. **Memoirs of the Life & Reign of George III,** 5 vols. London 1901.

Kitchener, William. **The Traveller's Oracle.** London 1822.

Knox, Vicesimus. **Liberal Education.** London 1781.

Knyveton, John. **Diaries,** ed. by E. Gray. **Diary of a Surgeon.** New York 1938.

    Surgeon's Mate. London 1938.

Man-Midwife. London 1938.

Malmesbury, James, Earl of. **Diaries & Correspondence,** 4 vols. Bentley 1844.

Mason, Charlotte. **The Ladies' Assistant.** London 1786.

Moritz, Karl Philip. **Travels in England 1782.** London 1789.

Pembroke Papers, 1780–1794, ed. by Lord Herbert. London 1950.

Purefoy Letters, 1735–1753, 2 vols. ed. by G. Eland. London 1931.

Rochefoucauld, F. de la. **A Frenchman in England 1784,** trans by S. C. Roberts. 1933.

Rose, George. **Diaries and Correspondence,** 2 vols. London 1859.

Savile, George. **The Complete Works of,** ed. by Walter Raleigh. Oxford 1912.

Shardeloe Papers, ed. by G. Eland. Oxford 1947.

Stewart, James. **The Whole Art of Hairdressing.** London 1782.

Thornton, Colonel Thomas. **A Tour of the Highlands.** London 1804.

Torrington Diaries (Tours of Col. the Hon. J. Byng. 1781-1794: later Viscount Torrington), 4 vols. ed. by C. B. Andrews. 1954.

Verney Memoirs, 2 vols. ed. by G. Verney. London 1907.

Walpole, Horace. **Letters,** 19 vols. ed. by Mrs. Paget Taylor. Oxford 1903–25.

Wentworth Papers, 1705–39, ed. by J. J. Cartwright. 1883.

Woodforde, James. **Diary of a Country Parson, 1758–1781,** 19 vols., ed. by J. Beresford 1924–31.

Young, Arthur. **General View of Agriculture in the County of Suffolk.** London 1787.

Autobiography, ed. by Bentham Edwards. London 1898.

BIBLIOGRAPHY
(Modern)

Bovill, E. W. **English Country Life, 1780–1830.** O.U.P. 1962.

Brewer, S. M. **Design for a Gentleman.** Chapman & Hall 1963.

Brooke, Iris. **Dress and Undress.** Methuen 1958.

Bryant, Arthur. **The Age of Elegance, 1812–1822.** Collins 1950.

Butterfield, H. **George III and the Historians.** Collins 1951.

Cunnington, C. Willett and P. **Handbook of English Costume in the 18th Century.** Faber & Faber 1957.

Clarke, John. **George III.** Weidenfeld & Nicolson 1972.

Edwards, Averyl. **Frederick Louis, Prince of Wales.** London 1947.

Fulford, R. **George IV.** Duckworth 1949.

Marshall, Dorothy. **English People in the 18th Century.** Longmans 1956.

Palmer, Alan. **George IV.** Weidenfeld & Nicolson 1972.

Trench, Charles Chevenix. **The Royal Malady.** Longmans 1964.

Trevelyan, G. M. **An Illustrated Social History of England,** 4 vols. 1942.

Villers, M. **The Grand Whiggery.** Murray 1939.

Watson, J. Steven. **George III.** Oxford 1960.

White, T. H. **The Age of Scandal.** Jonathan Cape 1950.

Williams, E. N. **Life in Georgian England.** Batsford 1962.

INDEX